Communication

An Introduction to the History of
Writing, Printing, Books and Libraries

Third Edition

by

Elmer D. Johnson

The Scarecrow Press, Inc.

New York and London   1966

Contents

		Page
1.	Communication and the library	5
2.	Early writing	12
3.	Ancient libraries	30
4.	Books and libraries in the Middle Ages	45
5.	Early printing	64
6.	European books and libraries, 1500-1900	82
7.	English books and libraries, 1500-1900	100
8.	Printing in Colonial America	118
9.	Libraries in Colonial America	132
10.	American libraries, 1775-1850	147
11.	A period of library progress, 1850-1900	169
12.	Books and printing since 1775	188
13.	Modern foreign libraries	201
14.	Modern American libraries	236
15.	The growth of the profession of librarianship	261
16.	Current trends in books and libraries	280
Index		291

I
Communication and the Library

In the history of man's cultural development, the communication of ideas ranks as one of his most significant achievements. Only when man learned to pass on knowledge that he had accumulated did he become distinguished from the lower animals. At first he could communicate through space only so far as sight and sound were perceivable; he could communicate through time only so far as human memory was reliable. Man learned to speak many thousand years ago; perhaps he developed complicated languages long before he learned to write. He may even have developed an oral literature that was handed down from generation to generation. He could teach his friends, his sons and his grandsons what he himself had learned, and he could even pass on to them the legends of his ancestors. But man's memory was imperfect, and so only the most simple tasks and the most elemental of stories could be passed on before the day of writing. But when man learned to perpetuate his thoughts through some means of writing, he added a new dimension to his means of communication - he could now communicate through both space and time. Assuming durable writing materials and sufficient time, a written message could be transmitted to the end of the earth if necessary; with reasonable care the same message could be preserved to the end of time. The ability to communicate graphically enabled man to transcend his physical limitations and extend the sum total of his accumulated knowledge - or any part of it - both to his contemporaries in space and to his descendants in time. Cultural advances did not need to be relearned by rote in every generation, or forgotten in every catastrophe, but could be preserved and passed on, so that each new generation could begin on the cultural plateau reached by its predecessors. With written records - graphic means of communication - man had reached the point where civili-

5

zation could begin.

A written record can serve to extend communication in
space without being preserved. A letter, an order, a bill of sale
- these often serve their purpose by being written and sent, received and read.   Once the information is received and put to use,
the message itself can be destroyed, its function performed. However, when information is to be transmitted through time, preserved for the use of readers yet to be born, then the library, or
its prototype, enters the scene. In its most elementary form, a
library is simply an organized collection of informative materials.
Although non-graphic materials such as museum objects, botanical
specimens, or archeological relics can also be informative, we
usually think of graphic forms of recorded information when we
think of a library.

The earliest 'keeper of the records" merely stored his materials in a convenient place for future use. As long as there were
only a few manuscripts, organization was no problem; when the
number made some arrangement necessary, he experimented, most
probably, with assortment by size, by shape, and later by form
and general subject. When the number of records stored passed
the limit of easy recollection, then a list of contents was made,
and the first library catalog or shelf-list was invented.

The earliest prototypes of libraries probably took several
forms.   The temple library developed as a means of preserving
religious scriptures, of standardizing rituals and ceremonies and
of making available enlightening commentaries and explications.
The business library began as a record of partnerships, commercial expeditions, properties owned, and tributes paid.   Palace and
governmental collections of records included tax lists, diplomatic
correspondence, royal proclamations, military adventures, and international treaties.   Even family records might approach library
status, with genealogical lists, private business records, deeds,
wills and marriage contracts.   Whatever the form of these earliest
libraries, they contained information that was preserved and used.
When succeeding generations could study the achievements and er-
rors of the past, then history began and man's prehistoric era was

ended.   Henceforth, the library and recorded history were to go
hand in hand down through the corridors of time.

The library, however, is only one of man's many means of
communication.   Man can pass on information to his fellow man
through a variety of methods.   Most elementary, of course, is the
simple gesture.   It was probably one of man's most original
means of communication.   Our earliest ancestors used the gesture
to beckon, to warn, to frighten, to welcome, to approve or to dis-
approve, and probably for many other purposes.   The American
plains Indians developed a system of signs and gestures that worked
very effectively between tribes who spoke entirely different languages.   Even today the gesture is much more widely used than
one would ordinarily imagine.   The policeman on the corner uses
a gesture to direct traffic.   Gestures are used as signals in a variety of sports, and in many forms of work, particularly in the
open or where there is much noise, they take the place of vocal or
written commands.   Next after the gesture in the methods of communication used by man comes the voice, ranging from a simple
cry of warning to a complicated speech system, employing thousands of words, and embellished with supplementary inflections and
intonations.   Primitive man used vocal but non-verbal means of
communication even before he developed recognizable speech.   His
cries of warning, screams of pain, grunts of approval, and squeals
of delight are still used by his civilized descendants when emotion
- or lack of it - precludes more formal expression.   After man
developed a spoken language it served him for thousands of years
as a most effective means of communication--within the range of
the human ear.   For amplification of the human voice nothing more
complicated than the megaphone, which primitive man approximated
with his cupped hands, was developed until the nineteenth century.
Now the telephone, the radio and television can extend the human
voice through almost unlimited space in instantaneous communication, while the various means of electronic recording, by disc, cylinder, wire or tape, can preserve the voice through almost unlimited time.

If man could not extend the range of his voice before his

discovery of electricity, he nevertheless did make excellent use of
other auditory means of communication. Various forms of the
whistle, the gong, and the drum can be found in almost all primitive societies, and these means were employed to convey information ranging from the most simple warning to a rather advanced
''drum language'' in use among certain African tribes. A little
more advanced form of sound communication came with the bell and
this device has been used for centuries to call worshippers together,
to warn citizens of danger, or to announce victories. Ultimately
from the auditory means of communication came the musical instruments - wind, string, and percussion. From the wooden whistle
have descended the flute and the trumpet, the oboe and the clari-
net and even the saxophone. The vibrating hunter's bow may have
given rise to all the stringed instruments from the lyre to the vio-
lin, and from the banjo to the grand piano. The hollow log, re-
sounding to the beat of pounding feet or fingers eventually led to
the drum and all of its varied percussion descendants. Altogether
these musical instruments added another dimension to men's ability
to communicate. If he could not convey ideas by musical means,
he could at least express his emotions in such a way that his fellow man could appreciate and enjoy them. Auditory but non-vocal
means of communication have always provided a considerable portion of man's facilities for reaching his fellow man.

Turning to visual means of communication, man has used
many means of conveying ideas, ranging from the notched tree des-
ignating a trail, or a pile of stones used for a property mark, to
the complicated system of ships' flags used to convey messages at
sea. Flags themselves constitute an entire field of symbolic communication, representing ownership, nationality, power, prestige,
rank and many more subtle meanings, depending upon their shape,
colors, or position upon a flagstaff. The semaphore and its related systems of light signalling constitute a vital means of communication for both sea and land transportation. Visual symbols
and signs are prolific in their relationship to religion, with the
cross in its various forms as a prime example. Business men
have long used signs, hall marks, trade marks and the like, to

identify their companies or products. Reasonably intelligent but illiterate customers would have little trouble in recognizing the products of their choice simply by product symbols. Such non-alphabetic representations can convey information, but they are restricted in their usefulness. Each one means one thing, or represents one service, but they cannot ordinarily be used together to convey added or related information. Two or more symbols used together are confusing if not absolutely meaningless. Unless an elaborate and prearranged code is available, communicating general information by signs and symbols is virtually impossible. But when such a code is known to sender and receiver, when each symbol or sign represents a specific word or sound, then we have a written language. Primitive man's early pictures became pictographs, his signs took on specific meanings, and so a written language was developed. And when those written records were preserved, they formed the basis of archives and libraries.

Approaching the general field of communication from another point of view, all methods of conveying information might be divided into two phases - static and dynamic. Dynamic communications is that which is in continuous process, usually instantaneous, such as human vision, human speech, radio, television, telephone and the like. If you miss a word in a public address, it is gone forever unless a recording has been made. If you miss an action in a circus scene, it is also gone unless it has been photographed by a motion picture camera. Dynamic means of communication are ephemeral without their static counterparts to preserve them. Static tools of communication are those that preserve the message in permanent form; writing, printing, pictures, photographs, sculptures, electronicly recorded impulses and the like. Information communicated by dynamic means lacks durability unless it is captured in some static form. But static means of communication in turn are only as durable as the media in which they are recorded. Furthermore, regardless of the durability of the recording medium, the information itself is useless or difficult to use unless it is arranged into some system for easy location of specific items. In other words, we come back to the library - the basic institution

for both the preservation of recorded information and its organization into a systematic and usable form.   Today's radio news is dynamic communication and today's newspaper is static communication; yesterday's news is available only if it has been preserved.
Thus the library, in its function of preserving recorded information in orderly and usable arrangement is a third and vital device
of communication.   Without it, the other two forms of communication are useful but are of ephemeral value.   Dynamic communication is less valuable to man because of its impermanence; static
communication is bewildering to him because of its increasing bulk
and confusion.   Only the library, or its counterpart in archive,
record file, or computer memory, can give permanence, order,
and reusability to man's accumulated communications of knowledge.
The library is a means of communication in the sense that it is a
storehouse of recorded information, so arranged as to be available
for continuous use over an indefinite period of time.   It is static
communication in its dormant, but potentially vital, form.   Just as
a motor cannot run without a source of energy, so the flow of communication cannot long continue without a source of information.
The library is the fundamental source of that information.

Essentially a library is a collection of recorded information.
But so is a bookstore, an attic filled with old letters, or a pile of
last weeks newspapers on a trash heap.   What distinguishes a library from other collections of recorded information is that it is
an organized collection, so arranged that like information is placed
together, or at least so arranged that every item has its definite
location so that it can be located as required.   To facilitate this
finding of books, the library must be indexed or cataloged.   The
more completely the information is indexed, the more valuable the
collection becomes.   The more readily available the information,
the more efficient the library; hence the more useful it becomes
to its public.   The library catalog with a dozen entries under
'horses" may satisfy the average reader who just wants to read
something about them, but even a hundred entries under the same
heading would be confusing, if not hopeless, to the person who
wants information on the diseases of the Percheron draft horses

used in Belgian coal mines during World War I.   It is precisely
this feature in the ultimate organization and cataloging of libraries
that has led the current generation to a new point in the history of
communication, a point possibly as significant as that reached with
the development of writing or printing.   In the midst of the "knowledge explosion" of the mid-twentieth century, the librarian and his
cohorts are no longer merely concerned with shelving and relocat-
ing books, but with the storage and retrieval of the information
they contain.   The scientist today does not want a book that might
contain the facts he needs; he wants the facts themselves, and he
is not overly concerned as to where the facts come from, so long
as they are reliable.   The whole nature of the field of human communication of factual knowledge is undergoing a revolution, but the
vital role of the library, in some form, in that field is unques-
tioned.

II
Early Writing

The development of writing, of books and of libraries has
been an evolutionary process. The trail from the earliest colored
pebbles to the latest electronic devices has been long but it has
been direct and meaningful. Each step has lead logically to the
next so that the ladder of man's achievements in communicating
with his neighbors has been clear and substantially continuous.
First came speech, then writing, then printing, and now electronic
communication. Each, in its way, has been a miracle.

It is quite probable that the earliest method of communication employed by man was the gesture, with or without accompanying vocal sounds. A clenched fist or an upraised arm conveyed a
threat, whereas an open palm outstretched could be used to signify
peace or friendship. An upraised finger indicated "one;" all fingers outstretched together could have meant "many." With dozens
of gestures of arms, hands, fingers, eyes and facial muscles,
many different ideas could be conveyed without uttering a sound.
With the addition of a few guttural grunts, most of the communication necessary for a primitive society was achieved. Today many
primitive and rural peoples still make full use of the gesture in
their language. Even with a well-developed language, modern man
uses the gesture considerably, all the way from a simple nod to
indicate agreement to the more elaborate motions of the public
speaker. The gesture, in all its forms, is fundamental to immediate interpersonal communication.

Along with the gesture, primitive man also developed a spok-
en language, at first combining the two, then gradually relying more
on the voice alone as he became more civilized. Just when or how
speech originated is lost in the prehistoric ages. Even the most
primitive humans known to history have had well-developed languages. Some authorities contend that man's first spoken words

12

were imitative, copying animal or other natural sounds.   Others
think that interjections, mere cries of alarm or fear, or to attract
attention, were man's first vocal expressions.   Undoubtedly nouns
and pronouns, the names of people and things and places, were
used very early in the development of speech, along with simple
verbs of action.   Adjectives and adverbs probably came much later,
beginning with those describing size, number and shape.   When he
could describe things that were not present, tell of things that had
happened in the past, and give vocal form to his imagination, then
man had developed a true language.

The spoken language, however, was at best only as durable
as sound waves and fickle memories.   Stories and legends could be
told and remembered and retold to successive generations, but each
story teller put his own personality into his version, so that no lis-
tener ever heard exactly what his grandfather had heard before him.
A history and a literature could be preserved without a written language, but it was a shadowy history and a changeable literature,
subject to the whims and imaginations of the tribal story-tellers.
In order to preserve history as fact instead of legend, a form of
writing was needed, and so the historian today separates the historic eras from the prehistoric at the point where written records began to be made and preserved.   It is quite probable that man
learned to write in an effort to stabilize his religious practices and
formalize his business contracts, rather than to record his history.

Before writing as we know it began, there were thousands of
years during which man used and kept some kind of account or record.   Perhaps his first attempt at graphic communication was a
simple sign, such as an arrow to point the way that a hunting party
had taken, or a clan symbol, marking the hunting grounds of one
tribe to distinguish it from others.   But very early, possibly
10, 000 to 15, 000 years ago, man began to draw pictures, and to
represent in pictorial form what he saw around him.   The cave
men drew the animals that he knew and hunted.   Some of these
drawings found in the caves of southern France and Spain are
thought to have been made around 10, 000 B. C.   They were elaborate and realistic and the artists made use of earth colors and ani-

mal fat to embellish their handiwork.   More often the primitive
drawings were crude and hardly recognizable as representations.
There is a question as to whether these drawings were a means of
communication or merely an expression of artistic impulse.   Was
the cave man indicating how many animals he had killed or simply
depicting something he had seen?   Or were there religious or symbolic meanings to these drawings?   Sometimes the presence of a
weapon or some numerical sign in the picture indicates clearly that
a story is involved and when this is so we may have an early form
of hunting chronicle.

Roughly contemporary with these early cave pictures are the
marked and colored stones, best known through the "Azilian pebbles," found in the Mas d'Azil area in Southern France.   These
small stones are marked with curious designs which may represent
numbers or other meaningful symbols, or which may have been
simply decorative.   Various suggestions have been made as to their
use and meaning.   Some scholars believe that they had some magi-
cal or religious value, but conveyed no specific meaning; others
consider them to be something like property markers, family or
clan signs or totems.   Still others think they may have been numerical records, indicating the number of animals owned, the number of days passed at some location, or the like.   Whatever their
purpose, they were an early attempt at graphic expression, and because of the durability of the stone, it is obvious that they were intended to be preserved.   Similar primitive paintings or engravings
on stone are found in many parts of the world.

Many other articles were used as mnemonic devices by
primitive peoples all over the world.   These are not means of communication, in the fullest sense of the word, but are merely memory aids, serving to remind the initiated of the main facts of a
record or story.   Among the best known of these mnemonic devices are the quipus or knotted cord records of the Peruvian Indians.   A quipu, using different colored cords, of different lengths
and knotted in different places, was a means of keeping property
records and historical chronicles.   The North American Indians had
a similar device in their belts of beads or wampum, in which the

color, size and location of the shell beads conveyed meaning. In
the Middle Ages, European peasants often used the clog calendar,
a notched stick of wood, to serve as a calendar and to remind them
of the church festivals and saints' days. In other parts of the
world primitive peoples have made similar use of carved wood,
bamboo or bone, stones or shells, woven cloth, and inscribed or
painted hides and bark. Whatever the form or material used, these
mnemonic devices were means of communication because they did
convey meaning to those who were trained to "read" them.

A step beyond the mnemonic device comes the first form of
what might be called true writing. This is the pictograph. The
North American Indian used the pictograph as little more than a
memory aid. For instance, the "winter count" kept by the Dakota
Indians from 1800 to 1870 was simply a series of 71 pictures inscribed on a buffalo robe. Each picture portrayed the most important event of a winter and it was enough of a reminder to the
tribal chronicler to allow him to describe a year's history of the
tribe. A step beyond this was the picture story or message. By
means of simple drawings, easily recognizable as men, animals,
sun, mountains, and other common objects, the Indian could convey
a love letter, a message about a hunting trip, a battle or even a
treaty between tribes. Other primitive peoples in South America,
Africa and Asia have used similar drawings to record events or
convey messages, but pictographs used in this manner still fall
short of being a workable system of writing.

On the other hand, some peoples, such as the Egyptians and
the Chinese, began with the same type of pictographs and gradually
developed them into true writing, capable of recording history,
transacting business or creating a literature. The Egyptian pictograph at first represented what it described and no more. Gradually, however, the pictograph became an ideograph, which conveyed an idea or meaning other than the object depicted. For example, the picture of a whip might mean "to dominate" or "to rule,"
while that of the sun could imply "day" or "time," while a figure of
a man with his hand at his mouth could mean "to eat." We still
use ideographs today, although we hardly ever think of them as

such.   Many highway signs are ideographs and so are the signs
used in mathematics and music.

The Egyptian advanced from ideographs to the next step in
the development of writing: the phonogram, in which the pictographic symbol took on a particular sound and conveyed that sound-
meaning even though the pictorial meaning might be different.   An
example in English would be taking a picture of a bee to represent
the verb "be."   Next, pictographs with established phonetic values
could be put together to form longer words, as if we were to por-
tray "belief" with pictures of a bee and a leaf.   The Egyptians
made good use of this rebus-like written language, but since they
had so many words that sounded alike but had different meanings
(homophones), they continued to use ideographic signs to distinguish
between them.   For example, if the spoken words for "river" and
"palace" were the same, they could add an ideograph for "water" to
the phonogram if they wanted it to be read as "river," and a
"house" ideograph if they wished it to be read as "palace."

If the Egyptians had gone one step further the phonograms
would have ceased representing syllables and would have retained
only their initial sounds, thus becoming a phonetic alphabet.   In
this case the pictograph for "bee" would represent only the sound of
the consonant "b," and that for the "leaf" would become the "l"
sound.   (These are not the origins of the letters in question, but
are only imaginary examples for purposes of illustration.)   While
the Egyptians never quite achieved a true phonetic alphabet, they
did develop a set of symbols for some twenty-five consonants and
some seventy-five other symbols that represented two consonants
each.   Both types actually represented syllables rather than letters
since vowels were to be understood.   The entire language could have
been written with these phonetic symbols, but the Egyptians preferred to continue using a combination of ideographs and phonograms.   The phonetic symbols were employed mainly in transcrib-
ing foreign words and for proper names.

The Egyptian pictographic writing is known as hieroglyphic
from the Greek words meaning "sacred carvings."   There are examples of hieroglyphic writing that date back more than 3000 years

before Christ. The earliest examples found were carved on stone
but very early in Egyptian history a writing material made from
the papyrus reed was developed. Thousands of pieces of Egyptian
papyri have been found, some dating back several thousand years.
Our word paper comes, through the Greek and Latin, from papyrus.
The hieroglyphic writing was strictly pictorial but, by about 3000
B. C., a modified form, less recognizable as pictures, was developed. This was the hieratic script which was more suitable for
rapid writing with brush and ink on papyrus. Still a third Egyptian script was developed about 700 B. C. This was the demotic
writing, a simplified version of the hieratic. Demotic script was
widely used in personal and business affairs. The hieroglyphic
script continued to be used, especially for official and religious
writings, until about the fifth century, after Christ.

Following the decline of Ancient Egypt the use of hieroglyphic writing gave way to Greek and Arabic scripts and for more than
a thousand years no one was able to translate the examples of it
that were found. Finally, in the early nineteenth century the Rosetta stone, a curiously inscribed plaque which had been uncovered
by French soldiers in Napoleon's attempt to conquer Egypt, was acquired by the British Museum. This stone carried three inscriptions, one in Greek, one in hieroglyphic, and one in demotic, all
apparently giving the same message. The Greek could be read,
but this did not immediately result in deciphering the Egyptian.
Several scholars studied the stone over a period of years and finally a young Frenchman, Jean François Champollion, discovered
the key to the hieroglyics. Champollion guessed that certain en-
closed groups of hieroglyphic characters represented proper nouns
and knowing these names from the accompanying Greek text, he was
able to begin assigning values to the hundreds of separate Egyptian
characters. It was a long task, and other scholars, English,
French and German, contributed to it, but Champollion is usually
given credit for first reading Egyptian hieroglyphics. Though our
knowledge of the Egyptian scripts is till not perfect, what we do
know has opened up a vast amount of information concerning the
life and history of the Nile valley peoples. It has also taught us

how one people devised a non-alphabetic system of writing that was
so successful that it was used for more than three thousand years.

Over in the Mesopotamian valley, in what is today Iraq, another civilization grew up simultaneously with that of ancient Egypt.
This was the Sumerian-Babylonian-Assyrian civilization which existed from before 3000 B.C. to about 500 B.C. These peoples also developed a system of writing based on pictographs, but showing
little similarity to that of the Egyptians. The Sumerians and their
successors had little stone and no papyrus, so they turned to clay
tablets for their writing materials. A short pointed stylus of wood
or metal was used to make impressions in soft clay, and the clay
was allowed to harden, or it was baked into bricks if a permanent
record was desired. The stylus-on-clay method of writing did not
lend itself to elaborate pictographs, and so the Sumerian writing
assumed the form of stylized diagrams made by short wedge-
shaped strokes in the clay. This writing, known as cuneiform
(Latin for wedge-shaped), was further simplified by the Babylonians
and Assyrians until it showed little or no resemblance to the original picture from which it developed. The Babylonians and Assyrians spoke different languages from the Sumerians but they employed the Sumerian cuneiform characters for writing, much as the
Japanese use Chinese characters for their quite different language.
Like the Egyptian, the cuneiform writing developed through the ideograph to the phonetic syllabary, and never developed into a true
alphabet. The number of phonetic symbols was, however, reduced
by the Assyrians to a few hundred. After the destruction of Assyria by the Persians in the seventh century B.C., the conquerors
took over the cuneiform script and further reduced it to a semi-
alphabet of some forty-three characters. Some of these characters
represented syllables, so it was not a true alphabet. It disappeared
in the fourth century B.C., and has had no lasting effect in the development of alphabetic writing.

The account of the deciphering and translating of cuneiform
is almost as romantic as that of the Rosetta stone. Examples of
the clay tablets had been known for centuries, and many scholars
had attempted to decipher them. Sir Henry Rawlinson, a British

army officer and scholar, was sent to Persia early in the nineteenth century to drill the army of the Shah.   In his spare time he
toured the ruins of ancient civilizations in and around Persia.   On
one of these expeditions he came upon an inscription chiseled into
the bare rock face of a high cliff.   This inscription, known as the
Rock of Behistun, was in three languages, Babylonian, Mede or
Scythian, and Old Persian.   The Persian could be read and after
many years of study and much aid from other scholars Rawlinson
finally deciphered the other two scripts.   The Babylonian was the
most difficult and the most important, because it opened up a vast
amount of knowledge that had been imprisoned in the clay tablets
and cuneiform inscriptions available in the Mesopotamian area.   The
deciphering of the Behistun inscription came within ten years of
Champollion's similar achievement with the Rosetta stone.

Many other ancient scripts have been discovered, and where
enough examples have been found, or where bilingual texts are
available, most of them have been deciphered.   For example, the
Hittites, who lived between the Egyptians and the Babylonians geo-
graphically, wrote their language both in a pictographic script, and
in a cuneiform script borrowed from the Babylonians.   The latter
has been deciphered, and much progress has been made toward
reading the pictographs.   The latest success in deciphering an ancient script came in the 1950's with the reading of the "Linear-B"
writing of the Mycenaens who lived on the island of Crete and the
adjacent Greek mainland about 1500 B.C.   Michael Ventris, a young
French scholar, deduced that the Linear-B language was Greek, or
at least an early form of Greek, and using modern cryptanalytic
methods managed to decipher it in 1952.   A similar script, also
found on Crete, is denoted "Linear-A" and, being apparently in another language, has not been fully deciphered.   In the Indus valley
of India a pictographic system of writing developed, possibly as
early as 3000 B.C., and this script also advanced to a system of
idiographs and phonograms, but there are too few examples of it
available for it to be deciphered.   Also at various other places
around the world, including Central America and Easter Island
in the southeast Pacific, examples of ancient and still unknown

forms of writing have been found.   The Mayan writing of Central
America, was in the form of elaborate hieroglyphs, and some of
the numbers and dates have been deciphered, although the language
itself remains almost unknown.   These and other undeciphered
scripts await another Rawlinson, Champollion or Ventris.   In most
cases there are so few examples of a particular type of writing
available that it is doubtful that an accurate reading will ever be
achieved.

Apparently every major civilization, in all parts of the
world, began its writing with pictographs.   This was true in China.
Like the Egyptians and Babylonians, the Chinese never developed
an alphabet.   However, unlike the Egyptian and Babylonian, Chinese is a living language and its script is used today not only by
hundreds of millions of Chinese but also by Japanese, Koreans, and
other Asiatic peoples who have adopted and adapted it as a written
form for unrelated languages.   The Chinese script began as pictographs, but by 1000 B.C. it reached a highly stylized form in
which the original pictures could seldom be recognized.   Actually
it developed as a system of phonograms, modified by ideographs,
somewhat as in the Egyptian, but the ensuing written language was
so successful that it has remained virtually unchanged for three
thousand years.   Only today, under Communist rule, are the Chinese attempting to substitute an alphabet for their more cumber-
some ideographic script, but they are apparently not too successful.

Most of the world today, however, uses some alphabetic
script, and most of these alphabets owe their origin to one developed in the eastern Mediterranean area somewhere between 2000
and 1000 B. C.   The origin of this Semitic alphabet, as it is usually called, is lost in antiquity, but there are many theories concerning it.   Many scholars have held that it was derived from the demotic script of the Egyptians.   There are similarities between
some of the Egyptian phonetic syllables, and the early forms of
some of the Semitic alphabetic symbols, but others are quite different.   Other students of the origin of the alphabet point to cuneiform
syllabaries used in the areas where the Semitic peoples lived as a
possible source for the alphabet, while still others point to early

scripts used on the islands of Cyprus and Crete. A cuneiform alphabet of 32 letters, discovered on clay tablets found at the site of ancient Ugarit, seems to have been an adaptation of an earlier Semitic alphabet for use on clay, and these tablets have been dated at about 1500 B. C. The question of just who first developed the phonetic alphabet is still unanswered, but it is known that several Semitic peoples used alphabets in the second millenium B. C. , and that around 1000 B. C. , the Phoenicians had a well developed alphabet of 22 letters. The Phoenicians were a trading people living on the coast of what is now Israel and Syria, and they engaged in a widespread commerce throughout the Mediterranean world. Being merchants, they had contacts with many peoples, including the Egyptians, Hebrews, Cretans, Cypriots, Hittites, and Babylonians, each of whom were in some respects more advanced than the Phoenicians. Perhaps because they needed a simple script in their business relationships they were among the first to make wide use of the alphabet. They spread it to other peoples, particularly the Greeks.

The Greeks took the phonetic alphabet, adapted it to their own language, and used it to create a great literature. The Phoenicians had used an alphabet consisting entirely of consonants, but the Greeks used some of the Phoenician letters as vowels, added others to represent phonetic values that were present in the Greek language and not in the Phoenician, and began the custom of writing from left to right. In addition, the Greeks developed different forms for the same letters, gradually producing something like our capitals and small letters, although their purpose was not the same. Their capitals were used generally for carving on stone or wood, and their small letters for ordinary writing. From Greece, the alphabet passed on to the Italian peninsula, probably first to the Etruscans and then later to the Romans. By the time that a Latin literature was flourishing, a few minor changes had been made, such as adding the letter F, and the alphabet achieved essentially the form in which it has passed down to the present. The alphabet as we know it in the English language is much the same as that used in the French, Spanish, Italian, Dutch and most other modern

European languages. Some modern eastern European countries also use the Latin alphabet, while others, including Russia, use an
alphabet developed from the old Cyrillic, which grew out of the ancient Greek in a different form from the Latin. The Arabic and
Hebrew alphabets, along with many other Near Eastern, North African, and Southeast Asian alphabets developed from the Semitic alphabet or from a common ancestor.

Writing Materials

In most ancient scripts, the form of the characters or letters varied with the material on which the writing was done. Thus
the Egyptian hieratic, the Babylonian cuneiform, and the Greek and
Latin capitals were developed to accommodate the materials on
which they were most effectively used: papyrus, clay, and stone,
respectively. The earliest writing materials were probably bone or
wood surfaces, marked with charred sticks or sharp stones, but
these materials do not lend themselves to preservation, so few examples of such writing are known. Later writing was done on
bark, particularly the inner bark of certain trees, and on animal
hides, sometimes tanned or treated. There was even writing on
early forms of textiles, but none of these products keep very well,
so only scraps of them have been preserved. But when man began
carving on stone, as the Egyptians sometimes did, a permanent
record resulted. Such carving was difficult and was used only for
the most important writings. The clay tablet, used by the Babylonians and others in their cuneiform writing, was also very durable, and thousands of these have survived.

For a plentiful and inexpensive writing material, the Egyptians turned to the wild papyrus reeds which grew profusely along
the Nile. While the papyrus was still young and green it was cut,
split, and the pithy inside core was removed and dried. This fibrous core was then pressed flat, laid in strips, and covered by another layer of strips at right angles. A glue or paste was then applied, and the whole was again pressed and dried. The result was
a thin sheet of rather porous but durable writing material. The
writing surface of the papyrus was then smoothed and polished with

a piece of ivory, bone, or shell. The resulting sheets were usually nine to eleven inches long, and five to nine inches wide, although other sizes were known. When larger sizes were needed,
sheets were pasted together, and rolled around a central core of
wood, metal or ivory. Rolls of more than a hundred feet in length
have been discovered, although fifteen to twenty feet was the length
of the average scroll.

The ink used for writing on papyrus was made from lampblack, or powdered charcoal, mixed with a gum solution, dried into blocks, and then thinned with water for use. Red inks were often used by the Egyptians, and these were made with a gum base,
colored by iron oxide or red lead. Other mineral sources were also employed occasionally to provide such colors as yellow (yellow
ochre), brown (limonite), or green (malachite). Reed pens, made
from dried reeds sharpened to a point, and with the point then
chewed or blunted to a soft brush tip, were the writing instruments
usually employed with the papyrus.

The papyrus reed was grown mostly in the fertile Nile valley, and hence most of the papyrus was made there. As the demand grew it was exported to the other Mediterranean countries.
Egypt had something of a monopoly on the production of papyrus and
its manufacture became an important industry. Papyrus was made
in several grades, and different names were applied to the various
types, according to thickness, finish and quality. Trade in papyrus
was an important business, and the Phoenicians considered papyrus
one of their most important items of commerce. Papyrus was the
most widely used writing material in classical Greece and Rome,
and although it declined in use after the fifth century A.D., it is
known to have been used as late as the eleventh century. All in
all, it must have served as a major writing material for over
4,000 years.

In addition to papyrus, the ancient world also knew and used
another fine writing material. This was parchment, the specially
treated hides of young cattle, sheep and goats. Dried or tanned
animal hides had been used for writing materials for thousands of
years, but parchment was a distinct improvement over ordinary

hides or leather in that it was thinner, whiter and smoother, and
could be used for writing on both sides.   Although tradition has it
that parchment was developed in the city of Pergamum, a Greek
colony in Asia Minor, as a competitor for the Egyptian papyrus
monopoly, the true story is more complicated.   Parchment was
more probably developed over a long period of time, and possibly
in several places.   However, Pergamum was a center of the parchment trade by the second century B. C., and the word "parchment"
is derived from the Latin name for Pergamum.   By the second
century after Christ parchment was widely used throughout the
Mediterranean world and it remained the major European writing
material throughout the Middle Ages.   Like papyrus, parchment
was made in many grades and the term vellum came to be applied
to the better grade made from calf-skin.   However, vellum and
parchment are often used interchangeably for all varieties of the
product.   Parchment could be dyed into exotic colors, and also
inks of various colors could be used for writing on it, so many
very beautiful manuscripts were produced with it.   Parchment also
could be folded better than papyrus, and so when the codex or modern book form came into use, it tended to replace papyrus and become the more common manuscript material.   It was widely used
in Europe and America as late as the nineteenth century for legal
manuscripts and is still occasionally employed for particularly fine
books and documents.

        The use of parchment brought a change in the writing imple-
ment.   The brush-tipped reed gave way to the sharpened, split-
point reed, and then to the split-feather quill.   The Romans made
good use of the quill and our word "pen" comes from the Latin
word for "feather."   The feather quill was used as a writing instru-
ment for at least 2,000 years, and the metal pen-point which we
use today is a faithful copy of it.

From roll to book

        The roll form continued in use long after the development
of parchment, but other forms were tried.   Smooth pieces of wood
could be written on with charcoal sticks, and this was an early

form of the schoolboy's "slate." Later this wooden slate was covered with a thin layer of wax. Then with a wood or ivory stylus
legible impressions could be made in the wax, which could be
smoothed over for reuse. This "tabula," from which we get our
word tablet, had many uses. It could be used for school practice
work, for figuring accounts in a business house, or for sending
letters. Such waxed tablets were widely used, and examples have
been found on wood, ivory and metal, from Egypt, Babylonia,
Greece and Rome. Sometimes the tablet was hinged to another,
and a "diptych" was then formed, looking something like the modern
book. A diptych presented two waxed surfaces, face to face, and
thus protected from damage. Sometimes, with very thin wood, or
metal, several waxed "leaves" could be hinged together and protected by outside covers. This closely approximated the modern
book form.

By about 100 A.D. another book form had become popular,
particularly in Rome. This was the codex, similar in form to the
multi-leaved tabula, and possibly suggested by it, but made of
papyrus or parchment. Several sheets were folded and then sewn
together along the folded edge to form a quire of eight, twelve, sixteen or more pages. If necessary, several quires could be sewn
together to form a thicker book. This form was much easier to
read than the roll, especially when several books were to be compared or consulted together. Although many papyrus codices have
been found, the form was better suited to parchment and as the
codex replaced the roll as the prevailing book form, parchment
rapidly replaced papyrus. When books and spines of wood or leather were added to the codex, it reached substantially the form of the
modern book. By the fourth century A.D., the codex was the most
widely used book form, but the scroll continued to be used for
some important documents down through the Middle Ages.

The origins of some words relating to books and libraries
are of interest. The English word "library" comes from the
French "librarie," which stems from the Latin "librarium," meaning "of books." This in turn comes from the word "liber" (book),
but the Latin "liber" originally meant "inner bark of a tree," used

as a writing material. The French no longer use "librarie" for library, but instead use it to designate a book shop. The French word for library is "bibliothèque," from the Greek words meaning, roughly, "book cabinet." Most of the European languages employ some form of "bibliothèque" for library, such as the German "Bibliothek." The English word "book," on the other hand, has an Anglo-Saxon origin, and comes from a word meaning "wooden tablet." This in turn is related to or derived from the word "boc," meaning "beechtree," also indicating an early use of wood or bark for writing.

Thus, long before the end of the ancient era, man had experimented with various forms of writing and writing materials, and, at least as far as the Mediterranean world was concerned, he had settled down to a system of written communication that was to remain virtually unchanged for a thousand years or more. This system included the phonetic alphabet in its Greek or Latin form, the parchment codex and the ink pen or quill. The physical ingredients were available for the writing and preserving of a great literature and the classics of the Greeks and Romans are eloquent proof that they were well used.

Bibliography

Books

American Council on Education: The story of writing. Washington, 1931. 64 p.

Baikie, James: Egyptian papyri and papyrus hunting. London, 1925. 324 p.

Barber, Charles L.: The story of speech and language. New York, 1965. 295 p.

Bodmer, Frederick: The loom of language. London, 1944. 692 p.

Brinton, Daniel G.: A primer of Mayan hieroglyphs. Boston, 1895. 152 p.

Budge, Ernest A.W.: The Rosetta stone in the British Museum. London, 1929. 325 p.

Bushnell, G.H.: From bricks to books. London, 1949. 160 p.

Bushnell, G.H.: From papyrus to print. London, 1947. 218 p.

Cerny, Jaroslav: Paper and books in ancient Egypt. London, 1952. 36 p.

Chiera, Edward: They wrote on clay: the Babylonian tablets speak today. Chicago, 1938. 235 p.

Clark, Cumberland: The art of early writing, with special reference to the cuneiform system. London, 1938. 151 p.

Clodd, Edward: The story of the alphabet. New York, 1938. 209 p.

Davies, Nina M.: Picture writing in ancient Egypt. Oxford, 1958. 78 p.

Denman, Frank: The shaping of our alphabet. New York, 1955. 232 p.

Diamond, A. H.: History and origin of language. London, 1960. 280 p.

Diringer, David: The alphabet, a key to the history of mankind. New York, 1951. 607 p.

Diringer, David: The hand produced book. New York, 1953. 603 p.

Diringer, David: Writing. New York, 1962. 261 p.

Doblhofer, Ernst: Voices in stone: the decipherment of ancient scripts and writings. New York, 1961. 327 p.

Driver, Godfrey R.: Semitic writing, from pictograph to alphabet. London, 1954. Rev. ed. 238 p.

Étiemble, René: The Orion book of the written word. New York, 1961. 114 p.

Gelb, I. J.: A study of writing. Chicago, 1963. Rev. ed. 319 p.

Goldberg, Isaac: The wonder of words. New York, 1938. 485 p.

Gray, Louis H.: Foundations of language. New York, 1939. 630 p.

Hogben, Lancelot: From cave painting to comic strip: a kaleidoscope of human communication. New York, 1949. 286 p.

Hunter, Dard: Papermaking: the history and technique of an ancient craft. New York, 1947. 611 p. (See especially pp. 3-48).

Irwin, Keith G. : The romance of writing, from Egyptian hieroglyphics to modern letters, numbers and signs. New York,
1961. 160 p.

Jespersen, Otto: Language, its nature, development and origin.
New York, 1964. 448 p.

McMurtrie, Douglas C. : The book, the story of printing and book-
making. New York, 1943. 676 p. (See especially, p. 1-
39).

Mallory, Garrick: Picture-writing of the American Indians. Washington, 1893. 822 p. (10th Annual Report of the Bureau of
American Ethnology.)

Mason, William: A history of the art of writing. New York,
1928. 502 p.

Moorhouse, A. C. : The triumph of the alphabet. New York,
1953. 223 p.

Ornstein, Jacob: The ABC's of languages and linguistics. Philadelphia, 1964. 205 p.

Pei, Mario: The story of language. Philadelphia, 1965. Rev. ed.
493 p.

Pumphrey, R. J. : The origin of language. Liverpool, 1951. 39 p.

Smith, A. M. : Printing and writing materials, their evolution.
Philadelphia, 1901. 236 p.

Sprengling, Martin: The alphabet, its rise and development from
the Sinai inscriptions. Chicago, 1931. 71 p.

Taylor, Isaac: The history of the alphabet. New York, 1899. 2 v.

Thompson, J. E. S. : Maya hieroglyphic writing: Introduction.
Norman, Okla. , 1960. 347 p.

Tsien, Tsuen-Hsuin: Written on bamboo and silk: the beginnings
of Chinese books and inscriptions. Chicago, 1962. 233 p.

Ullman, Berthold L. : Ancient writing and its influence. New
York, 1932. 234 p.

Van Hoesen, Henry B. : Bibliography. New York, 1928. 519 p.
(See pp. 259-313).

Waddell, Lawrence A. : The Aryan origin of the alphabet. London, 1927. 80 p.

Whitney, Elwood: Symbology: the use of symbols in visual com-
    munications. New York, 1960. 192 p.

Periodical Articles
Carpenter, Rhys: "The antiquity of the Greek alphabet," American
    Journal of Archaeology, XXXVII, (1933), 8-29.

Chadwick, John: "Decipherment of Linear B," Natural History,
    LXX, (1961), 8-19, 58-71.

Conder, C. R.: "Origin of alphabets," Edinburgh Review,
    CLXXII, (1890), 112-140.

Diringer, David: "The origins of the alphabet," Antiquity, XVII,
    (1943), 77-90.

Diringer, David: "Problems of the present day on the origin of
    the Phoenician alphabet," Journal of World History, IV,
    (1957), 40-58.

Edgerton, W. F. : "Egyptian phonetic writing, from its invention to
    the close of the nineteenth dynasty," Journal of the Ameri-
    can Oriental Society, LX, (1940), 473-506.

Hackh, I. W. D. : "History of the alphabet," Scientific Monthly, XXV,
    (1927), 97-118.

Hooke, S. H. : "The early history of writing," Antiquity, XI,
    (1937), 261-277.

Swanton, John R. : "The quipu and Peruvian civilization," U. S.
    Bureau of American Ethnology, Anthropological Papers,
    XXVI, 587-596.

Ullman, B. L. : "The origin and development of the alphabet,"
    American Journal of Archaeology, XXXI, (1927), 311-328.

III
Ancient Libraries

After civilized man began to make and keep written records, the formation of libraries was a logical development. The earliest form of library was what we would today consider an archive, since it was really a collection of government or religious documents. Ancient Egypt, as one of the earliest areas to develop writing, also developed some of the earliest libraries of which we have any record. These libraries were composed of papyrus rolls, and although the earliest ones known were official collections of legal or church records, some private and business libraries were also known to exist. Ancient Babylonia, in the Mesopotamian valley, also had libraries as early or earlier than those in Egypt.

The government archives contained mainly official records, correspondence and chronologies, accounting for the events in the reigns of various kings, or the accomplishments of officials in the collection of taxes or the building of monuments. Some records of court cases and chronicles of military expeditions have been preserved, along with some diplomatic correspondence between countries and kings. In the temples, the papyrus "libraries" included church records, religious ceremonies and rituals, and the lives of the various Egyptian gods.

Some of the wealthier Egyptian nobles and business men maintained private libraries, and since examples of these books were buried with their owners in their tombs, we know more about them than we know about the official archives. In tombs that archeologists have opened and examined, "books" of papyrus have been found, tightly rolled and sealed in pottery jars. Some of them contain family records and correspondence, but others include more exciting reading in the form of travel stories, tales of war and adventures, and books of magic. Occasionally there were a few rolls concerned with science, mathematics or medicine, usually associated with magic. The best known of all Egyptian books, and the one most widely found in private tombs was the "Book of the Dead." This was a book of religious ritual designed to guide the souls of the dead through the underworld to the hall of judgment, where one's permanent position in the next world was to be decided. The production of copies of the "Book of the Dead" was a profitable business, and the length and elaborateness, even the contents, of a copy varied according to the wealth and importance of the person for whom it was purchased. A copy now preserved in the British Museum is seventy-eight feet long and fifteen inches wide, and contains many colorful illustrations.

The "librarian" of the ancient Egyptian library was the palace or temple scribe, who helped to write and to preserve the papyrus rolls. In some cases the position of "keeper of the books" was hereditary, with the task descending from father to son. Wealthy nobles hired scribes to care for their books, or had servants trained for the task. In the library rooms, the papyrus rolls were kept in clay jars, leather sleeves, or metal cylinders, depending upon the value of the individual rolls. From one end of the container protruded a title label, with a few key words of the text for identification. These containers in turn were kept in coffers or on shelves, but little is known as to how they were arranged or cataloged. In some cases a list of the books in a library room were inscribed on the wall near the entrance. One such list can still be read on the walls of the Temple at Edfu, although the books themselves no longer exist.

Since Babylonia and Assyria made their books of baked clay, literally thousands of them have been preserved. Evidences of many government, religious and private libraries have been found in the ruins of the Mesopotamian cities. Considering that the major Egyptian collections were largely archival, the Assyrians may be said to have produced the first real library. We know that they and their predecessors achieved very large collections of clay tablets, systematically gathered and arranged, and including all types of literature. According to existing records, one scribe in charge of such a collection was given the title "Man of the written tablets,"

nearly two thousand years before Christ.   One of the Assyrian
kings, Assurbanipal (668-626 B.C.), is noted for his library.   Adding to a collection begun by his grandfather, Sennacherib, he gathered in his capital city, Nineveh, a library of many thousands of
clay tablets.   Under the direction of a royal librarian, a score or
more copyists and clerks were kept busy arranging and caring for
the tablets.   Some of the works were historical chronologies and
others were government records and correspondence, but there
were also works on grammar, poetry, history, science, mythology
and religion.   Dictionaries of earlier cuneiform languages were included to aid in the translation and copying of tablets that had been
preserved for hundreds of years by Assurbanipal's time.

The clay tablets in Assurbanipal's library were arranged
roughly by subject and lettered on the outside according to their
contents.   Longer works were written on several tablets consecu-
tively numbered, and sometimes kept together in a basket.   Occasionally a more important document would be written on one tablet,
and then encased in an outer clay shell that had to be broken before the inner one could be read.   Apparently works on different
subjects were kept in separate rooms, and a catalog or description
of the contents of each room was written on the door or nearby
wall, giving for each work the title or first line, the number of
lines, and for longer works the number of parts into which it was
divided.   Unfortunately the Assyrian civilization was virtually destroyed in wars during the sixth and seventh centuries B.C. and
the magnificent library of Assurbanipal was reduced to a pile of
rubble.   So indestructible were the baked tablets, however, that
many thousands of them were recovered from the ruins twenty-five
centuries later.   Most of these are preserved in the British Museum in London.   Other outstanding collections of clay tablets have
been found in the ruins of various Mesopotamian cities, including
Ashur, Ur, Nippur and Kish, indicating that there were probably
other public or private libraries dating back before 2000 B.C.   In
recent years discoveries of Hittite ruins to the west of Mesopo-
tamia have brought to light another ancient civilization that made
use of clay tablets and cuneiform writing.   A library of Hittite tab-

lets, including a few "catalog" tablets, or lists of writings, has
been found in what was apparently their capital or major city.
Still another library of cuneiform tablets has been found near the
Mediterranean coast in the ruins of the ancient city of Ugarit (mod-
ern Ras-Shamrah), and even the ancient Minoan civilization of
Crete used clay tablets.

      Although Greece's great age of literature was in the fifth
and fourth centuries B. C. , when Plato and Aristotle flourished, we
know relatively little of Greek libraries of that era.   A century
earlier, Pisistratus, tyrant of Athens from 560 to 527, is supposed
to have collected a private library of some size, but there is little
evidence of this.   The works of the philosophers and dramatists,
such as Plato and Euripides, indicate a wide acquaintance with earlier works, but the existence and size of their libraries is largely
conjecture.   For Aristotle's library, we are on somewhat firmer
ground, but even here we know little of its actual contents or final
disposition.   We do know that Aristotle collected books on many
subjects and made them available during his lifetime to his students and friends.   At his death he left his library to his follower,
Theophrastus of Lesbos, who in turn willed it to Neleus of Scepsis.
After that its fate is uncertain.   Part of it may have eventually
reached Rome or the Alexandrian Library, but if so the individual
manuscripts lost their identity in larger collections.   The fact that
it was kept together as long as it was indicates its value and its
importance as a collection.

      In addition to private libraries, there were also public col-
lections in ancient Greece.   There was a public library in Athens
in 330 B. C. , and it is interesting to note that it was a "popular"
library in that it contained copies of the current Greek dramas of
Aeschylus, Sophocles and Euripides, and made them available for
readers who could not afford to own copies.   The texts of the
dramas preserved in the public library were also "official" ones,
thus making it serve as something of a registry office as well as
a library.   By the next century, public, private and school libraries
were available in Athens and in the other larger Greek cities, so
that scholars from all over the Mediterranean world converged up-

on that area for study and research.

Libraries were also established in the Greek colonies in
Asia Minor, Egypt and Sicily, and it is an odd fact that more is
known about some of these colonial libraries than about those in
Greece proper. Antiochus the Great (223-187 B.C.) established a
library at Antioch in Syria, and Euphorion of Chalcis was appointed
librarian there. Archaeologists have uncovered the ruins of this
library building and have found there mosaic representations of
scenes from Homer and Euripides. Eumenes II, who lived from
197 to 149 B.C., and who reigned as king of Pergamum in Asia
Minor, established a library in his capital city. Book scouts were
sent to all parts of the Greek world to purchase or copy literary
works, and the library at Pergamum grew rapidly. According to
Plutarch, it contained over 200,000 rolls at its height, all housed
in a beautiful temple dedicated to the goddess Athena. The Roman
ruler Antony is supposed to have taken the Pergamum library as
spoils of war in 41 B.C. and presented it to Cleopatra of Egypt.

The greatest library stemming from Greek cultural domination grew up at Alexandria in Egypt in the third century B.C., under the Greek-Egyptian rulers Ptolemy I and II. Actually the
Alexandrian Library consisted in time of two collections. The
larger and more famous collection was in the Museum, a school or
assembly of scholars copied after Aristotle's school in Athens,
while the smaller was in a temple dedicated to the Egyptian god
Serapis. The former is sometimes called the Brucheium, while
the latter is termed the Serapeum. At their heights around 200
B.C. the collections are supposed to have contained several hundred thousand rolls between them. To enlarge the libraries, the
Ptolemaic emperors acquired books from all the known world, in
Egyptian, Greek, Latin, Hebrew and other languages. In most
cases translations were made into Greek, and different copies of individual works were compared and edited in order to achieve the
most authentic texts. In addition to obtaining copies of works for
research and preservation, scribes on the staff of the Alexandrian
libraries also made copies for sale, thus making the institution a
publisher as well as a library. One of the most important works

attributed to the Alexandrian scholars is the translation from the
Hebrew of the first Greek version of the Old Testament -- the
Septuagint, so-called from the seventy scholars who are supposed
to have worked on it.

Several outstanding names in Greek literature have been connected with the Alexandrian library. Demetrius of Phalerum, a
statesman and orator, was one of the early figures connected with
the library; he is in fact credited by some writers with having
planned and organized it. Zenodotus of Ephesus, a noted gram-
marian, was an early librarian, and so was Aristophanes of Byzantium, a lexicographer. One of the most important names connected with the Alexandrian library is that of Callimachus of Cy-
rene. It is not certain just what his connection was, but it is
known that he compiled a catalog or bibliography, probably of the
holdings of the library, that was widely known and used in his era.
The "Pinakes," as Callimachus' catalog was called, was an author
list, arranged into major subject or form groups, such as epic poetry, dramatic poetry, laws, philosophy, history and oratory. In
addition to the bibliographical details concerning each work, Callimachus added bits of information concerning the author, and short
excerpts or summaries of the works themselves. One author gives
the sub-title of the "Pinakes" as 'Tables of all those who were emi-
nent in any kind of literature, and of their writings." Though the
work, which was reported to have been contained in 120 rolls of
papyrus, has been lost, excerpts from it appear in the books of
later authors.

The ultimate fate of the Alexandrian Library is almost as uncertain as the names of its librarians. At its height it attracted
scholars from all over the Mediterranean world, and there are
many references to it in the works of classical authors. Apparently at least part of the Brucheium was burned in the fighting between the Egyptians and Romans around 43 B.C. After this the library from Pergamum may have been added to that of the Serapeum, since there was a flourishing library in Alexandria as late as
the second century A.D. Its significance declined, however, and
whatever was left was probably burned in 391 A.D. under the or-

ders of the Christian Emperor Theodosius. Tradition has it that
some of the library survived to be destroyed by the Moslem con-
queror Omar in 642 A. D. , but this is discredited. What Omar destroyed may have been a Christian library established on the site
of the Serapeum.

In the two centuries immediately before the Christian era,
libraries were present in most if not all of the major cities of the
Greco-Roman world. Athens had a flourishing book trade, and
copies of almost any known literary work could be purchased there.
The gymnasium or school founded there by the Ptolemies contained
a large library and on the Island of Rhodes a similar institution of
learning was built around a library. Fragments of a catalog of
this library have been found, indicating that the books were arranged by subject. An inscription found on the island of Cos shows
that a library there was built around donations of books and money
from the citizens of the island. Other Greek libraries of note were
located at Corinth and Delphi in Greece, and at Ephesus and Smyr-
na in Asia Minor. In the later Roman conquests, many of these
libraries were destroyed or carried off as spoils of war to Rome.

The Romans took from the countries they conquered many
cultural developments. Not only did they acquire the idea of libraries, but the books themselves were taken from Greece, Asia
Minor and Egypt to fill the shelves of the Roman libraries. In
many cases educated citizens were carried along as slaves to become the scribes, teachers and librarians of Rome. Roman culture was heavily indebted to Greece and Egypt, but in libraries as
in law the Romans improved on their predecessors.

In the second century B. C. , the Roman general Paulus, who
had defeated the Macedonians, brought home a Greek library as his
personal spoils of war, and in the next century, Sulla and Lucullus
did the same. Sulla set up his collection of manuscripts in a special room in his palace, and employed Tyrannion, a friend of Cicero, as his librarian. Lucullus went on from his conquests to become an ardent collector of books, and threw open his library to
all scholars who came to use it. A few years later Julius Caesar
drew up plans for a public library in Rome, patterned after the

great Alexandrian Library, and commissioned Varro, an ardent
book collector, to assemble it. Caesar's library never material-
ized, but it may have provided the plan for the library founded by
Caius Asinius Pollio about 39 B.C. on the Aventine Hill, and including many works from the collections of Sulla and Varro. The
Emperor Augustus, successor to Caesar, founded two public libraries, the Octavian Library and the Palatine Library. Each of
these, like most later Roman libraries, was divided into two sections, one each for Greek and Latin books. Following Augustus,
many of the later emperors founded libraries, either in Rome or
in other cities, so that by the middle of the fourth century, A.D.,
there were no less than twenty-eight public libraries in Rome alone.
Possibly the most famous of the classical Roman libraries was the
Bibliotheca Ulpiana, founded by the Emperor Trajan early in the
second century, A.D. Housed in the Forum of Trajan, this library consisted of two rooms, each 60 by 45 feet, on opposite
sides of a colonnaded court. Busts of important Greek and Latin
authors stood guard over their respective works. In the center of
the court was a huge stone replica of a papyrus scroll, symbolic
perhaps of Trajan's own history of his wars.

The public libraries in Rome approached our modern con-
ception of public libraries in that they were not only publicly owned,
but they were freely used by any citizen who could read, and it was
not uncommon to see both nobleman and slave using them at the
same time. In organization, the Roman libraries were apparently
patterned after those of Greece and Egypt, with the rolls arranged
according to subject or title on shelves or in bins. The average
book was rolled on a wooden core and preserved in a leather
wrapper, or perhaps in an earthen jar, but the more valuable and
more elaborate works were sometimes wrapped around an ivory
center and preserved in bronze cylinders. By the third century,
A.D., Roman libraries began to contain folded or book-form codices. Except in rare cases, books had to be used in the library
or in adjacent reading areas.

There were several grades of library workers in the Roman
libraries and under some emperors there was even an imperial

library administrator who supervised all the public libraries in
Rome.   Each library in turn had its own administrator or procura-
tor who apparently concerned himself with acquisition and administrative duties.   The more direct work with the books was done by
workers of various grades, including many slaves.   Some of them
worked only with Greek books, others with Latin.   Others
were copyists and transcribed additional works, while still others
were translators.   It is interesting to note that some of these library workers were women.

Many private libraries were almost as large and elaborate
as the public libraries.   Cicero had a large book collection of his
own, and Serenius Sammonicus, of the third century, A.D., was
reported to have built up a library of over 60,000 volumes.   Epaphroditus, who lived during the reign of Nero, left a collection of
30,000 manuscripts.   In the ruins of Herculaneum, a city destroyed
in the eruption of Mount Vesuvius in 79 A.D., there has been
found the remains of a large private library.   This collection of
some 1700 rolls was found in a room about twelve feet square with
the walls lined with book cases all the way to the ceiling.   The
rolls were charred and in very bad condition, but careful treatment has made many of them readable.   Apparently this collector
specialized in the works of the Epicurean philosophers, and there
is some evidence that the owner was the philosopher Philodemus.
The collecting of books and the building of private libraries became such a fad among the wealthy noblemen and merchants of
Rome that Seneca is supposed to have said, "Nowadays a library is
considered a necessary ornament with which to adorn a house,
along with hot and cold baths."   The libraries of the wealthier
noblemen had librarians of their own, usually slaves, trained to
keep them in order and to copy works from other sources.

Closely connected with libraries, then as always, was the
book manufacturer and the book seller.   In prosperous times, the
demand for copies of books was so great that the wholesale publishing of certain works became profitable.   An enterprising bookseller would hire a number of scribes, or perhaps purchase slaves
who could write a good hand, and set them to copying the book in

demand. One would read from the text, while ten or twelve
writers would copy, and a trained proofreader stood by to assure
the accuracy of their work.   There were a number of such book
manufacturers in Rome, some of whom were renowned for the
quality of their work.   There was no copyright to prevent anyone
from copying any work, but in many cases prominent authors allowed their works to be copied and sold by only one dealer, thus
making him in effect their publisher.   Adjoining the bookseller's
shops were posts on which lists of books for sale were posted.
On market days public criers were sometimes employed to stand
before the shops and proclaim the volumes for sale.   Some of the
larger bookshops had recital rooms where would-be authors could
read or recite their works to anyone who cared to listen.   If a lis-
tener was captivated enough by the recital to purchase a copy, a
scribe was set to work to produce it.

        The great era of Roman libraries lasted some five hundred
years, but like so many other ancient book collections, those of
Rome were all destroyed sooner or later.   Even while Rome was
still strong and powerful, accidental fires consumed several famous libraries.   In 80 A.D. a catastrophic fire destroyed the Octavian Library along with several temples and theatres.   In 192, the
great Palatine Library was burned, and also the library in the
Temple of Peace.   But the great destruction of Roman libraries
came in the fifth century with the fall of Rome itself.   Waves of
barbarians swept down the Italian peninsula, and virtually all ves-
tiges of the once great civilization were destroyed.   Most of our
knowledge about Roman libraries comes from brief statements
about them in the works of the great Roman writers that were preserved elsewhere, and in the ruins of ancient buildings such as
those in the buried cities of Pompeii and Herculaneum.   Fortunately, the writings of the Latin historians, poets and philosophers
were well known in Greece and Asia Minor, and it was largely in
those places that they survived when Rome itself was ransacked.

        A religious group thought to have been the Essenes main-
tained a monastic-like existence in Palestine roughly from 125
B.C. to 70 A.D., and the remains of a library of their writings

have been discovered. These "Dead Sea Scrolls" found at Qumran
were largely parchment rolls stored in clay jars, although some
were papyrus and at least one was on thin copper. After about
200 A.D. several Christian libraries were formed, including one at
Jerusalem, founded by Bishop Alexander, and one at Alexandria in
Egypt. Clement of Alexandria, writing about this time, quoted
from over 300 authors in his works, indicating that he had a rather
large library at his disposal. Eusebius, writing his history of the
Christian church about 330, used a library at Caesarea, and St.
Jerome used the same collection later. After 325, when the Roman Emperor Constantine recognized the Christian church and
founded the city of Constantinople, the collecting and preserving of
Christian literature proceeded in the churches and monasteries of
the eastern Mediterranean world. Some of them were destroyed
by the Moslems in the seventh century, but Constantinople itself
survived until 1453.

        After the Emperor Constantine transferred his capital to
Constantinople, many libraries of notable size were developed there.
A royal library was begun soon after 325 and within a decade contained over 4000 volumes. By the middle of the next century it
contained over 100,000 volumes, and was at that time probably the
greatest library in the world, but like its Roman counterparts, it
too suffered from a fire in 477 A.D. It was soon rebuilt, and
along with other libraries in the temples and schools of Constantinople, it made that city a cultural center for over a thousand
years. Though the Byzantine culture, as this civilization is called,
was more Greek than Latin, it still preserved copies of many Roman works, and excerpts from others in the many compends and
bibliographies compiled by its scholars. In fact, the great Roman
law code, the Code of Justinian, was really compiled at Constantinople rather than in Rome itself, although it was of course based
on the earlier Roman law.

        The libraries of Constantinople were rivaled in the seventh
and later centuries by the new ones springing up in the Moslem
world that developed to the east and south. The followers of Mo-
hammed esteemed the book second only to the sword, and although

for the majority of the people there was only one book, the Koran,
there were many scholars who translated, studied and preserved
the classical literature of the Greeks and Romans. As early as
689 a library and archival collection was established at Damascus,
then the center of the Moslem empire, and in the next century
there were libraries in most of the Moslem cities from central
Asia to Egypt. Baghdad, for example, had both public and university libraries, with the public one open to all who could read, and
the university library providing copying and translating services
for scholars. By the tenth century the Moslem culture had spread
throughout North Africa and into Sicily and Spain, and for several
centuries there were libraries and universities in an area stretch-
ing from Bokhara, east of the Caspian Sea, to Cordova in Spain.
The Moslem libraries contained books in scores of languages, and
representing hundreds of authors from India to England. Many of
their books, particularly copies of the Koran, were works of art,
beautifully written, decorated and bound. Unfortunately, these libraries too were destined to be destroyed by the fourteenth century. Civil wars, Christian crusaders, and the Asiatic hordes of
Genghiz Khan and Tamerlane all combined to destroy Moslem libraries, and scarcely one in a hundred of their books have survived in even a single copy.

To complete the library picture of the ancient world, we
should note that the Far East, too, had its cultural centers. China
had its schools and libraries long before the Christian era. Earlier Chinese rulers maintained archives of official documents but
the first national library was created about 100 B.C., when an attempt was made to obtain copies of all books in the empire to be
organized, cataloged and made available for government officials
and scholars. Critical bibliographies of Chinese literature were
compiled in the first century B.C., and earlier works were edited
and brought together in collections. When the Chinese capital was
moved about 50 A.D. from one city to another it was said that it
took 2,000 carts to move the books and manuscripts. Early Chinese writings were on bamboo and silk, but paper was invented in
China about 105 A.D., and although wars and revolutions destroyed

many Chinese libraries, a continuous cultural history has survived
for over two thousand years.

Generally speaking, the ancient library was a product of its
civilization. It appeared whenever a people had reached the point
where they had writing materials, a written language, and records
to preserve. It progressed in size, complexity and elaborateness
as civilization itself advanced. Books and libraries were spoils of
war, and centers of learning shifted as the tides of war built new
capitals on ancient ruins - and made ruins out of old capitals.
Whenever a civilization was overthrown by a more primitive people,
books and libraries disappeared and ignorance returned. If our
study of ancient libraries teaches us nothing else, it shows us that
books and libraries always accompany any advanced culture.

Bibliography

Books

Boyd, Clarence E.: Public libraries and literary culture in ancient Rome. Chicago, 1915. 69 p.

Brassington, William S.: A history of the art of bookbinding, with
some account of the books of the ancients. London, 1894.
270 p.

Budge, E. A. Wallis: The literature of the ancient Egyptians.
London, 1914. 272 p.

Bushnell, G. H.: The world's earliest libraries. London, 1931.
58 p.

Clark, J.W.: The care of books; an essay on the development of
libraries and their fittings. Cambridge, England, 1902.
352 p.

Cross, F. M.: The ancient library of Qumran and modern biblical
studies. New York, 1958. 196 p.

Dahl, Svend: History of the book. New York, 1958. 279 p.

Dunlap, Leslie W.: Alexandria: the capital of memory. Emporia,
Kansas, 1963. 25 p.

Fiore, Silvestro: Voices from the clay: a study of Assyro-Baby-
lonian literary culture. Norman, Okla., 1965. 254 p.

Hessel, Alfred: A history of libraries. New Brunswick, N. J.,
1955. 198 p.

Holliday, Carl: The dawn of literature.   New York, 1931. 367 p.

Johnson, E. D. :   A history of libraries in the western world.
New York, 1965. 418 p.

Kenyon, Frederic G. :   Ancient books and modern discoveries.
Chicago, 1927. 83 p.

Kenyon, Frederic G. :   Books and readers in ancient Greece and
Rome.   Oxford, 1932.   136 p.

Kramer, Samuel N. :   From the tablets of Sumer.   Indian Hills,
Colorado, 1956. 293 p.

Laessoe, Jorgen: People of ancient Assyria, their inscriptions
and correspondence.   New York, 1963.   169 p.

Lanciani, Rodolfo: Ancient Rome in the light of recent discoveries.
Boston, 1900.   329 p. (See pp. 178-205 on Roman libraries).

Maspero, Gaston: Life in ancient Egypt and Assyria.   New York,
1912.   376 p. (See pp. 287-302 on "Assurbanipal's Library".)

Myer, Isaac: The oldest books in the world.   New York, 1900.
502 p.

Nichols, C. L. :   The library of Rameses the Great.   Boston, 1909.
43 p. (Reprint, Berkeley, Calif. , 1964.)

Parsons, Edward A. :   The Alexandrian library.   New York, 1952.
468 p.

Pedley, Katharine G. :   The library at Qumran: a librarian looks
at the Dead Sea Scrolls.   Berkeley, Calif. , 1964. 23 p.

Pinner, H. L. :   The world of books in classical antiquity.   Leiden,
Netherlands, 1958. 2nd ed. 64 p.

Putnam, George H. :   Authors and their public in ancient times.
New York, 1894.   326 p.

Richardson, Ernest C. :   Beginnings of libraries.   Princeton,
1914.   176 p. (Reprinted, Hamden, Conn. , 1963.)

Richardson, Ernest C. :   Biblical libraries.   Princeton, 1914.
252 p. (Reprinted, Hamden, Conn. , 1963.)

Richardson, Ernest C. :   Some old Egyptian libraries.   New York,
1911.   93 p. (Reprinted, Berkeley, Calif. , 1964.)

Thompson, James W. :   Ancient libraries.   Chicago, 1939. 120 p.
(Reprinted, Hamden, Conn. , 1962.)

Van Hook, LaRue: Greek life and thought.   New York, 1923.
    329 p.   (See pp. 114-121 on "Greek libraries.")

Periodical Articles
Dunlap, Leslie W.:   "The Library at Nineveh," Stechert-Hafner
    Book News, XV, (1961), 81-83.

Highet, Gilbert: "The wondrous survival of records," Horizon,
    V, (Nov., 1962), 75-94.

Irwin, Raymond: "Callimachus," Library Association Record,
    LVIII, (May, 1956), 168-173.

Kleberg, Tonnes: "Bibliophiles in ancient Rome," Libri, I,
    (1950), 2-12.

Miller, Walter: "Hadrian's library and gymnasium," Art and
    Archaeology, XXXIII, (1932), 89-91.

Rau, R.V.:   "Did Omar destroy the Alexandrian Library?" Nine-
    teenth Century, XXXVI, (1894), 555-571.

Reichman, Felix: "The book trade at the time of the Roman Em-
    pire," Library Quarterly, VII, (1938), 40-76.

Root, Robert K.:   "Publication before printing," Publications of
    the Modern Language Association, XXVIII, (1913), 417-431.

Sperry, John A.:   "Egyptian libraries: a survey of the evidence,"
    Libri, VII, (1957), 45-55.

Weitemeyer, Mogens: "Archive and library technique in ancient
    Mesopotamia," Libri, VI, (1956), 217-238.

Witty, Francis J.:   "The Pinakes of Callimachus," Library Quar-
    terly, XXVIII, (1958), 132-136.

Wyss, Wilhelm V.:   "The libraries of antiquity," Living Age,
    CCCXVI, (1923), 217-249.

IV

Books and Libraries in the Middle Ages

After the fall of Rome in the fifth century, Europe entered almost a thousand years of the Dark Ages, and the cultural progress that Rome had made largely disappeared. True, in Greece, southern Italy, Sicily and Spain the nearness of, or actual control by, Byzantine and Moslem cultures provided a stimulus that kept libraries and learning alive, but for the great majority of Europe the denomination of the era as "dark ages" is correct. The classical libraries created by the Romans were destroyed or were allowed to decay, so that only a few copies remained of the thousands of manuscripts that had made Rome a center of learning. Not until the modern era would there again be libraries in most of Europe to compare with those of imperial Rome, and not until the Renaissance would there be very much added to the secular literature that Greece and Rome had left to posterity. Even before 500 papyrus had given way to vellum and parchment as writing materials, and the roll had been replaced by the codex, which became the major book form of the Middle Ages. From then until the coming of printing, there was no change made in the laborious process of writing and binding books by hand, although it must be admitted that this hand-making of books became an art. In illustrating or illuminating and in binding, the best medieval manuscript books equal or surpass anything produced today.

In the midst of the Dark Ages, there were several forces at work, though not always together, to preserve something of the culture of Rome and Greece, and to keep alive the learning of that advanced age. The institution usually credited with preserving books and learning during the Middle Ages is the monastery, and undoubtedly it did play a major role. Private book collectors also took part in preserving the classics, especially the secular ones. These private book collectors were wealthy merchants or noblemen,

particularly of Venice, Genoa, Marseilles and the other Mediterranean cities.   Many of them collected manuscripts for show and
prestige but, whatever their motives, they did acquire, preserve
and have copied many notable works.   After the eleventh century,
the medieval university took its place as an active participant in
collecting, editing and copying the earlier authors.   As already
mentioned, the Moslem world from Asia to Spain did its share in
preserving the writings of the classic era, as did also the Byzantine civilization around Constantinople.   Occasional enlightened
rulers, the Charlemagnes and Alfreds, whose reigns stand out like
beacons in an otherwise gloomy era, also aided in the preservation
of knowledge.

The monastery had its beginnings in the eastern Mediterranean area and in North Africa long before the fall of Rome.   In addition to the Essenes other Jewish and early Christian groups
found that religious worship could best be carried on in a relatively isolated community.   During the second century, A.D., monks
of the Coptic Christian sects were forming monasteries in Egypt
and manuscript collections of the early Christian writings formed
their libraries.   Several other Christian monasteries were formed
in the area from Egypt to Greece before the fourth century.   But
the significant movement in European monastic history began in
Italy in the sixth century.   One of the most important of these early Italian monasteries was that at Monte Cassino, founded in 529
by St. Benedict.   Just when a library was first established at
Monte Cassino is not known, but St. Benedict's rules of monastic
life included regular reading, especially at meals and during the
evenings, so books must have been available.   Cassiodorus, a
noble who had served with the ruler, Theodoric the Goth, retired
from his office in 554 to live as a monk on his estate in Calabria
in southern Italy.   Here at Vivarium, as he called his combination
of monastery, scriptorium and theological school, he began a library with his own collection of manuscripts and spent the remainder of his long life in promoting learning.   He continued to collect
manuscripts, both religious and secular, and trained monks in the
art of copying them.   Among his other works was a lengthy History

of the Goths. Another was a handbook of monastery rules and
regulations which included a section on the use of the monastery library. It also included a bibliography of literature available at
that time, and this may have been a catalog of the library at Vivarium.

Oddly enough, the spread of monasteries into the remainder
of Europe came not so much from southern Italy as from Ireland.
That island had been converted to Christianity in the fifth century,
and by the end of the sixth it was the cultural center of northern
Europe, with many flourishing monasteries and schools. Mission-
aries from Ireland established monasteries in England, France and
even in northern Italy. Among these monasteries were Lindisfarne
in England, Luxeuil and Corbie in France, St. Gall in Switzerland,
and Bobbio in northern Italy. Libraries were founded in each of
these institutions very early in its history, and by the seventh century they were cultural centers of their respective areas. Books
for these early monastic libraries were obtained from Ireland or
from the older religious libraries in southern Italy. The monks
who obtained or copied them often made long and dangerous trips
just to secure a needed text or even to compare one copy with another.

The spread of the monasteries, and hence of monastic libraries, was greatly encouraged by the establishment of the various orders of monks. The Benedictine order, one of the earliest,
was particularly interested in books and learning and each of their
branch monasteries was required to have a library. The Augustin-
ians and the Dominicans were also great lovers of books, and their
libraries ranked second only to those of the Benedictines. The libraries of the Cistercians were designed wholly to assist in their
religious studies, and contained almost no secular literature, but
those of the Carthusians were more worldly and as much as a
third of their works might treat of non-religious subjects. Even
the Franciscans, who disavowed most worldly goods, made an exception of books and their monasteries developed libraries equal to
those of other orders.

Whatever its order, the monastery usually included special

quarters for its library and scriptorium. The latter was a work-
room, where books were copied, illuminated and bound. In some
cases a group of writers or "scriptores" sat or stood at sloping
desks and copied, hour after hour, as another monk read to them.
More often, the copyist was his own reader, and only one copy
could be made at a time. A copyist would sometimes spend months,
or even a year, in copying one volume. After the text was copied,
the pages might go to an artist-monk who would illuminate or illus-
trate them with ornamental drawings for initial capital letters, and
along the borders. If these illuminations were in red, as they often were, they were termed "rubrications" and the artist was a
"rubricator." Other colors, including gold and silver were used in
more ornate works and sometimes the parchment or vellum itself
was tinted. The art of book illumination reached a high level during the later middle ages but many of the earlier works were also
noted for their beauty. The Lindisfarne Gospels, produced at the
monastery of Lindisfarne in north England about 700 A.D., survives
in the British Museum as an example of this era. Even more beautiful is the Book of Kells, a copy of the four Gospels made in an
Irish monastery about 800 A.D. This has been called one of the
most beautiful books ever produced. The bindings of the books produced in the monasteries also reached near perfection. They were
made of fine leathers and textiles, sometimes even of gold or silver.
Precious stones were sometimes set in bindings or into the metal
clasps that held the heavier books together. For larger books, the
covers were sometimes made of wood, covered with leather or
cloth. The leather bindings were ornamented with fancy toolings,
either "blind" as the plain toolings were called, or with colors or
gold foil pressed into the embossings. More valuable books were
sometimes chained to the tables or lecterns upon which they lay, or
fastened to shelves with chains long enough to reach a nearby desk
or table.

In the early Middle Ages, the books in the monastery libraries were still kept in chests rather than upon shelves. The chest
was known as an armarium, and thus the early monastic librarian
was known as an "armarius." The term "librarius" was also used,

and whatever he was called the librarian often directed the scriptorium and the book bindery as well as the library proper. In later periods, and in some monasteries, the position of librarian was combined with that of "precentor" or director of singing.

Catalogs of the monastic book collections were usually little more than accession lists. Some of them have survived, and from them we can tell a little about the contents of the average medieval library. The books of the Bible, usually in St. Jerome's translation into Latin, were always present, often in multiple copies. Next in importance came the commentaries on the Bible and the lives of the saints. The early Christian writings were usually present, with St. Augustine being a favorite. His City of God was probably the most popular single work other than the Bible. Secular works were usually kept separate from the works on theology but there were generally very few of them. Among these there would usually be works on philosophy, science and medicine, with even a few books on magic. Only a few of the classic authors were ordinarily present and these often varied widely from monastery to monastery. Cicero and Seneca were popular, along with Virgil and Horace and the Latin historians Sallust and Suetonius. In the later medieval period, the works of Ovid and Juvenal became more popular and Greek writers, particularly Aristotle became better known, at least in Latin translation. The Latin secular writers were studied by the monks in order to gain greater facility in reading Latin and thus to be able to read the religious works in that language more readily. Each monastery usually contained some works on local history and some writings of local authors but, for the most part, the monastery library in England was apt to be very similar to that in France or Italy. Sometimes secular works were preserved unintentionally when the parchment on which they were written was washed or erased, and a religious work written over it. The original writing would not be completely obliterated and could later be read after special treatment. Such accidentally preserved manuscripts are called palimpsests.

The usual method of acquisition for monastery libraries was by copying. A manuscript could sometimes be borrowed for copying, and on other occasions a monk would be sent from one monastery to another to copy literary treasures. Sometimes such trips would take a monk from Ireland to Spain, or from Poland to Italy, just to obtain a copy of a needed work. Copies of the more popular works could be bought, and generous friends sometimes donated books from their own libraries. Bequests of books on the death of noblemen, merchants and church officials often increased the size of monastic libraries. Sometimes these gifts were substantial and consisted of whole private libraries, but often they consisted of only one or two books. As monastery collections grew larger, methods had to be devised for arranging and separating the books. Separation by language, or into religious and secular groupings, or by size of volume were methods employed at various times and places, and later there were attempts to arrange books by major subjects. Occasionally collections were arranged solely by acquisition, thus keeping gift books together. Whatever the arrangement, the only "catalog" was a list of books, sometimes by author, sometimes by title or first line, and usually not even alphabetical. Ordinarily the books in the library were available only to the monks or their students, but there are accounts of "inter-library loans" between monasteries, and of borrowings of books by important personages. In the latter case, a sum of money or a book of like value might be left as deposit for the volume borrowed. In the early Middle Ages, when books were few, works were assigned to the monks for reading and almost the entire collection would often be in use. As collections grew in later centuries, the books often came to be divided into two groups, those that were chained and had to be used in one place, and those that could be taken to rooms or other points within the monastery for reading. The latter were usually duplicates or less valuable books.

In the midst of the Dark Ages, the reign of the Frankish emperor, Charlemagne (742-814), stands out as far as books and learning is concerned. Charlemagne himself was something of a scholar, and he felt a need to improve and spread learning in order to hold his large and sprawling empire together. He gathered a personal library of note but he is mainly remembered for the palace

library which he directed to be collected, not only from his realm
but from other lands. Important works in Italy and Spain were
copied for Charlemagne's library, and at least one volume came
from the imperial library at Constantinople. Once the books were
gathered, scholars were put to work collating and comparing texts
to test their authenticity and to remove interpolations added by
over-enthusiastic copyists. The style of writing was improved during this period and a new script, usually termed the Carolingian
minuscule, was developed for use by the court scribes. This
script proved so popular that it remained in use for several hundred years. The word "Carolingian" came from the Latin form of
the Emperor's name, while "minuscule" identified the script as being in small letters rather than the "majuscule" or capital letters
in general use since the days of the Romans. Libraries and learning went through a premature renaissance in the days of Charlemagne, and scholars from Greece to Britain visited his capital at
Aachen to use the palace library there.

Among the scholars attracted to Charlemagne's court was
the distinguished English monk, Alcuin (735-804). Alcuin had developed the monastery library at York, England, into one of the
best libraries in Europe, and had become renowned as a religious
leader and teacher. Charlemagne first called on Alcuin to direct a
school which had grown up around his court. This school seems to
have been something of an informal college for the training of officials and nobles, but it also attracted lay scholars and religious
leaders. Upon the success of this educational venture, Charlemagne encouraged the establishment of similar schools throughout
his realm, which then included most of western Europe. Alcuin
advised that if a library and scriptorium were established at any
given place a school would naturally grow up around it. Later Alcuin became the abbot at St. Martin of Tours, and there he established a model library for a religious institution. He made his
church library something of a source collection, where authorized
texts of the Bible and other religious works were kept for copying by
anyone who could visit or pay for a copyist. Charlemagne and Alcuin
stand out in the field of library history but, like others before them,

their efforts did not long survive. Charlemagne's grandson, Charles
the Bald, preserved the palace library, and even added to it. After his death the feudal wars and Viking invasions that swept much
of western Europe destroyed most of the schools and libraries that
Charlemagne had begun.

In the eleventh and twelfth centuries the monasteries of Germany and central Europe, especially those at Fulda, Corvey, St.
Gall and Regensburg, were active in building and preserving libraries. In these institutions, which were generally schools as well
as monasteries, the position of "librarius" became established as
the custodian of the books. It was the duty of this official to arrange the books, to see that sufficient copies of the more important
texts were available, to keep records of use, and in general to
carry out the usual functions of a librarian. The library cooper-
ated closely with the scriptorium, and books borrowed from other
monasteries could be copied for the collection. One of these eleventh century monastery librarians has left us a list of his sixty-
four readers and their reading for one Lenten season. Needless to
say, most of the works read were religious. Twenty-two monks
chose works of the early Christian writers, such as St. Jerome and
St. Augustine. Twelve chose commentaries on the Bible written by
medieval scholars, while eleven more took works on monastic life
and discipline. Nineteen were reading works of church history,
such as those of Bede, Orosius and Eusebius, or other theological
works. Only one individual was reading a secular writer, and he
was perusing the works of the Roman historian, Livy.

Closely akin to the monastery library was the cathedral library which developed largely after the eleventh century. Since the
cathedral was the seat of a bishop and a religious center, it was
often connected with a theological school and its library was for the
use of students as well as for the church officials. The cathedral
library at Canterbury in England is said to have had more than
3000 volumes in the twelfth century, which would have been fairly
large for its time. Most of the medieval monastery and cathedral
libraries of which records have survived numbered their literary
treasures in the hundreds rather than the thousands. The monas-

tery library at St. Gall in Switzerland had only 300 volumes in the ninth century, while that at Reichenau in Germany had only 413. The famous Benedictine monastery at Bobbio in northern Italy possessed only 650 books three centuries after its founding, and in the twelfth century that at Cluny in France had only 570. Of course, it must be remembered that these bound volumes contained ten or twenty times as much written matter as the classic papyrus roll and this must be kept in mind in comparing the size of the medieval library with those of the ancients.

In considering the intellectual history of medieval Europe, the Moslem civilization in Spain and Portugal should not be ignored. Following the conquest of that peninsula by the Moslems in the eighth century, a highly developed civilization emerged, and cities such as Toledo, Seville and Cordova became centers of learning. The University of Cordova in the tenth century was one of the three great Moslem universities, and there were lesser colleges at several other Spanish cities. No less than seventy important libraries were reported in Spain during the tenth to twelfth centuries, many of them filled with rare and beautiful books. Book collectors, both official and private, obtained their literary treasures from as far away as India and England. The technique of paper-making entered western Europe through Spain as did also the ornate Morocco leather book bindings. The Spanish Moslems were not only collectors of books, they were writers as well, and they produced many of the important medieval works in science and philosophy. By the late twelfth century, however, Moslem civilization in Spain was on the decline and there were political and religious leaders who ordered that books be destroyed and who banned writing contrary to the prevailing religious beliefs. Later on the wars between the Christians and Moslems in Spain destroyed still more books and libraries. By the sixteenth century, when King Philip II was gathering materials for a royal library, he found that the only source for books on the Moslem history of Spain was North Africa, because all Arabic books in Spain had been destroyed.

From the fall of Rome to the twelfth century, education in western Europe was mostly in the hands of the monasteries. Ca-

thedral schools developed after the tenth century, but their emphasis was largely on religious education.   Even in the monasteries
most of the instruction beyond the elementary years was theological, but it was usual for the monks to give the rudiments of school-
ing to the sons of neighboring noblemen, and sometimes to promis-
ing children of poorer parents.   Some of the monastic orders encouraged education particularly.   During the reigns of some enlightened monarchs there were brief periods of educational progress.   In the later middle ages, schools for the training of clerks
for the growing business firms were founded in some of the cities;
but reading, writing and arithmetic were about the extent of their
studies.   Whatever the type of school, lessons were memorized
and recited by rote; independent thought or reading outside the prescribed texts was not encouraged.   The quality of teaching was usually poor, and the few great teacher-scholars, such as Peter Abe-
lard (1079-1142) in Paris, and John of Salisbury (d. 1180) at Canterbury, stand out far beyond their fellows.   By the late eleventh century a few of the schools were reaching into higher education, and
in Paris degrees of bachelor of arts were being given at the com-
pletion of a prescribed series of studies.

    The development of the medieval universities, in the twelfth
century and later, changed this pattern and raised the level of
learning in western Europe to a point where the Renaissance could
begin.   The earliest universities of note were those in northern
Italy at Bologna and Padua, and these grew largely out of informal
groups of students who hired learned men to teach them.   Law,
both civil and religious, and medicine were subjects that were much
in demand and competent teachers were scarce.   When a group of
teachers, each teaching a different subject, met with their students
with some regularity in one location a "university" was born.   Later
on, the power to grant degrees was obtained from civil or religious
authorities or both, and a more formal course of studies was required.   Generally speaking, however, the medieval university student usually studied under one teacher until he felt that he had
learned all he could from that source, and then went on to another.
Before a degree could be received, however, an examination before

a group of the masters or teachers had to be passed. The university idea spread throughout all of Europe, and by 1500 there were
some fifty or sixty of them, scattered from Spain to Scandinavia
and from England to Poland.

In these early universities there were no libraries as such
at first, in fact there were no campuses or stately buildings such
as are usually associated with universities. Each master had a
collection of books which he might lend or rent to his students.
Each student, in turn, had to buy not only his own textbooks, but
also any other book he might wish to read, unless he could borrow
or rent it from a master or bookseller. Only the most wealthy of
students could afford to own all the texts he might wish to study so
the book rental trade was brisk. Usually the university authorities
controlled the book trade in order to guarantee the authenticity of
the texts and the booksellers or "stationarii" were licensed by them
as were the dealers in parchment and other writing materials.

As the universities grew in size, they usually came to be divided into colleges, and it was in these colleges that the earliest
academic libraries were founded. It became usual for each college
to provide books for its students, and wealthy alumni often donated
books to the collections. At the collection of colleges that came to
be known as the University of Paris, the library of the Sorbonne
College was an early outstanding one. By 1322 the Sorbonne Library had over a thousand volumes, and by 1400 it had established
a circulating collection which could be taken from the library by the
students after the payment of a deposit. By 1480, this library was
housed in a separate building, with a main reading room twelve by
forty feet. A set of rules for the use of the Sorbonne Library has
been preserved. Some of them may sound odd today, but many of
them are still familiar. A few of these rules (adapted from Nathan
Schachner: The Medieval Universities, p. 329) were: No student
could enter the library unless wearing cap and gown. Each student
had a key to the library and no one else could enter the library except with a member. It was forbidden to write on the books, or
tear out leaves. As far as possible, silence was to reign in the
library. Books containing condemned doctrines could be read only

by professors of theology and then only when necessary.

The university library was similar in organization to the monastery library, except that its books were kept in divisions according to the subjects taught in colleges or faculties. At first there were no sub-classes within these groups. Books were arranged according to size and accession. In handling the books, the change from chests to lecterns and bookshelves was gradual but by the end of the middle ages, as books became more common and more widely used, shelves were in general use. Subject catalogs were of course unknown, but book lists, similar to those in the monastery libraries, were maintained and a number of these have survived down to the present. In the Sorbonne Library, and probably in others, the different faculties were distinguished by colors, and each book was marked with the color of its appropriate faculty. Sometimes additional letters or numbers were employed to indicate the shelf or section where a book was shelved. Interestingly enough, there was an attempt at a "union catalog" in fourteenth century England. Some unknown librarian, possibly a Franciscan monk in London, compiled a Registrum Librorum Angliae, which was an attempt to list all of the known copies of the works of some ninety authors and the libraries in which they could be located. Some years later the list was extended by another scholar to include the works of about 600 writers located in 180 different libraries. This work contained not only authors, titles and locations, but a short biographical account of the author as well. This is a treasure of English bibliography prior to 1400.

In addition to the early universities at Paris and in Italy, other notable ones with important libraries were those at Cracow (1364), Prague (1366), Heidelberg (1386), Oxford (1412), and Cambridge (1425). The dates given are those in which general libraries are known to have been functioning and are not necessarily those of the founding of the universities. Both Oxford and Cambridge had college libraries functioning long before the general university libraries appeared. University College at Oxford, for example, claims to have had a library as early as 1280. Richard de Bury, Bishop of Durham, planned to leave his library to Dur-

ham College, Oxford, but unfortunately his death resulted in the
scattering of most of his books. De Bury was a leading religious
figure of his day, and an ardent book collector. He collected
books through dealers in London and in Europe, through his
trips to the continent, and through gifts of his many friends and
co-workers. His account of why and how he collected books is
told in his work entitled Philobiblon, or, The Love of Books,
written about 1345. Thomas Cobham, the Bishop of Worcester,
planned a general library for Cambridge University as early as
1327, but it was nearly a century later before one was effectively functioning there. Among other notable English libraries of the
fifteenth century was the Guildhall Library, founded in London
about 1425. This library resulted from a bequest of the Lord
Mayor Richard Whittington and was a public collection open to all
serious students.

As the Middle Ages progressed and declined, a number of
important private libraries were developed in various parts of Europe. Notable among them were those of the Italian authors Petrarch and Boccaccio and of several members of the Medici family.
Petrarch (1304-1374) began collecting books as a boy, and covered
much of Europe in his search for manuscripts in his later life. He
is particularly noted for his part in rescuing and preserving some
of the works of Cicero and Virgil and for donating much of his library to the city of Venice. Poggio Bracciolini (1380-1459) was another noted Italian book collector who learned Greek and visited
Constantinople in order to enrich his library. Cosimo de Medici
(1389-1464) founded several libraries during his lifetime, including
the noted one at San Marco, to which he gave 400 books. Many
of his books came from the library of Nicolo Niccoli (1364-1423),
who had spent a lifetime collecting rare books, and whose treasures
included many unique volumes. Federigo, Duke of Urbino, founded
the famous Urbino Library of Greek and Latin classics in the fifteenth century, largely with gifts from his own private collection.
For both the Medicis and Duke Federigo, Vespasiano de Bisticci
(1421-1498) served as book agent and collector. Vespasiano was
something of a scholar and editor as well as an international book

dealer, and he kept a staff of writers busy making copies of important works which he found in his travels throughout Europe.

In Hungary, King Matthias Corvinus who ruled from 1458 to 1490, collected a remarkable library for his time and area. It was reported to contain 50,000 separate items. Although this is probably an exaggeration, there is no doubt that he did amass a sizable library. He maintained groups of copyists, illuminators and binders in both Buda, his capital, and in Florence, in order to provide for his collection the finest copies of the most authentic works available. Although most of his books were destroyed by the Turks when they invaded Hungary in 1526, some 125 volumes have survived. Charles V of France (1337-1380) collected a library which was housed in the Chateau du Louvre in Paris, and which was administered by a full time librarian. Another French ruler, Philip the Good, Duke of Burgundy (1396-1467) was also a noted collector. He founded libraries at Dijon, Paris, Bruges and Antwerp. His stated goal was to acquire the largest and finest library in the world and to that end he employed a regular staff of copyists, illuminators and translators.

Many private collectors donated their libraries to university or public libraries. Robert de Sorbonne, in 1250, gave his library to the college that took his name in Paris, and Humphrey, Duke of Gloucester, gave his library to Oxford University early in the fifteenth century. His contemporary, William Gray, Bishop of Ely, made a collection of Greek and Latin classics and later donated them to Balliol College, also at Oxford. Many of these libraries, whether private, university or church, were later destroyed or scattered in political and religious wars. Neglect and abuse added to the toll, so that today in most cases only a few volumes survive from what were once large and magnificent libraries.

One library of the Middle Ages that deserves special notice was the Library of the Popes in the Vatican at Rome. Tradition has it that the early popes had begun a Vatican library even before the end of the Roman empire, but the history of these early papal collections is obscure. We know that there was a papal library from the sixth century on, and that particularly under Pope Za-

charias (741-752) it received important accessions from the earlier
monastery libraries.   Because of the struggles within the Church
in the thirteenth and fourteenth centuries few if any of the original
volumes were preserved.   A new Vatican Library was begun in the
early fifteenth century, and this library grew into importance under
the direction of Pope Nicholas V (1447-1455) who had been a book
collector of note before becoming Pope.   Nicholas added his own
volumes, particularly of Greek classics which he had translated into Latin.   At his death the collection contained some 1200 volumes
and it was further increased by Pope Sixtus IV (1471-1484) to about
3500 volumes.   About this time the collection was divided into a
main library for the use of monks and scholars and a smaller private library for the Pope.   The papal library served as the central
library of the Roman Catholic Church and as such it preserved the
most authoritative texts of all the major Christian writings.   Copies
of religious works were made continuously for distribution to
churches and monasteries throughout the Catholic world, and duplicates were kept for loan or deposit in other church libraries.
Though the Vatican library never reached great size before the
modern era, the high quality and value of its holdings made it one
of the most important libraries in the world.

        A significant adjunct of the medieval library was the com-
mercial book maker and bookseller.   Although the majority of books
were in the hands of religious or official libraries, there were private book collectors and there was business to be carried on in
providing books for libraries, schools and scholars, particularly
after the tenth century.   The professional copyists, the book publishers of their day, might not rival the monks in the accuracy or
artistic perfection of their works, but they could compete in school
texts.   Also, the private book makers produced most of the secular
literature of the day--even though there was comparatively little of
it.   The copyist usually flourished in the towns, and by the later
middle ages he could be found, usually along with book-binders and
illuminators, in organized guilds or companies.   In London, for instance, there were, by 1400, separate and powerful guilds for the
text-writers or copyists, for the limners or illuminators, and for

the binders.   The bookseller, on the other hand, was often a lone
hand, although he might have agents in other cities.   Usually he
could be found in the larger towns, or around universities and monasteries, and he often added to his income by renting books to students who culd not afford to buy their own texts.   In 1323, there
were no less than 28 booksellers in the vicinity of the University
of Paris, some of them offering as many as 125 texts for rent.
On a higher level, commercially speaking, were the international
book dealers, sometimes really smugglers, who could obtain for a
Paris or London customer a rare text from Constantinople or Cordova and who handled books and manuscripts in the same manner
that they would costly fabrics or works of art.   Some of these book
men, for example, Vespasiano, were scholars and by securing the
texts of the classics from the East and making them available in
Western Europe they contributed substantially to the beginning of
the Renaissance.

Even ordinary books were luxuries in the early Middle Ages.
It has been estimated that in current values, an average volume as
late as the twelfth century would have sold for about two hundred
dollars.   Many relatively wealthy and scholarly people acquired only a few books in a life time and wills have been preserved that
mention ten or twenty books as a valuable bequest.   A tenth century
sale of a single book of sermons brought a price of 200 sheep and
three barrels of grain, while a complete Bible was traded for a
house and lot.   In the fourteenth century, a two volume Missal was
sold for 200 gold francs and a century earlier another was traded
for an extensive vineyard.   It should be pointed out that these were
probably extra-illuminated and ornately bound works, but the fact
remains that almost any book was expensive.   Also, one element in
the value of medieval manuscript works was the degree of accuracy
of its contents.   A book that had been carefully collated with more
than one other copy or one whose authenticity had been certified by
a reputable scholar, was obviously of greater value since it could
be used as a master work from which other copies could be made.

Despite the scarcity of books and the smallness of libraries,
the cultural centers of the Middle Ages did bridge the gap between

the ancient and the modern worlds. Whether in monastery or cathedral, university or bookshop, a representative proportion of the classics were preserved despite the ravages of wars and time. There is much that we do not know about Rome and Greece - and about medieval Europe - but we would know much less if it were not for the influence of medieval libraries in preserving books. The art of communication through the written word declined considerably after the fall of Rome, but it was never completely lost. The western world owes an eternal debt of gratitude to the scholarly monks, the princely book collectors, and the industrious copyists who preserved the records of the past.

Bibliography

Books

Addison, Julia D.: Arts and crafts in the Middle Ages. Philadelphia, 1908. 398 p. (See pp. 326-364 on books and manuscripts.)

Beddie, J.S.: Libraries in the twelfth century; their catalogs and contents. Boston, 1929. 23 p.

Brassington, William S.: A history of the art of bookbinding with some account of the books of the ancients. London, 1894. 270 p.

Cassiodorus Senator: An introduction to divine and human reading. New York, 1946. 283 p.

Clark, J.W.: The care of books. Cambridge, England, 1902. 352 p.

Clark, J.W.: Libraries in the medieval and renaissance periods. Cambridge, England, 1894. 61 p.

DeBury, Richard: Philobiblion, or, The love of books. London, 1925. 148 p. (Originally published 1473; many other editions.)

Diringer, David: The hand produced book. New York, 1953. 603 p.

Duckett, Eleanor Shipley: Alcuin, friend of Charlemagne. New York, 1951. 337 p.

Dunleavy, Gareth W.: Colum's other island: the Irish at Lindisfarne. Madison, Wisc., 1960. 149 p.

Guppy, Henry: Stepping stones to the art of typography. London,
    1928. 45 p.

Herbert, John A.: Illuminated manuscripts. London, 1912. 135 p.

Hessel, Alfred: A history of libraries. New Brunswick, N.J.,
    1955. 198 p. (See pp. 9-37).

Holzknecht, Karl J.: Literary patronage in the Middle Ages.
    Philadelphia, 1923. 258 p.

Humphreys, K.W.: Book provisions of the medieval Friars. Am-
    sterdam, 1964. 150 p.

Johnston, Edward: Writing and illuminating and lettering. New
    York, 1939. 500 p.

Ker, Neil R., ed.: Medieval libraries of Great Britain: a list of
    surviving books. London, 1964. 2nd ed. 424 p.

Kibre, Pearl: The intellectual interests reflected in libraries of
    the 14th and 15th centuries. New York, 1946. 40 p.

Kibre, Pearl: The library of Pico della Mirandola. New York,
    1936. 330 p.

Laurie, S.S.: The rise and early constitution of the universities.
    New York, 1891. 293 p.

Madan, Falconer: Books in manuscript. London, 1920. 208 p.

Merryweather, Frederick: Bibliomania in the Middle Ages. New
    York, 1900. 322 p.

Middleton, J.H.: Illuminated manuscripts in classical and medie-
    val times. Cambridge, England, 1892. 270 p.

Mitchell, Sabrina: Medieval manuscript painting. New York,
    1965. 212 p.

Norris, D.M.: A history of cataloging and cataloging methods,
    1100-1850. London, 1939. 256 p.

Ogilvy, J.D.A.: Books known to Anglo-Latin writers from Ald-
    helm to Alcuin, 670-804. Cambridge, Mass., 1936. 108 p.

Orcutt, W.D.: In quest of the perfect book. Boston, 1926. (See
    especially pp. 109-150.)

Putnam, G.H.: Books and their makers during the Middle Ages.
    London, 1896. 2 v. (Reprint New York, 1964.)

Savage, Ernest A. :   Old English libraries; the making, collecting
    and use of books during the Middle Ages.   London, 1911.
    298 p.

Savage, Ernest A. :   The story of libraries and book-collecting.
    New York, n. d.   230 p.

Schachner, Nathan: The medieval university.   New York, 1938.
    388 p.

Taylor, Archer: Renaissance guides to books.   Berkeley, Calif.,
    1925.   130 p.

Thompson, J.W. :   The medieval library.   Chicago, 1939.   694 p.
    (Reprinted, New York, 1957.   702 p.)

Thornton, J. L. :   Chronology of librarianship.   London, 1941.
    266 p.

Weitenkampf, Frank: The illustrated book.   Cambridge, England,
    1938.   264 p.

Periodical Articles

Beddie, J. S. :   "Ancient classics in the medieval libraries," Specu-
    lum,   V,   (1930),   3-20.

Connolly, Brendan: "Jesuit library beginnings,"   Library Quarterly,
    XXX,   (1960),   243-252.

Garrod, H. W. :   "The library regulations of a medieval college,"
    The Library,   VII,   (1927),   312-335.

Buksh, S. K. :   "The Islamic libraries," Nineteenth Century, LII,
    (1902),   125-139.

Koch, Theodore W. :   "New light on old libraries,"   Library Quar-
    terly,   IV,   1934.   244-252.

Laistner, M. L.W. :   "The library of the Venerable Bede," in his
    Intellectual heritage of the early middle ages.   Ithaca,
    N. Y. ,   1957,   pp.   117-149.

Mackensen, Ruth S. :   "Four great libraries of medieval Baghdad,"
    Library Quarterly,   II,   (1932),   279-299.

Schutz, Geza: "Bibliotheca Corvina," Library Quarterly,   IV,
    (1934),   552-563.

Winger, Howard W. :   "Regulations relating to the book trade in
    London from 1357 to 1586,"   Library Quarterly, XXVI,
    (1956),   157-195.

V
Early Printing

The fifteenth century saw the coming of the second most important event in the history of books and libraries. The first, of course, was the development of writing; the second, the development of printing. Ordinarily we say that Johann Gutenberg invented printing around 1450 in Mainz, Germany. However, there is much more to the story than that; there were others involved besides Gutenberg, and we should say "printing from movable type" in order to be reasonably accurate about the date. Actually, if we define printing in its simplest form as making an impression of intelligible characters by one object upon another, then printing began long before the Christian era. The Babylonians and Egyptians used metal or wooden seals for impressing pictures and pictographs upon clay or wax. The Babylonians even used a seal-cylinder, by means of which an entire paragraph could be rolled out on a clay tablet with one turn of the embossed cylinder. The Chinese used similar seals for centuries, and by the fifth century after Christ they were using inked seals for printing on paper, rather than the plain seals for making impressions on clay or wax. These inked seals were made of wood and hence produced a primitive form of woodcut. A variation of this came from stone inscriptions, from which paper copies could be made by rubbings. In 770 A. D. , the Empress Shotoku of Japan ordered the distribution of a million Buddhist charms, produced by "printing" from a wood-cut. These charms were on paper eighteen inches long by two inches wide, containing about 150 characters, and they were designed to be placed in shrines throughout the country. Since the date of this Japanese charm is fairly well authenticated, it is certainly one of our earliest known examples of printing.

Wood-cut printing continued to develop in China in the eighth and ninth centuries until it reached a rather high degree of perfec-

tion.   Carefully carved wooden blocks could contain an illustration
and a half page or more of Chinese characters, so that the appearance of a modern page could be achieved.   Several pages, side by
side on a long sheet of paper could produce a printed "book" or
roll.   The earliest known book printed in this manner is the "Diamond Sutra," printed in 868.   A sutra was a Buddhist holy book,
and this particular one was printed on a roll sixteen feet long and
one foot wide.   It was carefully and neatly done, indicating that
such printing was an accomplished art by that time.

The Chinese not only originated block printing, but also an
early form of printing from movable type.   Since the Chinese written language was based on a phonetic syllabary rather than on an
alphabet, one piece of type could be used to print a whole word.
Experiments with individual pieces of type for each character, with
the type made of baked clay, were made as early as the eleventh
century.   These types were locked together in a metal form, inked
and pressed upon the paper much in the manner of modern printing.
Fonts of the clay type were kept on hand, but unusual and little
used characters could be carved and baked relatively quickly as
needed.   Some two centuries later the Chinese printers were trying
movable types made of tin or wood, but printing from wood blocks
remained the usual form of duplicating written materials in China
and movable type did not gain acceptance until much later.   The
Chinese were able to do a remarkable amount of printing by means
of wooden blocks, including many-volumed encyclopedias and sets of
reference works.   They also printed paper money in millions of
copies, especially from the ninth to the thirteenth centuries.   Korea
borrowed printing from the Chinese and by the fifteenth century,
still long before Gutenberg, the Koreans were printing hundreds of
copies of books from movable metal type.   But the Koreans, like
the Chinese, used type slugs containing a whole word rather than a
single letter, so they fell short of the workable system later developed in Europe, and printing in Korea fell into disuse in the same
century that saw it rise.   There are surviving examples of printing
from movable types in China and Japan in the sixteenth and seventeenth centuries, but most printing in those countries continued to

be done from wood-blocks until European presses and printing methods were introduced in the nineteenth century.

The knowledge of wood-block printing spread gradually westward from China, first to Mongolia and central Asia, then to Persia, and finally to the Moslem countries at least as far west as Egypt.   Paper money was printed in Persia in 1294, and scraps of printed materials found in Egypt may date from an even earlier period.   It is uncertain whether block printing eventually reached Europe from Asian sources or whether the Europeans developed the art independently but it is known that the art was practiced in Europe by the fourteenth century.   One interesting product for which block printing was employed was playing cards.   The origin of the card games is undoubtedly Chinese, where they were first called "sheet dice."   They were in use there by the tenth century if not earlier.   Playing cards may have reached Europe through the returning Crusaders, who had first seen them in Asia Minor, or they may have come through the Russians who were under the influence of the Mongols in the late thirteenth and fourteenth centuries.   At any rate, block printed playing cards were in use in western Europe in the fourteenth century and along with them block printed religious items, such as pictures of the Saints.   Whether cards or pictures, these block prints were single items, made from a single rather crudely carved block but they did provide multiple copies of a graphic work.   As such, they were the immediate forerunners of printing.

Whether or not there is a direct connection between early printing in Europe and that developed in China, there is no doubt about the spread of another phase of book-making from East to West.   This was the manufacture of paper.   Papyrus, parchment and vellum were all comparatively expensive, and for a process that made hundreds of copies of a work in a short time, a cheaper writing material was necessary.   It has been estimated, for example, that it would have taken the hides of five thousand calves to provide the vellum necessary for printing just 35 copies of the Gutenberg Bible.   Many surfaces had been tried in various countries for writing, including wood, clay, stone, metal, hides, cloth, silk, bamboo, papyrus and bark, but all were either too scarce or too bulky for use in mechanical printing. Several primitive peoples, including the natives of Mexico and the Southwest Pacific, developed sheets of matted vegetable fibers that were elementary forms of paper, but the Chinese were the first to make a really perfect product. As early as the second century A.D., they had experimented with paper made from silk, tree bark, and hemp. [Later cotton and linen rags were used, and by the fifth century paper of good quality was commonplace in China. This paper was made by soaking and pounding the raw materials until the individual fibres were separated. A thick mixture of these fibres with water was spread and then a fine meshed screen was dipped into the mixture. As the screen was lifted a thin layer of the fibres adhered to the screen, and when this layer was dried and peeled off it made a single sheet of paper. Later the paper was pressed and sometimes rubbed with stone to give it a smooth hard finish.]

Traveling westward along the trade routes, the art of manufacturing paper had reached Samarkand in Central Asia by 750, and Baghdad by 793. By 900 paper was being made in Egypt, and by 1100 in Morocco. The first paper manufactured in Europe was in Moslem Spain about the middle of the twelfth century, and in Italy about a century later. No paper was manufactured in northern Europe until the fourteenth century, and none in England until 1494, but of course paper was being used in each of these places for many years before it was actually manufactured there. The oldest extant paper document of European record comes from Sicily and is dated 1209. In the fourteenth and fifteenth centuries, France became the most important paper-maker in Europe. The source materials used were rags, sometimes of cotton or silk, but more often, of linen or hemp and the process was much the same as that employed for centuries in China. Oddly enough paper did not receive a warm welcome in Europe despite its comparative cheapness as a writing material. Religious and governmental leaders opposed its use, particularly on important documents, and for many years it was illegal to use paper for official manuscripts.

From the playing card and religious print, it was only a

short step to the block printing of small books, with each page being made as a single print. As in the early block printed books in
the Far East, these pages usually consisted of a large picture and
a few words.   The earliest known European block books date from
around 1428, although it is quite possible that others were made
earlier.   The process of making the block book began with the
wood-cut of picture or text or both.   The block was inked and the
paper pressed upon it and rubbed lightly to insure a clear impression.   This block-printing process was used for small books that
could be produced relatively cheaply and distributed widely.   Many
of them were on religious themes, such as the "Pauper's Bible,"
a collection of Bible verses with pictures, designed for children or
near-illiterates.   Other block books were elementary school texts,
particularly Latin grammars.   Such works continued to be printed
for some time after the development of printing from movable type,
and apparently they were well used since only a few of them have
survived.   Though it was only a poor beginning, block book making
undoubtedly pointed the way for the printed book which followed it
by only a generation or two.

One other predecessor of printing that should be mentioned
is textile printing.   It seems that wherever textile fabrics have
been developed, methods of impressing designs on them have soon
been achieved.   Primitive textile printing was practiced in Egypt
early in the Christian era, and examples dating from the sixth to
eighth century have been found in Egypt, India, China, and Germany.   However, the art of textile printing was apparently lost in
Europe for centuries, and re-discovered around 1300.   This process of printing upon cloth was very similar to that of printing upon paper, that is it was done by pressing a carved inked block upon cloth supported by another wooden block.   It appeared in Europe along with the early wood-block prints, or possibly earlier,
and although it was a matter of printing patterns and designs rather
than words and pictures, it was still a form of transferring an impression, and it was, for many years, far more widely used than
printing on paper.

The development of printing from movable metal type centers

around the activities of Johann Gutenberg and in order to under-
stand his role in his historic occasion it is necessary to know a
little about the man himself.   He was born about 1400 in Mainz,
Germany and seems to have come from a fairly well-to-do family.
About 1430 he left Mainz and took up his home in Strasbourg, where
he entered into a partnership with several craftsmen, workers in
gold and other metals.   During his years in Strasbourg, Gutenberg
became involved in several lawsuits, both in business and domestic
matters (he was sued for breach of promise by one Strasbourg
lady), and thus his presence there is a matter of record.   However, just when he began work on a printing press is uncertain.
About 1440, he was sued by two of his ex-partners for failing to
teach them a secret process, unnamed but usually thought to have
been printing.   There are a few fragments of printing which some
authorities believe were printed by Gutenberg in Strasbourg, but
there is no general agreement on these.   In 1448, however, Gutenberg was back in Mainz, and by 1450, he was definitely in the
printing business as several of his contemporaries later recorded.
In 1452, already indebted to one Johann Fust, Gutenberg took that
gentleman into partnership with him.   By this time, the press was
in operation, but apparently it brought little remuneration to Gutenberg, for by 1455, he was so indebted to Fust that he made over
his share of the printing equipment to Fust and another partner,
Peter Schoeffer.   From this press there came, in or before 1456,
the famous Gutenberg Bible, sometimes called the 42-line Bible
from the number of lines of type per page.   This edition of the
Bible was no experimental affair; it is undoubtedly one of the finest
pieces of printing ever done.   It does not seem reasonable that a
first printed book could be such an example of perfection, so it
must be assumed that many years of experimentation and trial and
error were necessary before a printing press could be developed to
do such fine work.   Apparently those years of experiment without
income impoverished Gutenberg and his creditors and business successors reaped the benefits of his work.

No single piece of printing actually bears the imprint of
Gutenberg, but from careful study of the available records most

authorities agree in crediting him with several items, and of course
it is quite possible that dozens of minor books, pamphlets, and
broadsides printed by Gutenberg may have been lost or worn out in
later years.   The first dated piece of printing was an indulgence,
a broadside church form, printed in 1454, apparently by a Gutenberg press in the hands of Peter Schoeffer.   The 42-line Bible was
probably printed in or completed by 1456, because, although it
bears no date itself, a copy was illuminated and bound by Heinrich
Cremer in the summer of 1456, according to a note in the copy
still preserved in the Bibliothéque Nationale in Paris.   This so-
called Gutenberg Bible was most probably completed and sold by
Fust and Schoeffer, but the press, the type and possibly even the
composition of the Bible were Gutenberg's handiwork.

Did Gutenberg really invent the printing press?   The best
evidence indicates that he did.   At least he put together the first
workable press using movable metal type and developed it mechanically to the point where excellent printing could be achieved.   A
skilled metal-worker, he developed methods of typecasting that
made it possible to cast large numbers of precisely-made, uniform
type.   Since the water-soluble ink used in wood-block printing was
not satisfactory for press-work, Gutenberg also encouraged the development of an ink that was thick and yet quick-drying for use on
the presses.   Finally, he developed the press itself, no doubt using
for a prototype the screw-press that had long been used in leather
curing and winemaking.   The finished product made it possible to
print large numbers of copies from the same type, uniformly inked,
and on both sides of the paper -- quite a change from the old block-
printing methods.   Putting all these things together, and making
them work, constituted Gutenberg's "invention," and its perfection
was definitely a notable achievement in man's history.   Gutenberg's
later life is obscure, although it is generally believed that in 1465
he became a pensioner at the court of Count Adolph of Nassau and
that he died in Mainz in 1468.

Other European countries also claim the invention of printing.   The Netherlands in particular have a case for one Laurens
Koster or Coster, who is alleged to have used a printing press with

movable type as early as the 1430's.   There is little proof to support this claim, although there is evidence that someone was experimenting with printing in the Netherlands about the same time that Gutenberg was developing his press.   One other interesting claimant to Gutenberg's fame has come from France, where in 1444-1446 at Avignon, one Procopius Waldfoghel, a silver-smith, was experimenting with "alphabets of steel," with which he claimed to be able to "write artificially."   There is no evidence to show that Waldfoghel ever did any printing.   Other, even more vague and unsubstantiated, claims to the invention of printing come from other cities in France, Germany, Italy and Czechoslovakia.   Until and unless some more substantial discovery is made in the history of early printing, Gutenberg's position seems secure.

Whatever doubts there may be about Gutenberg's printed works, there is no doubt that successful printing was in operation in the city of Mainz either before or shortly after 1450, and that from this city it spread fairly rapidly to the rest of Europe.   In 1462 a feudal war between two competing claimants for the archbishopric of Mainz resulted in the capture of the city by one force and the disruption of the printing industry there, at least temporarily.   Some of the printers, trained in the shops of Fust and Schoeffer, were unemployed and had to look elsewhere for jobs. Others may have been forced to leave because they had opposed the victorious bishop.   At any rate, they left Mainz and carried their knowledge of the art of printing to other parts of Europe.   A French writer described this exodus in 1470:

> There has been discovered in Germany a wonderful new method for the production of books, and those who have mastered this method are taking their invention from Mainz out into the world somewhat as the old Grecian warriors took their weapons from the belly of the Trojan horse.   The light of this wonderful discovery will spread from Germany to all parts of the earth.   (Putnam, G.H.: Books and their makers during the Middle Ages, I, 359, reproducing a letter from Wilhelm Fichet to Robert Gaguin.)

It was natural that the nearby German towns should receive printing shortly after it had been perfected in Mainz, and this

seems to have been the case.   There were printers in Strasbourg
by 1460, in Bamberg by 1461, and in Cologne by 1465 or earlier.
Some of the German printers crossed the Alps and set up the first
presses in Italy.   Conrad Sweynheym and Arnold Pannartz left
Mainz and started a printing establishment at Subiaco, near Rome,
either late in 1464 or early in 1465.   Later they moved on to Rome
and became the first printers in that city.   Other Italian cities had
printing presses in the 1470's, including Venice, where the industry flourished, Naples, Florence, and Genoa.   Basel in Switzerland
had printing by 1465, Paris in 1470, Utrecht in the Netherlands in
the same year, and even Cracow, in Poland, by 1475.   The art
was slower in reaching the Baltic countries and the Balkans.   It
was the 1480's before there were presses in Denmark, Norway and
Sweden, and not until 1494 did printing reach Constantinople.   The
first printing in England was done in 1476 or early in 1477 and in
Spain in 1474.   There were reports of three printers going to Moscow in 1490 but the first known printing in Moscow was not done until 1563.   By 1500 more than 1700 presses had been in operation in
over 300 cities of western Europe and they had turned out over
40,000 separate works or editions in more than 15,000,000 copies.
These works printed before 1500 are known as incunabula, from the
Latin word for "cradle," referring to the books produced in the infancy of the art of printing.

Even before 1500, many printers had become outstanding artists in their profession and some of the most beautiful works of
typography ever produced had appeared.   Italian printers early assumed a lead in the new industry, and among them Nicholas Jenson
and Aldus Manutius stand out.   Jenson's press was in Venice.   He
produced more than 150 different books, all printed in a clear,
very legible type which he designed himself.   Just as Gutenberg's
type was based on the gothic handwriting then prevalent in Germany,
so Jenson based his "roman" type on the script used by the human-
ist scholars of northern Italy.   Aldus Manutius, also of Venice, was
known for his development of italic type, and for the printing in
small, well-made but relatively cheap, editions of the Greek and
Latin classics.   Most early printers preferred the large, folio for-

mat for their books or at least the quarto, but Aldus turned to the octavo, a small, hand-sized, volume that was easy to hold and to read.   Most modern books are in the octavo size.   More than any other of the early printers, Jenson and Aldus were responsible for popularizing the printed book and thus helping to spread learning. Both men were scholars as well as printers and they edited the books that they published.   One of the greatest achievements of Aldus Manutius was the collection of the many fragments of Aristotle's works into as nearly complete an edition of his works as was then possible.   He is also remembered for the founding of the Aldine Academy for the study of the Greek and Latin classics, but this did not survive long after his death in 1515.

Among the early German printers, the Koberger family of Nuremberg stand out for the quantity if not for the quality of their work.   They printed on a large scale, running several presses, with a large number of workmen each trai ned in a special task. They tended to specialize in religious works and in textbooks, and by 1500 had twenty-four presses in operation in Nuremberg and nearby towns.   Many of their books were profusely illustrated with wood cuts.   One of the Kobergers' most famous works was the Nuremberg Chronicle, which was an illustrated history of the world. It was very elaborate, with almost two thousand illustrations, but it was so carelessly done that the same wood-cut was often used several times to depict different people or different scenes.   The Kobergers promoted their business effectively with published catalogs, and used salesmen to peddle their books throughout Europe. Johann Snell, of Lubeck, Germany, had a similar but smaller establishment with branches in Denmark and Sweden.

Among other early European printers of importance were several generations of the Estienne family of France.   Beginning with Henri Estienne in 1502, and for nearly 150 years, this family produced, in Paris and Geneva, some of the finest books ever published.   Another famous printing family was the House of Plantin, in Antwerp, which lasted for some 300 years and was noted for excellent printing from the sixteenth to the nineteenth century.   The Elzevir press, in Leiden, produced over 1600 books in five different languages in a little over a century of operation. Switzerland considers Johann Froben, who printed in Basel from 1491 to 1527, one of its greatest printers. Froben surrounded himself with scholars, including Erasmus, and undertook to produce only the best of printing and the most authentic of texts. Among his most notable publications was a Greek New Testament in nine huge folio volumes. Froben also published some of the earliest works on medicine and science, part of which were illustrated with woodcuts by Hans Holbein.

Closely associated with printing throughout its history has been the art of type-founding. Early printers like Gutenberg and Jenson were also type-founders, but by the sixteenth century, type designing and founding was becoming a separate trade and types were being created specifically for printing. Two Frenchmen stand out for their contribution to type designs in the sixteenth century. One of these was Robert Granjon, who specialized in italic type faces, and the other was Claude Garamond, who developed a clear, open roman character, based somewhat on the Jenson type. Both styles of type were widely used by contemporary printers, and after a revival of interest in the nineteenth century, adaptations of these types are still popular.

Printing was relatively late in reaching England, with the first printing there coming late in 1476 or early 1477. The first English printer was William Caxton, a wealthy merchant who had been living in Bruges, Belgium. He apparently learned the art of printing during a visit to Cologne, Germany, and took it up at first as a hobby. At the request of Margaret, Duchess of Burgundy, who was English born, Caxton had translated from the French a popular book on the Trojan wars, entitled Recuyell of the Historyes of Troye, and he printed some copies of this in Bruges in or before 1475. Thus the first book printed in English was not printed in England. Caxton decided that printing could be a profitable trade and so in 1476 he returned to England and set up his printing business at Westminster Abbey. There his first dated printing was another translation, The Dictes or Sayengis of the Philosophers, 1477. There were probably earlier publications in pamphlet or

broadside form from the Caxton press, but none of them has survived. Before his death in 1491, Caxton printed more than a hundred different works, including the poems of Geoffrey Chaucer, virtually a contemporary, and other works of English literature.   As
a printer, Caxton was not an artist and his works fall short of perfection, but as an editor and publisher he did much to standardize
the English language and preserve its literature.   Caxton used several type-faces at different times, but the one for which he is best
remembered is the Old English black-letter, a heavy almost gothic
type that is still sometimes used.

Caxton's successor was Wynken de Worde, who had been his
assistant almost from the first.   Wynken de Worde was in many
ways a better printer than Caxton and his output in numbers was
large, but his importance in the early history of English printing is
overshadowed by that of Caxton.   Both Caxton and Wynken de Worde
printed in Westminster Abbey, then a separate village but now a
part of London.   The first printer in London proper was John Lettou, in 1480.   William de Machlinia, Richard Pynson, and Julian
Notary also printed in London before 1500, and other presses were
established in Oxford and St. Albans before the turn of the century.
All were foreigners except Caxton and possibly the printer at St.
Albans, whose identity is unknown.   On the whole, early English
printing is typographically undistinguished when compared to that
produced on the continent during the same period.   With the possible exception of Wynken de Worde and Richard Pynson, the early
English printers seem to have been journeymen rather than masters
and never to have brought their trade to perfection.

The total product of the fifteenth century presses is astound-
ing numerically and equally amazing is the quality and variety of
the matter printed.   Although many works have undoubtedly been
lost, it is apparent that practically every extant piece of literature
in the western European languages, or in Latin or Greek, plus
many in Hebrew, must have been printed in that prolific half-century.   There were nearly 500 editions of the Bible, or its parts,
with several hundred more religious works such as Breviaries,
Hymnals and Prayer-books.   With the various editions of the works

of the Saints and those of the early Christian philosophers, the
grand total of religious works formed about half of the output of
the fifteenth century presses.   About ten per cent of the incunabula
were books of church or civil law, including commentaries and text-
books.   Another twenty per cent or so were works of literature,
both classic and medieval, while all the sciences together made up
not quite another ten per cent.   The remainder were divided among
elementary text-books (mostly Latin grammars), history, travel,
and miscellaneous.

Some of the authors and titles that enjoyed popularity before
1500 might be of interest.   They included, among the Latin classics,
the works of Cicero, Virgil, Ovid, Seneca, Horace, Juvenal, Per-
sius and Terence, in roughly that order.   In the Greek, there were
the works of Aristotle, Aristophanes, Aesop, Homer, Galen, Theophrastus, Theocritus, and Euripides.   Among the medieval writers,
Petrarch, Boccaccio, and Dante, with the works of the first named
going through some 40 editions prior to 1500.   In history, the Nuremberg Chronicle was one of the most important books produced
but there were similar contemporary works.   In the sciences there
were volumes on agriculture, astronomy, mathematics, medicine
and botany, with many more on the pseudo-sciences like astrology
and alchemy.   Several contemporary romances were published, including an early best-seller by Aneas Sylvius, entitled Concerning
Two Lovers.   Christopher Columbus' Letter Concerning the Newly
Discovered Islands was a popular item in the 1490's, and went
through twelve editions, despite the fact that it was only a four-
page leaflet.   Of English authors published before 1500, perhaps the
most significant was Geoffrey Chaucer, whose Canterbury Tales
were printed by Caxton.

All things considered, the art of printing made great progress in its first half-century.   The first collophon, giving publisher and date of publication, appeared in 1457 in a Psalter
printed by Fust and Schoeffer in Mainz.   Wood-cut illustrations
were added to books printed from movable type in 1461, and copper
engravings were used as early as 1476.   The first elementary form
of a title-page appeared in 1463, the first table of contents in 1470,

and even attempts at indexes were made by 1480. The printing press itself had reached a form by 1500 that was to change very little in the next three hundred years, and typography in general had reached a stage of near perfection that has been improved upon only in the last century. Though the making of books was still a laborious job, involving much hand work, it was far superior to handwriting, and the literate world would no longer be handicapped through lack of reading material. The invention of the printing press brought about a cultural revolution hardly surpassed by any other single development since the beginning of writing. Henceforth communication of man's ideas through either space or time would have a rapid and relatively inexpensive vehicle, so that a Martin Luther could begin a Reformation, and a Thomas Jefferson could prepare the way for a new nation with a Declaration of Independence. Books, pamphlets and broadsides, journals, magazines and newspapers, all the products of the presses, were to play a major role in changing history. And the accumulation, preservation and distribution of this mass of printed material was to radically change the character of the library and the librarian.

Bibliography

Books

Aldis, Harry G. : The printed book. Cambridge, England, 1951. 142 p.

Bland, David: The illustration of books. New York, 1954. 160 p.

Bliss, Douglas P. : A history of wood-engraving. London, 1928. 256 p.

Blum, Andre: On the origin of paper. New York, 1934. 79 p.

Blum, Andre: The origins of printing and engraving. New York, 1940. 226 p.

Buehler, Curt F. : The fifteenth-century book: the scribes, the printers, the decorators. Philadelphia, 1960. 195 p.

Buehler, Curt F. : University and the press in fifteenth-century Bologna. South Bend, Indiana, 1958. 109 p.

Bullock, Warren B. : The romance of paper. Chicago, 1940. 154 p.

Butler, Pierce: The origin of printing in Europe. Chicago, 1940.
    154 p.

Carter, Thomas F. : The invention of printing in China and its
    spread westward. Rev. ed. New York, 1955. 293 p.

Davenport, Cyril: The book, its history and development. New
    York, 1930. 258 p.

DeVinne, T. L. : Notable printers of Italy during the fifteenth cen-
    tury. New York, 1910. 210 p.

Diringer, David: The illuminated book: its history and produc-
    tion. New York, 1958. 524 p.

Dowding, Geoffrey: Introduction to the history of printing types.
    London, 1961. 278 p.

Duff, E. Gordon: Fifteenth century English books. Oxford, 1917.
    123 p.

Goldschmidt, E. P. : The printed book of the Renaissance. Cam-
    bridge, England, 1950. 92 p.

Greenwood, David: Chronology of books and printing. New York,
    1936. 186 p.

Hamilton, Frederick W. : A brief history of printing. Chicago,
    1918. 2 v.

Handover, P. M. : Printing in London from 1476 to modern times.
    Cambridge, Mass. , 1960. 224 p.

Hind, Arthur M. : An introduction to a history of woodcut. New
    York, 1935. 2 v.

Hunter, Dard: Paper making; the history and technique of an an-
    cient craft. New York, 1947. 611 p.

Jennett, Sean: Pioneers in printing. London, 1958. 196 p.

Johnson, Henry L. : Gutenberg and the Book of books. New York,
    1932. 24 p.

Laufer, Berthold: Paper and printing in ancient China. Chicago,
    1931. 33 p.

McKerrow, Ronald B. : An introduction to bibliography for literary
    students. Oxford, 1927. 359 p. (See pp. 38-144.)

McMurtrie, Douglas C. : The book: the story of printing and
    bookmaking. New York, 1943. 676 p.

Orcutt, William D. : The book in Italy during the fifteenth and six-
     teenth centuries. London, 1928. 220 p.

Orcutt, William D. : Master makers of the book. New York,
     1928. 271 p.

Oswald, J. C. : A history of printing. New York, 1928. 403 p.

Peddie, Robert A. : Printing, a short history. London, 1927.
     389 p.

Pollard, Alfred W. : Fine books. London, 1912. 331 p.

Scholderer, Victor: Printers and readers in Italy in the fifteenth
     century. Oxford, 1949. 23 p.

Smith, A. M. : Printing and writing materials, their evolution.
     Philadelphia, 1901. 236 p.

Steinberg, S. H. : Five hundred years of printing. New York,
     1955. 277 p.

Stillwell, Margaret B. : Incunabula and Americana. New York,
     1931. 483 p.

Updike, Daniel B. : Printing types, their history, forms and use.
     Cambridge, Mass. 1946. 2 v.

Winship, George P. : Gutenberg to Plantin: outline of the early
     history of printing. Cambridge, Mass. , 1926. 84 p.

Winship, George P. : John Gutenberg. Chicago, 1940. 38 p.

Winship, George P. : Printing in the fifteenth century. Philadel-
     phia, 1940. 158 p.

Wroth, L. C. , ed. : A history of the printed book. New York,
     1938.

Periodical Articles

Currier, C. W. : "Early labors of the printing press," Catholic
     World, LXIII, (1896), 59-70.

Daniel H. : "The Koreans were ahead of Gutenberg," Natural His-
     tory, LX, (1951), 376-378.

Deland, Judson: "The evolution of modern printing," Journal of
     the Franklin Institute, CCXII, (1931), 209-234.

Jackson, Katherine: "The printer of the fifteenth century," South
     Atlantic Quarterly, VIII, (1909), 361-369.

Prostov, Eugene V. : "Origins of Russian printing," Library Quarterly, I, (1931), 255-277.

Uhlendorff, G. A. : "The invention of printing and its spread till
1470," Library Quarterly, II, (1932), 179-231.

Table I

The Spread of Printing in Europe

Date	Country (Modern name)	City	Printer
1445-1453(?)	Germany	Mainz	Johann Gutenberg
1454 (?)	Germany	Mainz	Fust & Schoeffer
1458 (?)	Germany	Strasbourg	Johann Mentelin
1461	Germany	Bamberg	Albrecht Pfister
1464 (?)	Italy	Subiaco	Sweynheym & Pannartz
1465	Germany	Cologne	Ulrich Zell
1466 (?)	Switzerland	Basle	Berthold Ruppel
1467 (?)	Italy	Rome	Sweynheym and Pannartz
1468	Germany	Augsburg	Gunther Zainer
1468	Czechoslovakia	Pilsen	(Unknown)
1469	Italy	Venice	John of Spires
1470	Germany	Nuremberg	Johann Sensen-schmid
1470 (?)	Italy	Venice	Nicolas Jenson
1470	France	Paris	Martin Crantz, Ulrich Gering, & Michael Fri-burger
1470	Netherlands	Utrecht	Gerardus Leempt & Nicholas Ke-talaer
1471	Italy	Milan	Antonio Zarotti
1471	Italy	Naples	Sixtus Riessinger
1471	Italy	Florence	Bernardo di Cen-nini
1473	France	Lyons	Wilhelm Konig
1473 (?)	Hungary	Budapest	Andreas Hesse
1473 (?)	Belgium	Louvain	John of West-phalia
1474	Poland	Cracow	Casper Hochfeld-er
1474	Spain	Valencia	Lambert Palmart
1476 (?)	England	Westminster	William Caxton
1478	England	Oxford	Theodoric Rood
1480	England	London	John Lettou
1482	Austria	Vienna	Stephen Koblinger
1482	Denmark	Odense	Johann Snell
1483	Sweden	Stockholm	Johann Snell

Date	Country (Modern name)	City	Printer
1489	Portugal	Lisbon	Rabbi Elieser
1491	England	London	Richard Pynson
1491	Westminster	England	Wynken de Worde
1491	Switzerland	Basle	Johann Froben
1494	Turkey	Constantinople	David ibn Nachmias
1494	Italy	Venice	Aldus Manutius
1502	France	Paris	Henri Estienne
1515	France	Paris	Geoffrey Tory
1555	Belgium	Antwerp	Christopher Plantin
1563	Russia	Moscow	Ivan Fedorov

VI
European Books and Libraries, 1500-1900

The total cultural effect of the invention of printing can hardly be over-estimated. The coming of printing revolutionized communication and made it possible for the dissemination of new ideas
to thousands of people instead of a few score. Information on new
discoveries could be made quickly available, but also the age-old
truths of the classics and the Scriptures could reach more people.
Learning, long shut up in monasteries and in a few schools,
emerged to become something that anyone with interest and initiative could pursue. Printing furthered the Renaissance that had already begun, and facilitated the Reformation that soon followed.
With more books being printed and read and more people becoming
educated, the Dark Ages rapidly came to an end. The printing
press, probably more than any other factor, was responsible for
the beginning of the modern era.

In particular, the printing press changed the world of books.
This change was achieved gradually over a period of a half-century
or more as the products of the presses were increasing and filling
the book-shelves of Europe. The bookseller ceased being a dealer
in manuscripts, scarce and costly, and could instead stock and sell
the newly printed books in large numbers. Journeymen booksellers
peddled their wares from town to town and from village to village.
Later on, with the publication of cheaper works, the chapman followed with his penny chap-books to sell to the poorest reader.
The new trades of printer, bookbinder, paper-maker, woodcut artist, type-maker, copper-plate engraver and bookseller added numbers to the rapidly growing middle class. Though few publishers
became really wealthy, the book business was economically as well
as culturally a successful innovation.

In the library itself, the coming of the printed book brought
many changes -- but not at first. In fact, many fifteenth century

82

librarians and book-collectors refused to have the printed books in
their libraries. In their eyes, the printed page was merely a poor
imitation of the real thing. Gradually, however, the book replaced
the manuscript and in time the latter became a valuable rarity
rather than an object of ordinary use. When they did come into
the libraries books were kept on open shelves rather than in chests
and on lecterns. The library was separated from the scriptorium
and, indeed, the latter disappeared, with some monasteries acquiring printing presses instead. Printed books were plentiful enough
to be loaned for use outside the library walls, and hence the public
circulating library became a possibility. The typical sixteenth century library became the oblong room with books around the wall,
and with tables for readers in the center, or perhaps cases for dis-
playing historical objects in the place of the tables. The library
room came to have stipulated times for opening, with a librarian
or keeper on duty. With books in larger numbers, new methods of
classification and arrangement had to be devised and various experiments were made in this direction. Whatever the system used,
whether by subject, size or source, something in the way of a catalog or finding list was usually available. Many libraries now numbered their holdings in thousands rather than hundreds, and by 1600
at least a beginning had been made toward the modern library.

The books themselves varied widely in content and size in
the early centuries after the beginning of printing. Many of them
were still huge folios, resembling the bound volumes of manuscripts, but there were also the small popular books printed by Aldus Manutius in Italy, by the Elzevir Press in Holland, and by
others. Religious works still outnumbered the others and the classics were still popular, but contemporary works ranging from science to superstition and from travel to romance were also widely
published.

The medieval wood-cut gradually gave way to the copper-
plate engraving, but this did not happen until after the wood-cut
had reached a high stage of perfection under such artists as Hans
Holbein and Albrecht Durer. Bookbindings ranged from the paper
back through the simple unlettered vellum to the highly ornate gold-

embossed leathers. Printing types were changed, except in Germany, from the black-letter or gothic types to lighter, more legible ones. Printing as an art tended to decline in Italy, Germany and England, but it flourished in France and the Low Countries, reaching a high point in those areas in the seventeenth century. In the printing of the Plantin and Elzevir families the copperplate engraving came into its own.

Since the Renaissance had begun in the Italian peninsula, and since the printing industry had achieved an early popularity there, it is only natural that Italian libraries prospered in the fifteenth and sixteenth centuries. Several outstanding libraries were begun long before the printing press but these were joined by others as books became more plentiful and the profitable trading centers of Venice, Genoa, Florence and Naples produced merchant princes with sufficient interest and funds to collect books and endow libraries. A few wealthy nobles, who had searched monastery libraries from Greece to England to purchase, purloin or copy writings for their collections, now added printed books to their libraries and opened them to the public or gave them to public institutions. The book and manuscript treasures of the Medici family found their way into the Laurentian Library, for which a building was designed by Michelangelo. It was opened in Florence in 1571. Another great Italian library was that of St. Mark (Biblioteca Marciana) in Venice. It was based on the collection of Cardinal Bessarion and was housed in its own building about 1550. In 1609, the Ambrosian Library (Biblioteca Ambrosiana) was opened to the public in Milan, largely through the efforts of the scholarly Archbishop of Milan, Federigo Borromeo. This library, which grew to contain many thousands of books, was open to any and all who wanted to come there to study. It was connected with a "College of Doctors" which was really a group of scholars engaged in research, and a printing press was provided to make available to all the results of their studies. The National Library of Florence had its beginnings in 1714 in a gift to the city of books from the library of Antonio Magliabechi while that in Turin was founded in 1723 by Vittorio Amadeo II. Bologna's central university library was founded in 1721 by Count Marsigli, while Girolamo Casanate opened his library to the public in Rome in 1701. In the eighteenth and nineteenth centuries public and school libraries remained almost non-existent in Italy, but a few university and endowed libraries continued to grow and by 1900 they were among the most valuable libraries in the world.

Among theological libraries, the most important by far was that of the Vatican in Rome. After many vicissitudes in the Middle Ages, the Vatican Library began to grow rapidly in the sixteenth and seventeenth centuries. Many treasures from monastery libraries found their way to the Vatican as gifts to the various Popes, and occasionally whole libraries were added at once, as for instance in 1600 when Fulvio Orsini bequeathed his library to the Vatican. In 1623, Maximilian, Duke of Bavaria, took the Palatine Library of Heidelberg as spoils of war and gave it to Pope Gregory XV. In 1658, the Library of Urbino, founded by Duke Federigo some two centuries earlier, passed into the hands of the Pope, and was added to the Vatican collection. Still another great collection, the library of manuscripts and books collected by Queen Christina of Sweden, was added a generation later. From this period onward, the course of the papal library has been one of continued improvement in size and value, except for a brief set-back early in the nineteenth century. At this time the French under Napoleon seized many of the most valuable books in the Vatican Library, but most of them were returned after the Emperor's fall from power. The Vatican librarians have been generally of very high quality, numbering among them several outstanding writers and scholars, such as the seventeenth century church historian, Baronius. Other Vatican librarians began the task of cataloging the valuable contents, and took steps to preserve the thousands of manuscripts already centuries old. Printed books were separated from the manuscripts, and among the latter the codices were separated from the rolls. Further division was made by languages, and the more valuable tomes were enshrined in separate cases. By 1900 the Vatican Library was easily one of the most important in the world. It contained then over 400,000 printed books including 4,000 incunabula;

more than 30,000 Latin, 4,000 Greek, and 3,000 Oriental manuscripts, with the latter division including Hebrew. So important
has the Vatican Library been considered in the development of the
Catholic Church that many of its most important leaders have been
honored with the post of chief librarian, and several of these have
been promoted, in time, to the position of Pope.

The libraries in France after 1500 owed much to Italian pre-
cedents, just as did its medieval libraries. The French tended to
improve or broaden the Italian beginnings, and to promote a profession of librarianship that was hardly achieved in Italy. France
had the advantage over Italy of being a unified nation, at least after
the sixteenth century and this gave rise to a French national library. At least since the days of Charlemagne the rulers of
France had owned royal private libraries and under several of them,
particularly Charles V (1337-1380) and Louis XI (1423-1483), important collections were made. Francis I, (1494-1547) strengthened
the Bibliothèque du Roi, as it was then called, by ordering that one
copy of each book printed in France be deposited there and by establishing the position of royal librarian. One of the first to hold
this position was Guillaume Budé, a noted scholar, who is generally given credit for organizing the royal book collection into a true
library. Although the Royal Library grew slowly, it suffered from
several moves both in and outside of Paris, and not until 1731 did
it find a permanent home on the Rue Richelieu. After that growth
was more rapid, with important additions made by gift, by purchase
and occasionally by confiscation. The first printed catalog in 1622
listed some 6,000 volumes, of which over half were manuscripts,
but after that most of the growth was in printed books, and by 1700
there were over 70,000 volumes. During the French Revolution,
the Royal Library became the Bibliothèque Nationale, and its size
was increased considerably by books seized from the nobility, the
suppressed monasteries, and from churches. Military conquests
under Napoleon I brought additional volumes, many of great value,
so that by 1815 the French national library contained over half a
million volumes. Some of these were later returned to their original owners, but the nineteenth century saw continued growth so

that by 1900 the Bibliothèque Nationale was probably the most important library in the world. Its growth in organization and usefulness paralleled its growth in size, and directly or indirectly, it served as a model for research libraries all over the world.

An early rival of the French national library was the Bibliothèque Mazarine under the direction of the librarian, Gabriel Naudé. Naudé (1600-1653) had book agents search all over Europe for books and manuscripts to add to the Cardinal's Library, and by 1650 it contained some 40,000 volumes, most of them richly bound in leather and stamped with Cardinal Mazarin's seal. This library was open for reference use to the public, or at least to those students who had the Cardinal's favor. Naudé, in addition to cataloging and arranging the Mazarin library, also wrote one of the earliest books on library science. This was his Avis pour Dresser une Bibliothèque, or Advice on Establishing a Library, published in 1627. In this work, Naudé proclaimed the necessity for having all types of books in a library, new and old, rare and common, religious and profane. He recommended a system of classification based on the faculties or branches of knowledge commonly taught in the universities but he subdivided these into smaller classes for convenience. He hoped the Bibliothèque Mazarine would become a universal library, preserving the literary heritage of all peoples, and he set out to make it so. Unfortunately, the library was virtually destroyed in the 1650's by Mazarin's political enemies, only to be reconstituted a decade later. After the Cardinal's death, his library was bequeathed to the Collège de Mazarin and still later it became the property of the French government. It became one of the major libraries of Paris and by the end of the nineteenth century it contained over 250,000 volumes.

Elsewhere in France, most of the notable libraries of the sixteenth to nineteenth centuries were either those of the universities or of the nobles. Some of the towns developed publicly owned collections at an early date, such as the Bibliothèque Municipale of Troyes, founded in 1651, but these were more in the nature of museums than libraries. Some of the monastery libraries underwent transformations and emerged as university or other institutional li-

braries.   One of these is the Bibliothèque Ste. Geneviève, in Paris,
which began as the library of the Abbey of St. Genevieve in 1624,
and grew until by 1900 it was a national reference library of over
300,000 volumes.   During the French Revolution, many religious
libraries, both monastic and cathedral, were confiscated by the
state and since that period most of the library development has
been on a national basis, except for a few private universities and
endowed institutional libraries.   Some of the confiscated volumes
were made available to municipalities for the formation of public
libraries, but the movement was largely a failure.   Such "public"
libraries as developed, either before or after the Revolution,
tended to be the reference, non-circulating type, and although scholarly and valuable they were of little use to the general public.
Public library service as it is known in America today was virtually unknown in France before 1900.

In Germany, there was no national unity until the nineteenth
century, so each German state developed its own library, and
many of them were deservedly famous.   The State Library of
Brandenburg, (later the Royal Library of Prussia and the Imperial
Library of Germany) was founded in Berlin in 1661 by Frederick
William, the Great Elector.   Before his death he had built this
collection to more than 20,000 volumes and 1,500 manuscripts, all
catalogued and classified by the librarian, Christoph Hendreich.
This library had many ups and downs, but it was strengthened under Frederick William I of Prussia to about 75,000 volumes by
1740, and under Frederick the Great to about 100,000 volumes by
1790.   In the nineteenth century it grew rapidly, especially through
purchase and gift of several large private libraries, so that by
1900 it contained well over a million volumes and more than 30,000
important manuscripts.   Earlier Prussian princes had set up at
Königsberg the so-called "Silver Library," where the bindings were
ornately tooled in silver.   Duke Albrecht V (1550-1579) founded the
State Library of Bavaria at Munich with his own private library as
a nucleus.   It was housed in a separate building in 1575, and contained over 20,000 volumes by 1600.   Julius, Duke of Brunswick,
founded the Duke's Library at Wolfenbütttel in 1558, and in the next

century, Duke August compiled a catalog of this library that contained nearly 4,000 pages.   In the seventeenth century, the philosopher Gottfried Wilhelm Leibniz was librarian at Wolfenbüttel for a
few years, and in the eighteenth century the dramatist Gotthold
Ephraim Lessing held the same position.   By the eighteenth century the other German states and principalities also had libraries,
usually founded by the nobility, and many of them grew into considerable size by the nineteenth.   Their holdings included many valuable early printed works and manuscripts, making them important
research collections.   Ulrich Fugger (1526-1584), merchant of Augs-
burg in southern Germany, added to a collection begun by his father
and grandfather.   His descendants continued to enlarge this family
library, and eventually parts of it went to three major libraries,
the Austrian National Library, the Bavarian National Library, and
the Palatine Library at Heidelberg.   In the eighteenth century, Johann Frederich von Uffenbach collected books systematically, buying
them on tours all over Europe until he had amassed a collection of
several thousand volumes.   On his death his library was given to
the University of Göttingen.   Collecting books became the vogue for
wealthy men and even for some of those not so wealthy, if current
accounts can be relied upon.   The presses turned out the books in
volume; booksellers and the great annual book fairs at Leipzig and
Frankfort made them readily available and for those with means it
was easy to accumulate sizeable libraries.

One phase of library history that was common down to the
nineteenth century was the confiscation of books as spoils of war by
conquering armies.   Sometimes, of course, books were destroyed
by pillaging soldiers who did not appreciate their value but often
they were carefully gathered by agents of the victorious king or
prince and carried off with full honors to become parts of the cap-
tor's library, or of some institutional collection where he chose to
place them.   The fate of the Palatine library of Heidelberg has already been mentioned, and other examples are not rare.   The armies of Gustavus Adolphus, King of Sweden in the seventeenth century, collected books from libraries all the way from Finland to
Czechoslovakia and presented them to Swedish libraries, especially

that of the University of Uppsala. Napoleon was another collector
of books as spoils and libraries from Denmark to Spain were rav-
aged at his command. In other wars and revolutions literally thousands of books changed hands and thousands more were destroyed,
with monastery and church libraries suffering particularly in the
religious wars that followed the Reformation. Some of the important library moves were made voluntarily, as when Queen Christina
of Sweden took with her into exile a large part of the royal library
and eventually gave it to the Vatican.

Besides the state libraries in Germany and the private collections already mentioned, there were other types of libraries developing in the sixteenth and seventeenth centuries. The Protestant
church libraries replaced the monastery libraries to some extent.
Martin Luther taught that everyone should read the Bible and he
translated it into German so that it could be read. He encouraged
the Lutheran churches to provide books for the people to read and
popular libraries, small but useful, grew up in the local churches.
These were quite different from the old monastery collections in
that they consisted of printed books, and they were apparently well
used. Another type of popular library was the municipal or "alder-
man's" library. One of these was founded at Nüremberg in 1445,
but most of them date from later centuries. In the larger cities
these collections often grew through the years to become the important municipal reference libraries of the nineteenth century, but in
the smaller towns they just as often remained small and comparatively unused. At Jena, Heidelberg, Göttingen, and Königsberg, to
mention only a few of the more prominent universities, there developed scholarly libraries far superior to those in most other European countries. At Göttingen, for example, the university library
was founded about 1737, reached about 60,000 volumes before 1800,
and over half a million by 1900. The university library at Leipzig
was founded in 1543, and with the addition of many valuable private
collections over the centuries it too had reached a half million printed volumes by 1900, with thousands of valuable manuscripts in addition. Not only were the university libraries valuable in terms of
holdings, but they were well organized and directed by scholar-li-

brarians who operated them according to definite library procedures, and kept their treasures available for use.

Among the German scholars who gave at least a portion of
their time to librarianship was Gottfried Wilhelm Leibniz, (1646-
1716), also noted as a philosopher, mathematician, theologian and
diplomat.   Leibniz became acquainted with libraries during a stay
in Paris (1672-1676) and he may have worked for some time in the
royal library there.   At any rate he later went to Hanover as librarian and privy counsellor to the Duke of Brunswick.   Still later
he was librarian at Wolfenbüttel, and at that library he created an
alphabetical catalog and directed the construction of one of the earliest buildings ever designed strictly for library use.   Leibniz was
a theoretical as well as a practical librarian, and he is remembered for his general philosophy of librarianship.   In his writings
on librarianship he recommended strong financial support of libraries by their patrons or the state and presented the public library
as both a popular reading collection and a research center.   He de-
plored those who judged a library by its numbers only, or by its
bindings, and said that the only true evaluation of a library was by
the quality of the books in it and by the extent to which they were
used.   In addition to his alphabetical catalog of authors, he recommended a subject catalog or index and also a chronological index
by date of publication.   Many of Leibniz' ideas about library service were more fully realized by German librarians of the eighteenth
and nineteenth centuries.

An outstanding German librarian of a later era was Fritz
Ebert, who headed the Wolfenbüttel Library in the early nineteenth
century.   In his book on The Training of the Librarian, Ebert was
rather critical of the average library of his day.   In particular, he
found the usual university library to be poorly organized, in charge
of inexpert personnel, and filled with treasures that were   all but
lost for the average scholar who used the library.   He was a little
more charitable to the municipal libraries, but these too he felt had
suffered from maladministration and untrained workers.   He urged
that librarianship be raised to the status of a full-time, trained profession, but unfortunately few people agreed with him at that time.

Ebert was something of a perfectionist and a bit over-critical perhaps, but his points were well taken. Like Leibniz, he was ahead
of his time.   The German dramatist, Johann Wolfgang von Goethe
(1749-1832), was for a time in charge of the libraries at Weimar
and the University of Jena, and took an active interest in their
growth and organization.

Despite Ebert's criticism, the German libraries of the nineteenth century were probably the best in the world.   The variety in
kinds of libraries, the numbers of all types, the size of the major
ones, the professional interest and ability of the librarians, and
the financial backing afforded by church, state and wealthy patrons,
all combined to make this possible. By the early nineteenth century, German librarians were familiar with such library developments as circulating libraries, popular reading rooms, published
bibliographies and catalogs, inter-library loans, and even union catalogs.   It must be admitted, however, that libraries for popular
use lagged considerably behind those designed for scholarly and reference service.   By 1900, all types of libraries, even children's
collections, were present in Germany, and most of them were well
used.   As an example, there were in that year some 268 libraries
containing more than 5,000,000 volumes in Berlin alone.   In Munich, a much smaller city, there were 46 libraries, with more than
2,000,000 volumes and 60,000 manuscripts.

In other parts of Europe libraries progressed in varying degrees after the coming of printing, with the west and north in general being far ahead of the east and south.   In Austria, the Royal
Library was founded by the Emperor Maximilian I in 1493, although
parts of it date from even earlier years.   It was reorganized and
enlarged by Ferdinand I about 1564, and by 1600 it contained about
1500 manuscripts and 10,000 printed books.   One of its early librarians was Enea Silvio Piccolomini, who later became Pope Pius
II.   In the eighteenth century the Emperor Joseph II closed many
Austrian monasteries and gave their books to the Royal Library and
to provincial collections.   In 1808 a royal decree ordered that one
copy of each book printed in Austria-Hungary should be deposited
in the Royal Library and after that it grew fairly rapidly.   By 1900

it contained over 1,000,000 volumes, along with an important manuscript collection, and one of the largest groups of Egyptian papyri in existence.   Other important libraries in Austria were developed at the universities of Vienna, Graz, and Innsbruck.   Empress Maria Theresa opened the library in Innsbruck in 1746, while that at Vienna dates back to a joining of faculty libraries at the university in 1545.

In Belgium, the Royal Library at Brussels was founded in 1837, but it was based on the library of the Dukes of Burgundy, dating back to the fifteenth century.   It progressed rapidly and by 1900 it contained over 500,000 printed books and 28,000 manuscripts.   The municipal library at Antwerp was opened in 1609, and is one of the oldest continuously operating public libraries in Europe.   There were important university libraries at Ghent and Louvain, and large municipal libraries at Brussels and Liege. Most of the other Belgian towns had small municipal collections, but like those in comparable German towns they were largely reference and little used.   In the Netherlands, the Royal Library was founded in 1798 on the basis of the library of the Princes of Orange and several smaller collections.   Its holdings in incunabula were especially valuable, and it too reached the half million mark by 1900.   The University of Utrecht Library was begun in 1636, but many of its books came from a municipal collection gathered by the town fathers nearly a century earlier.   The University of Leiden was virtually built around a library donated by the first William of Orange in 1575, and the University of Amsterdam library grew out of a theological collection dating back to the fifteenth century. Some of the older and more important libraries in the Scandinavian countries are: The University of Copenhagen Library, founded in 1482; The Royal Library of Denmark, 1539; The Free Public Library of Oslo, 1780; the University of Oslo Library, 1811; and the Royal Library of Sweden, Stockholm, 1585.   The University of Uppsala, probably containing the oldest library in Sweden, was founded in 1477, and greatly enlarged by Gustavus Adolphus in 1620.   In all the Scandinavian countries, the movement toward popular libraries and reading rooms in towns and provinces became particularly strong after 1850.

In Spain and Portugal, the private libraries of the medieval
scholars declined after the Moslems were driven out of the country
in the fifteenth century, and although the monasteries and the
Church developed libraries afterward, they did not compare with
those of France or Germany. The National Library at Madrid was
founded by Philip V in 1711, and became the most important library in Spain in size and quality of collection. By 1900 it contained some 600,000 printed volumes and over 20,000 manuscripts.
Also in Madrid, the Central University Library, founded in 1508,
was noted for its collections on Spanish history and literature. One
of the most noted libraries in Spain is that of the monastery at San
Lorenzo del Escorial, near Madrid. This institution was founded
by Philip II in 1565, and its library received his personal attention.
Many fine private libraries were added to it in its early years,
some by gift and some by purchase. Later it suffered losses in
wars and fires, but it remained one of the most important libraries
in Spain because of the value of its 30,000 books and 5,000 manuscripts, many of them unique. In Portugal, the National Library,
founded in Lisbon in 1786, is the most valuable single collection,
although the Municipal Library at Oporto almost equalled it in size
in the nineteenth century. Several universities in Spain and Portugal had notable collections of books and manuscripts in the nineteenth century, including those at Seville, Barcelona, Salamanca
and Coimbra, although lack of staff and organization often left their
services inadequate. Many private libraries in these countries
compared favorably with those in northern Europe, but interest in
public and college libraries lagged considerably behind that in the
other countries of western Europe.

In Russia, the greater libraries date for the most part from
the eighteenth century, growing out of private collections or from
libraries taken as spoils of war. The Imperial Library in St. Petersburg began with the seizure of several libraries in Latvia in
1714 by Peter the Great. It was little more than a royal private
library, however, until 1794, when Catherine the Great added to it
a library of nearly 300,000 volumes seized in Warsaw at the time

of the dismemberment of Poland. In the nineteenth century the
Russian Imperial Library was enlarged by the legal deposit of two
copies of each book printed in Russia, and through the acquisition
of other large collections donated by merchants or nobles. By
1900 it was one of the largest libraries in the world, with nearly
two million volumes and over 30,000 manuscripts. Other important
libraries in Russia before 1900 included the Academy Library in
St. Petersburg founded in 1725; the Goruyi Institute Library there
(1773); the University of Moscow Library (1755); and the Public Library of Moscow, which evolved from a library founded in 1689.
Other large Russian cities, such as Odessa and Kharkov, also began municipal libraries in the nineteenth century, the former in
1830 and the latter in 1886. The University of Helsingfors (Helsinki) in Finland began a library in 1640, while that of Cracow in
Poland goes back to 1400 or even earlier. Elsewhere in Eastern
Europe, libraries, whether public or college, private or religious,
were far behind those in the western countries, at least down to
1900. The same was true in the Balkan states where Turkish domination or influence lasted well into the nineteenth century. There
were a few scholarly libraries, scattered and small, but nothing to
resemble the collections in western Europe.

Along with the development of libraries, the invention of
printing spurred several other developments in the world of books,
including particularly the publishing of periodicals and encyclopedias.
The periodical began with the pamphlet of the sixteenth century, developed into a sporadic series of related pamphlets, into annual or
biennial "registers" of the news, and finally, by the late seventeenth
century, into the regular periodical. Three of the earliest periodicals were the Journal des Scavans, which began publication in
France in 1665; the Transactions of the Royal Philosophical Society
in England in the same year, and a journal in Latin, the Acta
Eruditorium, which began in Germany in 1682. The newspaper developed from the news-sheet or broadside of the sixteenth and seventeenth century and had become fairly common by the early eighteenth century. As early as 1548, a newsletter was issued by a
Frankfurt printer for a short time, and several "Zeitungs" or news-

papers were printed elsewhere in Germany by 1600. Newspapers
and periodicals together added a new element to the field of communication, the element of "news," the most recent information of
military developments, or of science and literature. The impact of
the printed word was spread farther than ever, and the ambitious
printer had a new source of income.

The encyclopedias, created by almost a school of writers in
the seventeenth and eighteenth centuries, were an outgrowth of ancient and medieval attempts at collecting all available knowledge into one book or set of books. In 1630, Johann Heinrich Alsted published in Switzerland what was probably the first modern encyclopedia. He arranged his reference book topically, under seven major heads with some thirty-five subdivisions. Later in that century, two Frenchmen, Pierre Bayle and Louis Moreri, both produced encyclopedias, with that of Bayle being usually considered
the most authoritative. In 1704, John Harris published his Lexicon
Technicum, or An Universal English Dictionary of Arts and Sciences,
arranged alphabetically. In 1728, Ephraim Chambers, with the aid
of many other English scholars, produced his two volume Cyclopedia, which was more complete and scholarly than that of Harris.
Using a French translation of Chambers, as a base, Denis Diderot
and other continental scholars produced the famous Encyclopédie
which appeared in thirty volumes in Paris between 1750 and 1780.
By the end of the eighteenth century the encyclopedia had reached
virtually its modern form, complete with illustrations, long articles by authorities, alphabetic arrangement and cross references.

Generally speaking, the sixteenth and seventeenth centuries
brought the art of printing to a stage of perfection that was not
surpassed in the eighteenth and nineteenth. The copper-plate engraving largely replaced the wood-cut in the sixteenth century, but
it was not until the nineteenth that other methods of reproducing
pictures were developed. Printing in more than one color was
tried even before 1500, but perfection in this type of work was not
achieved until some three hundred years later. The center of
Europe's printing industry moved from Germany to Italy and then
in the seventeenth century to France and the Low Countries. The

whole era from 1500 to 1800 saw only slow progress in the book world, including libraries. After the library had adapted itself to the changes brought on by printing, there was relatively little improvement in functions or services and not much more in the numbers of libraries. The major libraries grew gradually but usually in a haphazard manner. In the nineteenth century the industrial revolution brought tremendous changes in the printing industry and the growth of democracy and education brought improvements just as important to the world of libraries. Books were being printed by the millions, and libraries were preserving them by the hundreds of thousands but, more important, the libraries were coming to be used more than ever and the library was being recognized as a popular educational institution rather than a store-room of rare books.

Bibliography

Books

Burton, Margaret: Famous libraries of the world: their history, collections and administration. London, 1937. 458 p.

Cotton des Houssayes, Jean Baptiste: Duties and qualifications of a librarian. (Originally printed, 1780.) Chicago, 1906. 56 p.

Ebert, Friederich A. : The training of a librarian. (Originally printed 1820.) Woodstock, Vermont, 1916. 39 p.

Dahl, Svend: History of the book. New York, 1958. 279 p.

Edwards, Edward: A statistical view of the principal libraries of Europe and America. London, 1849.   48 p.

Edwards, Edward: Libraries and founders of libraries. London, 1864. 503 p.

Edwards, Edward: Memoirs of libraries. London, 1859. 2 v.

Hessel, Alfred: A history of libraries. New Brunswick, N. J., 1955. 198 p.

Johnson, Alfred F. : French sixteenth century printing, London, 1928. 32 p.

Johnson, Elmer D. : A history of libraries in the western world. New York, 1965. 418 p.

Koch, Theodore W. :   The Imperial Public Library at St. Peters-
       burg. New York, 1915.   35 p.

Krieger, Bogdan: Frederick the Great and his books.   New York,
       1913.   24 p.

Lipsius, Justus: A brief outline of the history of libraries. (Orig-
       inally printed 1627.) Chicago, 1907.   121 p.)

Lomeier, Johannes: De bibliothecis... (Chapter 10 translated by
       John W. Montgomery as: A seventeenth century view of
       European Libraries. Berkeley, Calif. , 1962. 181 p.

Naudé, Gabriel: Advice on establishing a library. (Originally
       printed 1650.) Berkeley, Calif. , 1950.   110 p.

Norris, Dorothy M. :   A history of cataloging and cataloging meth-
       ods, 1100-1850. London, 1939.   246 p.

Ogle, J. J. :   The free library, its history and present condition.
       London, 1897.   344 p.

Orcutt, W. D. :   The magic of the book.   Boston, 1930.   315 p.
       (See pp. 63-104.)

Orcutt, W. D. :   Master makers of the book.   New York, 1928.
       271 p.

Pollard, Alfred W. :   Early illustrated books.   London, 1917.
       256 p.

Pottinger, David: The French book trade in the Ancient Regime,
       1500-1791. Cambridge, Mass. , 1957.   363 p.

Rice, James: Gabriel Naudé. Baltimore, 1939.   134 p.

Savage, Ernest A. :   The story of libraries and book collecting.
       New York, 1909.   230 p.

Thornton, J. L. :   Chronology of librarianship: an introduction to
       the history of libraries and book-collecting.   London, 1941.
       266 p.

Tisserant, Eugene: The Vatican Library.   Jersey City, N. J. ,
       1929.   31 p.

Periodical Articles

Christiansen, Claude H. :   "Classification and cataloging in the
       Scandinavian countries," Library Quarterly, I, (1931), 436-
       454.

Garnett, Richard: "Librarianship in the 17th century," in his Es-
       says in librarianship and bibliography, London, 1899,

pp. 174-190.

Gosnell, Charles F.: "Goethe the librarian," Library Quarterly, II, (1932), 367-374.

Hoffman, Herbert H.: "Co-operative acquisition in German research libraries, 1800-1930," Library Quarterly, XXXIV, (1964), 249-257.

Maass, Ernest: "Leibniz' contributions to librarianship," College and Research Libraries, IV, (1943), 245-249.

Montgomery, John Warwick: "Luther and libraries," Library Quarterly, XXXII, (1962), 133-147.

Munthe, Wilhelm: "The library history of Norway," Library Journal, XLV, (1921), 19-24, 57-62.

Reichman, Felix: "Three hundred years of the Prussian State Library," Library Quarterly, XXXII, (1962), 225-230.

Rostenberg, Leona: "The libraries of three Nuremberg patricians, 1491-1568," Library Quarterly, XIII, (1943), 21-33.

Rostenberg, Leona: "The library of Johann Albrecht, Duke of Mecklenburg, 1526-1568," Library Quarterly, XV, (1945), 131-138.

Schwiebert, Ernest G.: "Remnants of a Reformation library," Library Quarterly, X, (1940), 494-531.

Spratt, H. P.: "Some libraries of Northern Europe," Library Quarterly, IV, (1934), 467-486.

Stummvoll, Josef: "Austrian libraries, past and present," Library Quarterly, XX, (1950), 33-38.

Trenkler, Ernest: "History of the Austrian Nationalbibliotek," Library Quarterly, XVII, (1947), 224-231.

Wehmer, C.: "History of German university libraries," Library Trends, XII, (1964), 496-506.

VII

English Books and Libraries, 1500-1900

Until the sixteenth century libraries in England developed much the same as those on the continent. There were the early monastery libraries, the beginning of the university libraries and a few private collections worthy of note. After about 1500, however, English library history began to develop in a manner of its own.

Both the book arts and libraries in England were severely retarded in the 1530's and 1540's by the Act of Dissolution, which under Henry VIII separated the Church of England from the Roman Catholic Church. Much of the property of the Church was transferred to the King, and in the process, many monastery libraries were broken up and their contents sold or destroyed. The cathedral libraries at York and Canterbury managed to escape much of this damage but in these as in many other libraries, all books that were considered pro-Catholic were removed and destroyed. The printing trade was heavily censored, and nothing could be printed without the approval of the government. When this literary purge was over, the Cambridge University Library contained only nineteen manuscripts of 330 previously held, while Oxford lost almost all of its library. All over England it was estimated that at least a quarter of a million books were destroyed. The accession of Queen Elizabeth I in 1558 brought an end to this tragic period but not until after many literary treasures had been lost and library development in England had received a costly set-back.

The Elizabethan period saw a considerable revival in the English literary world and a period of progress for libraries. By 1560 collectors were beginning to regather the scattered volumes, to obtain copies of others from Europe and to reprint many of the scarce printed works. Oxford University's library, for example, was greatly enlarged and strengthened through the activities of Sir Thomas Bodley. Bodley, having achieved success in business and diplomacy, retired in 1587 and devoted himself to building up the collection at Oxford. So effective were his efforts that in later years the Library took his name, and to this day it is known as the Bodleian Library. By 1602, Bodley had built the Oxford Library to about 2,000 volumes. In 1613, it had grown so that an annex was needed, and by 1620 the first regular librarian, Thomas James, could report that the library contained 16,000 volumes. Many important accessions came in the seventeenth century, including 1300 manuscript volumes from the collection of Archbishop Laud, and 8,000 volumes donated by John Selden, a lawyer. By 1700, the Oxford University Library was by far the largest and most important in England.

The Cambridge University Library did not fare as well in the seventeenth century as did the Bodleian, but it did grow. In the late sixteenth century it had received a valuable gift of books and manuscripts from the Library of Matthew Parker, Archbishop of Canterbury, and in 1632, a large group of Arabic manuscripts from the collection of Thomas Erpenius of Leiden was added. During the Civil War and Commonwealth period, 1641 to 1660, the fortunes of the Cambridge Library varied, sometimes losing, sometimes gaining a few volumes. After the Restoration of King Charles II it received some royal attention, and in 1606, Bishop Tobias Rustat presented an endowment of Ł1000, the proceeds from which were to be used for the purchase of books. Henry Lucas bequeathed a collection of 4,000 volumes to Cambridge, and several other important gifts and bequests of books were received before 1700. Cambridge and Oxford also had libraries of note in their constituent colleges. In many cases, these college libraries had endowments of their own, and were better off financially than the central collections. The college library contents were usually more restricted in subject than the University Library and their use was generally limited to the students and faculty of the particular college.

The University of Glasgow Library, founded in 1453, was an important educational asset in the sixteenth and seventeenth centuries. The University of St. Andrews in Scotland is known to have

had a library as early as 1478, but its organization as a univer
collection dates from 1611. Edinburgh University Library was
founded in 1583, due largely to a gift of funds and books from
Clement Little, a wealthy merchant and lawyer. A fourth Scotti
university, at Aberdeen, had a college library in operation in 14
and a university general library by 1634, but it never equalled t
others in size or importance. In Ireland, the library of Trinity
College at Dublin was begun with a gift of books by the English a
after a victory over the Irish at the battle of Kinsale in 1601.
1604 this collection had 4,000 volumes, and it grew steadily afte
that to become the most important library in Ireland. James
Usher, later primate of Ireland, directed the early growth of thi
library, and on his death in 1655, willed his own library of 7,0
volumes and 600 manuscripts to it.

In the eighteenth and nineteenth centuries, the story of E
lish university libraries was one of slow but steady progress.
many cases the college libraries merged with those of the univer
ties, or at least came under central direction, but in others the
retained their separate identities. In 1715 George I presented t
the Cambridge University Library a collection of some 30,000 b
and magazines, and in the nineteenth century Lord Acton's libra
of over 50,000 volumes was added. At Oxford, major gifts included 4800 manuscripts donated by Dr. Richard Rawlinson in 17
and a sum of L36,000 presented by Rev. Robert Mason in 1841
the purchase of books. Cambridge moved its library into a new
building in 1755. Oxford University Library, after several move
expanded into the remodelled Radcliffe Camera building in 1860.
By 1900, each library contained well over a half million volume
and each occupied parts of several buildings. Elsewhere in Eng
land and Scotland, several new colleges and universities began i
the nineteenth century, and each of these in time built up imposi
libraries. Some of these were the University of London (1837);
University of Durham, (1832); Victoria University at Manchester
(1851); and the University of Liverpool (1882).

The national library of England, the British Museum, has
had a long and interesting history. The early rulers of England

had acquired collections of books, particularly Queen Elizabeth I, whose library was noted for the beauty of its bindings. In 1570, Sir Humphrey Gilbert, a favorite of Elizabeth's, drew up a plan for a Royal Academy and Library, and similar ideas were advanced by Roger Ascham, who was the royal librarian. Neither of these plans was successful, however, and the Royal Library remained simply a private collection. Throughout the Civil War and Commonwealth period following the execution of Charles I, the Royal Library was kept intact, largely through the efforts of its librarian, John Dury. Dury took his position seriously, and even published a booklet in 1650, entitled The Reformed Librarie Keeper, probably the first book on library science in English. Dury had some surprisingly modern ideas. He considered the librarian to be an educator, rather than a mere keeper of books, someone who would be a cultural missionary and bring books and readers together. He called for the use of alphabetized catalogs, preferably printed in book form, and for the liberal use of all materials. In 1662, the Royal Library, by act of Parliament, was allowed to claim one copy of every book published in England, and Richard Bentley, who became Royal Librarian in 1694, enforced this act strictly. He built up the library considerably and made the collection semi-public. To carry out his ideas for the Royal Library, he wrote a pamphlet on A Proposal for Building a Royal Library and Establishing it by Act of Parliament. He wanted governmental aid to build the Library up to at least 200,000 volumes and to support it permanently as a public institution. His plan was good but premature and it was not until a half-century later that a similar plan was put into effect.

Sir Hans Sloane, a physician and scientist, is the man most directly responsible for the founding of the British Museum. During his life he collected books and manuscripts and museum pieces ranging from botanical specimens to antique furniture. On his death, he made his collection available to the nation on condition that it be suitably housed and displayed to the public. In 1753, Parliament accepted this offer and united the Sloane Collection with two others, the Cottonian and Harleian Libraries, to form the be-

ginnings of the British Museum, which was finally opened to the
public in 1759.   The Cottonian Library was largely the collection of
Sir Robert Bruce Cotton, whose grandson donated the library to the
government in 1701.   In 1707 much of the Royal Library was joined
with it in the Cotton House.   The Harleian collection was purchased
by Parliament from the heirs of Sir Robert Harley, who gathered
it early in the eighteenth century.   Harley had brought together a
private library of over 50,000 books and 7,500 manuscripts, but only the latter were obtained by the government, while the printed
volumes were dispersed through various sales.   In 1760, shortly
before his death, King George II donated his private library, including the remains of the earlier Royal libraries, to the Museum.
George III, who reigned from 1760 to 1820, was a noted book collector himself, and his agents scoured England and Europe for book
treasures.   After his death the library was reputed to contain more
than 100,000 volumes, and most of them, along with rare manuscripts and works of art, were later added to the British Museum
by George IV.   Other notable accessions to the Museum were the
Burney Library of 13,500 volumes purchased in 1818, the Banks
collection of 16,000 volumes on natural science donated in 1820,
and the Grenville Library of 20,000 volumes given in 1846.

Although the British Museum was the national library, it was
still a museum, and its main purpose was to display the curios
and rarities collected over the years by the various donors.   Hence,
Montagu House in London, the first home of the Museum, was
largely a show place for the scientific collections, and the books
were shelved in rooms off the main display hall.   Would-be users
of the books found it difficult to get to them and almost impossible
to study them once they were reached.   Moreover the first three
directors of the Museum were all scientists and the book and
manuscript collections did not receive the attention they merited until well into the nineteenth century.   The librarian who was to
transform the Museum into one of the greatest libraries in the
world was, oddly enough, not even an Englishman.   He was Anthony Panizzi, an Italian political refugee, who in 1831 became an
assistant librarian in the Museum thanks to a friendship he had

formed with a member of the Board of Trustees. While he knew
little of library work before his appointment he was well learned
in European languages and literatures and became expert in bibliography as well.   Although he was Head Librarian only from 1856
to 1866, his entire thirty-five years on the staff were spent in improving the book and manuscript collections and in making them
more useful to the public.   He drew up rules for cataloging the
books, and began the lengthy process of organizing and cataloging
the thousands of volumes.   He pointed up the weaknesses in the collection, and urged larger appropriations to fill in the gaps.   He
enforced strictly the deposit laws which required publishers to supply the library with copies of all British publications.   Probably
more than anything else, Panizzi is remembered for designing the
circular reading room which was opened to the public in 1857.   It
was a milestone in library architecture and served as a model for
other buildings in many countries.   When Panizzi joined the staff
of the Museum it was the seventh largest library in Europe, but
when he resigned it was the second only to the Bibliothèque Nationale.   It was said of him that he took a book collection and made it
into a library, and it might be added that in so doing he made of
himself one of the world's greatest librarians.   After Panizzi's re-
tirement, the Museum continued to grow rapidly in size and service, and perhaps its greatest achievement in the late nineteenth century was the production of the printed British Museum catalog which
was completed in 1905.   It represented book and pamphlet holdings
up to 1900, and by this date there were over 2,000,000 volumes to
be included.   In addition to the printed books, there were over
5,000,000 items in the Museum, including prints, maps, broadsides, papyri, clay tablets and other exotic book forms, pictures,
art works and museum objects.

The most important library in Scotland, and the one that became officially the Scottish National Library after 1925, was the
Advocate's Library, founded in 1682 in Edinburgh.   Originally a
legal library, it early began to specialize in Scottish literature and
history as well.   In 1709 it was granted depository rights for all
books published in Great Britain, and under the librarianship of the

historian, David Hume, it grew to be a collection of some 30,000
volumes by 1750.   In later years gifts of books and funds have secured steady growth, and by 1900 the Advocate's Library was approaching 500,000 volumes.   Wales also has a national library
founded in 1873 at Aberystwyth, and Ireland has one which was begun in Dublin in 1877.

The private collection has played a major role in English library history, particularly since the seventeenth century.   At first
the collectors were largely nobles and clergymen, but later they
were joined by merchants and scholars, many of whom amassed
libraries of considerable size.   Many of these private collections
later became a primary part of or a substantial addition to important public and university libraries.   A few examples of the more
notable private collections, many of them gathered by several generations of the same family, will serve to indicate their importance.
The Earls of Balcarres developed the Biblioteca Lindesiana, of
which the most valuable parts were eventually given to the John Rylands Library in Manchester.   This collection comprised more than
100,000 books and 6,000 manuscripts by 1900.   The Rylands Library also contains the Biblioteca Spenceriana, another nineteenth
century private library of nearly 40,000 volumes.   The Dukes of
Marlborough developed at Blenheim a library which had 20,000 volumes in the early 1800's.   The historian, William Camden, left a
large library at his death in 1623, and this eventually ended up in
the British Museum.   In 1678, the Reverend James Nairne gave
2,000 books to the University of Edinburgh Library.   And so the
story goes -- book collectors competing with each other to acquire
books and manuscripts and in the end bequeathing, donating or selling their libraries to some institution.   Not all of the great English
private libraries came into public hands; many of them were sold at
auction, with the more valuable items simply going into the hands
of other collectors.   Furthermore, not all of them remained in
England.   Many were acquired by American buyers and others went
to European collectors, particularly French and German.

A number of English professional libraries had reached notable size and importance by the eighteenth century.   Lincoln's Inn,

a legal corporation that was noted as a training school for lawyers, had a professional library dating from 1508. Gray's Inn and the Inner Temple, similar legal organizations, had large libraries by 1750, and the latter was open to the public as well as to its own lawyers and students. The Royal Society, a scholarly scientific organization, had an important library from its founding in 1667. It specialized in transactions and publications of learned societies, largely obtained in exchange for its own publications, and by 1800 it numbered over 75,000 volumes. In Edinburgh, the Signet (law) Library was founded in 1755, and in the other larger cities legal, religious and scientific libraries were known before 1800 and fairly common in later years. Professional libraries were particularly numerous in London, where there were large collections in medicine, natural history, archaeology, geology, geography, chemistry, botany, zoology and the fine arts. The nineteenth century also saw the development of special libraries in the various government offices in London. Particularly notable were those of the Foreign Office (established 1782), the Public Records Office (1838), the Patent Office (1855), and the Colonial Institute (1868).

There were a few early attempts to provide public library service for the average reader, but it was not until the late nineteenth century that much was accomplished in this direction. A public library was established in Coventry in 1601, but it did not survive. A parish library was founded at Langley Marish, in Buckinghamshire for public use in 1623, and a public library was reportedly founded in Leicester in 1632. One established in Manchester in 1654 has survived almost intact, indicating that it was little used. The library at Dundee, Scotland, dates from 1601, and that of Bristol, England, from 1613, but there is some doubt as to the public character and use of these institutions in their early years. They were indeed public property, but their book collections were small, the caretakers were often indifferent, and the amount of public interest in them is questionable. Possibly of more use were the parish libraries founded by the Reverend Thomas Bray and his associates around 1700. These libraries were placed in the parish churches for the use of ministers and church

members, and were mostly religious in nature, but they apparently
had considerable use for a few years. After Bray's death, the libraries tended to decline and those that survived usually became
ministerial collections, more professional than public in nature.
That there was an interest in public library service, and an attempt in that direction, is evidenced by a pamphlet published in Newcastle-on-Tyne in 1769. It was hopefully entitled A Scheme for
Founding and Supporting a Public Library in Alnwick, Addressed to
All Readers in that Place and Neighbourhood.

In the latter half of the eighteenth century two types of semi-
public libraries became fairly common in England. These were the
proprietary and subscription libraries. The former were usually
connected with some organization and operated on a non-profit basis, while the latter were more often commercial. An example of
the proprietary type was the mechanics' library, designed to provide educational and recreational reading matter for apprentices
and workers in particular locations or trades. Others were formed
by co-operative societies, working-men's clubs, and trade unions,
and many of them eventually formed the bases of local public libraries. They usually included trade manuals, textbooks, religious
and political pamphlets, and occasionally more serious literary and
historical works. They were usually open only to members. The
subscription library, on the other hand, was open to anyone who
could pay the relatively small fee. These were more in the nature
of book clubs or rental book services and often were connected
with book stores or publishers. They may well have had their origin in the coffee-house libraries of the seventeenth century. In
that era the more popular inns or coffee-houses around the universities and in the larger towns began to keep book collections for
their patrons. These books could be read on the premises, or borrowed for a small sum. Regular patrons paid an annual rental for
the use of the books, and in at least one case this rate was only a
shilling for a year. The popularity of these collections stemmed
from their contents: political pamphlets, poems and plays that
were available nowhere else except by purchase. Needless to say,
the contemporary booksellers complained of this service, arguing

that it deprived them of sales. The subscription library was a
popular means of obtaining reading matter, patronized by scholar
and noble along with many a worker and tradesman. By the nineteenth century the subscription libraries had become larger and
more highly organized, with sizable collections of books housed in
permanent quarters. The Liverpool Lyceum, the Bradford Library
and Literary Society, and the Newcastle Library and Philosophical
Society are examples of some of the larger ones, and their names
indicate the widening circle of activities that went along with the libraries. Something in the way of rural libraries were the "itinerat-
ing libraries" established in 1817 by Samuel Brown of Haddington.
These small collections of 25 to 50 books, left in the homes of rural citizens for circulation in the neighborhood, met a popular demand and the system was copied in other areas to some extent.
This system did not survive its founder, who related his adventures as a library promoter in his pamphlet, Some Account of Itin-
erating Libraries and Their Founder, published in 1856.

The development of the modern English public library actually had its beginning in 1847. In that year, following numerous requests from churchmen, social reformers, and trade union leaders,
Parliament passed an act appointing a Committee on Public Libraries to consider the necessity of establishing them throughout the
nation. Two years later this Committee presented a very full report on the conditions of library service then available, and the
need for a tax-supported free public library service. In 1850, as
a result of this report, the Public Libraries Act was passed, allowing cities of 10, 000 or more population to levy taxes to support library service. Subsequent laws extended the Library Act to Scotland and Ireland, and made library tax levies permissable for
smaller towns and rural areas. In 1870, the passage of the Glad-
stone-Forster School Law, which made communities responsible for
the establishment and maintenance of free public schools, greatly
increased the number of readers and consequently the demand for
public libraries. Seventy-seven cities had formed public libraries
by 1877, following the lead of Norwich, which adopted the Act in
September, 1850, and opened its public library officially in 1857.

By 1900 there were over 300 public libraries established under the Act and many of them already had several branches. Generally speaking, however, public library service was poorly supported in England prior to World War I, and there was little in the way of library extension for rural areas. On the brighter side of the picture was the fact that the growth of public libraries came just as many of the great private libraries were being broken up, and some of their most valuable treasures found their way into public collections. For this reason, among others, the larger British public libraries compare very favorably as research centers with the university libraries, and indeed with any but the very largest libraries in the world.

Two subjects closely connected with the history of books and libraries are copyright and legal deposit. The first refers to the author's or publisher's legal rights to a published work, and the latter to the legal requirement that one or more copies of all published works be deposited in certain designated libraries. In England the subject of copyright can be traced at least as far back as 1557, when the Stationers' Company was incorporated in London as an association of printers and publishers representing all such tradesmen in England. In effect it was a monopoly of the publishing business because non-members were unable to get government permits for operation. Previous to this time, what amounted to a copyright might be obtained by securing a "privilege" from the King for printing a book. In later years, the entry of a book title in the register of the Stationers' Company gave the publisher exclusive rights to his publication for an indefinite term. In 1662, the first Copyright Law, in the form of a licensing act, replaced the Stationers' Register, and this act, revised in 1709, 1801, and later, has continued in operation to the present. By the nineteenth century, British copyright was held to be for the life of the author plus fifty years. Legal deposit originated in 1610, when Thomas James, librarian at Oxford, through Sir Thomas Bodley, induced the Stationers' Company to place one copy of each book published by their members in the Library of the University. This practice was made legal and permanent in the Licensing Act of 1662, and two other libraries, that at Cambridge University and the Royal Library, were added to the deposit list. In the eighteenth century legal deposit was extended to other English, Scottish and Irish libraries, but during the nineteenth century the number was curtailed considerably. It had been found that deposit laws were being consistently evaded and when a stronger copyright law was passed in 1852, deposit was required only for the British Museum, while four other major libraries could obtain free depository copies by requesting them in writing.

England saw little progress in the printing arts in the sixteenth and seventeenth centuries. After a good beginning under Caxton and his fellows of the late fifteenth century, English printing felt the burden of censorship and unsettled political and economic conditions for a century and a half. There were many printers but their output was closely watched by both government and religious censors and it was not until after the Restoration of the Stuart kings in 1660 that much progress was made in either quantity or quality of printing. Typography was a trade and not an art in England and even the printing of the Shakespearean plays was poorly done. The types used were often old and worn, margins were small, title-pages were poorly designed, and illustrations were often so carelessly printed as to be hardly recognizable. A few fine books were printed, such as Thomas Roycroft's Polyglot Bible of 1657, which was an excellently executed six volume folio. It was sold by subscription in advance of publication; a new idea in the business of bookselling in England, and one that was to be used often in later years for major publishing ventures.

After 1700, printing in England took on new life, and by the middle of the century it had come to be among the best in Europe. About 1720, William Caslon, a type-founder, began to develop new type faces designed especially for the English alphabet. Taking his patterns from the better Dutch printers and improving on them, Caslon produced a type that was clean and precise. He employed a combination of curves and angles that was pleasing to the eye. John Baskerville took the Caslon type-forms, adapted them moderately and with them produced some of the most beautiful books in

printing history.   Baskerville not only improved upon the type he
used, but upon the press, paper and ink as well.   He printed some
67 different books, but probably his best known book is his edition
of the works of Virgil.   Baskerville's books were expensive, even
for his day, and they were designed largely for the collector, or at
least for the appreciator of fine books.   Whatever their purpose,
they set a standard of perfection and even of elegance in printing
that has influenced the book world ever since.

The output of the early English printers consisted for the
most part of religious works, political pamphlets, and the classical
authors, although the latter were never printed as extensively in
England as they were on the continent.   In the sixteenth century
came more pamphleteering, more works by English authors and a
few government publications.   Early in the seventeenth century came
the King James Bible, the largest publishing venture in England to
that date.   Still later in the same century came the first periodicals, usually folded sheets of four to eight pages, giving the latest
political or military news along with some contemporary literature
and the editor's views on a variety of subjects.   Usually these early journals were short-lived unless they enjoyed political or governmental support and their fortunes varied with the political and social prestige of their editors.   By 1750, the periodical had become
fairly common and newspapers, magazines and yearbooks were in
general use among the upper classes.   There were general and
news magazines, such as the Gentleman's Magazine; literary periodicals like the Spectator and important yearbooks of current history, such as the Annual Register.   Many scientific books and journals joined the literary output of the English presses in the late
eighteenth and nineteenth centuries, and, in general the press of
England became and remained as free and prolific as any in the
world.

Although they were not printed in large numbers before the
nineteenth century, there were a few children's books published.   In
1477 Caxton published his Boke of Curteseye, or book of manners
for young people, to instruct the young Englishman on how to act
in church and at home, and also on what to read.   The Schoole of

Vertue and Book of Good Nurture for Children and Youth to Learn
Their Duty By was a similar work, written by F. S. Seager and
printed in 1577.   About 1600 there appeared the horn book, the first
elementary printed matter designed for the child's own reading.
The horn book was really a single page, fastened to a wooden pad-
dle and protected by a transparent cover of horn.   It usually contained the alphabet and a short sentence or verse of simple reading.
The World in Pictures, first printed in England about 1658, has
been considered the first picture book for children.   About 1750
John Newbery became the first publisher to be particularly interested in children's books.   He published a collection of Mother
Goose Rhymes and when this proved to be popular he printed Oliver
Goldsmith's History of Margery Two-Shoes, probably the first story
in English written especially for children.   In all, Newbery published more than a hundred small books for his juvenile readers,
and was himself the author of many of them.   He was also one of
the first publishers of annual gift-books, an item which was to become very popular in the nineteenth century.

      One other publishing development of the eighteenth century is
worthy of note.   This was the compiling and publishing of multi-
volumed encyclopedias.   Ephraim Chambers' Cyclopedia..., published in 1728 contained only two volumes, but it was followed by
the first edition of the Encyclopedia Britannica in 1771.   This work,
which was to become the standard in its field, was a major under-
taking, with many authorities contributing to it and with its three
volumes appearing in as many years.   Such reference works were
often sold by subscription, and issued in numbers or parts which
could be later bound into volumes.   Often two or more printers
would combine their efforts in order to print an encyclopedia or to
issue the complete works of a popular author.

      In book illustrations, the wood-cut continued popular in Eng-
land well into the seventeenth century, although the copper engraving was known there as early as 1588.   In the days of Baskerville
and Caslon, the copper engraving was generally used, but in the
nineteenth century it was replaced by the steel engraving.

      In bindings, English books progressed from the rather simple

leather and vellum backs of the sixteenth century through the more
ornate tooled and decorated leathers of the seventeenth and eighteenth centuries, and down to the cloth and boards of the nineteenth.
Generally speaking, English bindings were never quite as fancy as
those preferred by the French and Italian collectors.

Although types, illustrations and bindings progressed noticeably over the years, the printing press itself changed little between
1500 and 1800.   In the nineteenth century came revolutionary changes
in the printing process, including the rotary press, the lithograph,
the linotype and the high speed power presses, to mention only a
few.

Late Victorian England was a literate world and the market
for books, whether the six-penny thriller or the twenty-guinea collector's item, was extensive.   The English printer and publisher
not only met this demand at home, but spread his wares throughout
the world and the twentieth century owes much to the nineteenth
century bookmen for both the quantity and the quality of their product.   The power of the printing press as a vital means of popular
communication is nowhere better illustrated than in the last few
centuries of English history.

Bibliography

Books

Altick, Richard: The English common reader: a social history of
      the mass reading public, 1800-1900.   Chicago, 1957.   430 p.

Bennett, William: John Baskerville.   Birmingham, England, 1937-
      1939.   2 v.

Birmingham Public Library: Notes on the history of the Birming-
      ham Public Libraries, 1861-1961.   Birmingham, England,
      1962.   26 p.

Blagden, C.:   Stationers' company, a history, 1403-1959.   London,
      1960.   321 p.

Boulton, W.H.:   The romance of the British Museum.   London,
      1931.   242 p.

Craster, H.H.E.:   A history of the Bodleian Library, 1845-1945.
      Oxford, 1952.   372 p.

Curwen, Henry: A history of booksellers. London, 1873. 483 p.

Duff, William G. : William Caxton. Chicago, 1905. 118 p.

Durkan, John, and Ross, Anthony: Early Scottish libraries. Glasgow, 1961. 196 p.

Dury, John: The reformed librarie keeper. (Originally printed 1650.) Chicago, 1906. 71 p.

Edwards, Edward: A statistical view of the principal libraries of Europe and America. London, 1849. 48 p.

Edwards, Edward: Free town libraries, their formation, management and history in Britain, France, Germany and America. London, 1863. 371 p.

Fagan, Louis: The life of Sir Anthony Panizzi. London, 1880. 2 v.

Esdaile, A. J. K. : The British Museum Library. London, 1946. 388 p.

Great Britain, Parliament: Report from a select committee on public libraries. London, 1849. 317 p.

Greenwood, Thomas: Public libraries; a history of the movement in England. London, 1890. 586 p.

Irwin, Raymond: The heritage of the English library. New York, 1964. 296 p.

Irwin, Raymond: The origins of the English library. London, 1957. 272 p.

Jayne, Sears: Library catalogues of the English renaissance. Berkeley, Calif. , 1956. 226 p.

Kaufman, Paul: Borrowings from the Bristol Library, 1773-1784. Charlottesville, Va. , 1960. 138 p.

Kaufman, Paul: Reading vogues at the English cathedral libraries of the eighteenth century. New York, 1964. 70 p. (Originally appeared in New York Public Library Bulletin.)

Kronick, David A. : A history of scientific and technical periodicals. New York, 1962. 274 p.

Library Association: A century of public libraries, 1850-1950. London, 1950. 27 p.

McColvin, Lionel R. : The public library system of Great Britain. London, 1942. 218 p.

Minto, John: A history of the public library movement in Great
    Britain and Ireland. London, 1932. 366 p.

Moran, John: Wynkyn de Worde, father of Fleet Street. London,
    1960. 56 p.

Munford, W. A. : Penny rate; aspects of British public library his-
    tory. London, 1951. 150 p.

Oldman, C. B. : English libraries, 1800-1850. London, 1958.
    78 p.

Partridge, R. C. B. : The history of legal deposit of books through-
    out the British Empire. London, 1938. 364 p.

Plomer, Henry R. : A short history of English printing, 1476-
    1898. London, 1900. 345 p.

Predeek, Albert: A history of libraries in Great Britain and North
    America. Chicago, 1947. 177 p.

Rawlings, G. B. : The British Museum Library. London, 1916.
    231 p.

Rees, Gwendolen: Libraries for children; a history and a bibliog-
    raphy. London, 1924. 260 p.

Ricci, S. de: English collectors of books and manuscripts, 1539-
    1930. Cambridge, England, 1930. 203 p. (Reprinted, Lon-
    don, 1960.)

Savage, Ernest A. : Old English libraries. London, 1911. 298 p.

Streeter, B. H. : Chained libraries, a survey of four centuries in
    the evolution of the English library. London, 1931. 368 p.

Thornton, John: Classics of librarianship; further selected read-
    ings in the history of librarianship. London, 1957. 203 p.

Thornton, John: A mirror for librarians; selected readings in the
    history of librarianship. London, 1948. 207 p.

Wiles, R. M. : Serial publication in England before 1750. Cam-
    bridge, England, 1957. 391 p.

Wormald, Francis: The English library: studies in its develop-
    ment before 1700. London, 1958. 273 p.

Periodical Articles

Borden, H. K. : "Libraries and cultural renaissance," Library
    Quarterly, IV, (1934), 28-35.

Ditzion, Sidney: "The Anglo-American library scene," Library
    Quarterly, XVI, (1946), 281-301.

"The foundation of libraries," Cambridge History of English Liter-
    ature, IV, 474-497.

Garnett, Richard: "Librarianship in the 17th century," in his Es-
    says in Librarianship and Bibliography, (London, 1899), 174-
    190.

Hamlyn, Hilda M. : "Eighteenth century circulating libraries in
    England," The Library, 5th series, I, (1947), 197-222.

Houlette, W. D. : "Thomas Bray," Library Quarterly, IV, (1934),
    588-609.

Kaufman, Paul: "Community lending libraries in 18th century Ire-
    land and Wales," Library Quarterly, XXXIII, (1963), 299-
    312.

Lyle, Guy R. : "A royal book-collector, George III," Library Quar-
    terly, III, (1933), 180-191.

McCue, George S. : "Libraries of the London coffee-houses," Li-
    brary Quarterly, IV, (1934), 624-627

Oates, J. C. T. : "The Cambridge University Library, 1400-1600,"
    Library Quarterly, XXXII, (1962), 270-286.

Wellard, James H. : "The state of reading among the working
    classes of England during the first half of the nineteenth cen-
    tury," Library Quarterly, V, (1935), 87-100.

VIII
Printing in Colonial America

The development of printing came only a half century before the discovery of America and it is not surprising that printing followed closely as European civilization spread to the New World. The Spanish were the first to secure permanent colonies, and their motives in settling them were both economic and religious. They intended to Christianize the natives, and since the printed word was an effective means of spreading and preserving Christianity, a printing press was a logical supplement to the early missionary's equipment. Thus the first printing press in the Americas was established in Mexico City sometime in the 1530's. The exact date of the first printing, and the name of the first printer are both uncertain. It may have been Pedro Varela in 1531, or Esteban Martin in 1536, but proof for both is lacking. On the other hand, the coming of Juan Pablos to Mexico City in 1539 is well documented. He was an agent of Juan Cromberger, a leading printer of Seville in Spain, and from his press there came a number of works in the early 1540's. Most of his publications were religious works but he also printed primers for children, and official publications for the government. By 1550, a typefounder had joined Pablos' printing crew, and the type and make-up of his publications improved considerably thereafter. Printing did not thrive in Mexico and there were few presses outside of Mexico City until the nineteenth century.

The second American country to have a printing press in operation was Peru. In 1584, Antonio Ricardo, formerly of Mexico City, opened his printshop in Lima and began his printing with a four-page Royal proclamation, a copy of which still exists. Printing spread very slowly to the remainder of Latin America. Ecuador had a press in such good condition as to print a seven hundred page folio volume by 1627 but how much earlier it had been operating is not known.   Guatemala had a press by 1660, but most of the other countries were without printers until the eighteenth century. Argentina's printing history began about 1705, Brazil's about 1747, Chile's about 1748, and Venezuela's about 1764.   Bolivia and Panama did not have printers until the nineteenth century, and there were no presses in the West Indies until after 1700.

In the English colonies of North America the first printing was done in Massachusetts.   The Reverend Jose Glover, who thought that a printing press in the new colony would further the causes of both the Puritan church and the new Harvard College, arranged for the shipment of a press and an experienced printer to Cambridge.   This press was set up and in operation by early 1639, with young Matthew Day as the printer.   Matthew's father, Stephen Day, is sometimes given as the first American printer but it is now thought that the elder Day was the mechanic who set up the press while his son was the actual printer.

The first piece of printing known to have come from the Day press was a broadside, The Freeman's Oath, and the first pamphlet was An Almanack for the year 1639.   Not a single copy of either has survived.   The oldest known book printed in what is now the United States appeared from the Day press in 1640.   It was the celebrated Bay Psalm Book, or The Whole Books of Psalmes Faithfully Translated into English Metre...   The Day family operated the press until 1649, when upon the death of Matthew Day it came under the operation of Samuel Green, who continued it until 1692. Up to that date more than two hundred books and pamphlets were published by this one press.   They included almanacs, items connected with Harvard College, and books and pamphlets of a religious nature.   In 1675 the town of Boston acquired its first printing press when John Foster set himself up as a printer there. Foster was also a wood engraver and he illustrated some of his books himself.   Interestingly enough, one of the earliest American printers was an Indian who took the name of James Printer.   He learned the trade at the press of Samuel Green and his name appears as printer on at least one book.

The second of the English colonies to acquire a printing es-

tablishment was Pennsylvania, where in 1685 young William Bradford appeared as a printer sponsored by the colony's founder, William Penn. Bradford's first Pennsylvania imprint was also an almanac: America's Messenger, Being an Almanack for the Year of
Grace, 1686. Bradford did not remain long in Penn's good graces,
however, and in a few years he moved to New York, where in
1693 he established the first press in that colony. His first known
publication there was a slap at the Pennsylvania leaders who had
opposed him, and was entitled: New-England's Spirit of Persecu-
tion Transmitted to Pennsylvania... Bradford remained in New
York until his death in 1752, printing more than 400 books and
pamphlets during his lifetime. He is noted as one of the colonial
era's outstanding printers, having produced the first New York paper
currency, the first American Book of Common Prayer, the first
history of New York, and the first copperplate map of New York.
Bradford also had a share in the establishment of the first paper
mill in America, and established the first printing press in the colony of New Jersey in 1723. His sons and grandsons continued the
family printing business until well into the nineteenth century.

        The colony of Virginia had a printing press for a brief peri-
od in 1682, and it is possible that one or two items may have been
printed then but if so there is no record of them. Instead, the
printer, William Nuthead, was ordered by the English government
to pack up his press and return to London, which he did. Nuthead
later turned up in Maryland where, by 1686 or possibly earlier,
he operated a press at St. Mary's City, making this colony the
third to have an active printing establishment. Virginia did not
have a permanent printing press until 1730 when William Parks set
up his operations at Williamsburg. South Carolina followed, with
a printing press in operation at Charleston in 1731 and from that
date until the Revolution that port city was one of the most active
printing centers in the colonies. Three printers, in fact, set up
shop in Charleston in 1731 and 1732, but they did not survive very
long. Instead it was Lewis Timothy, a protegé of Benjamin Franklin, who became South Carolina's first important printer after he
arrived there in 1733. In North Carolina, James Davis was the

first printer in 1749, and in Delaware James Adams set up the
first press in 1761. Georgia had no printer until James Johnston
arrived in 1763. No printing was done in Canada until 1751, when
Bartholomew Green, Jr., a grandson of Samuel Green of Massachusetts, set up his shop in Halifax, Nova Scotia. A year later,
John Bushell, another New Englander, began the first newspaper
published in Canada, also at Halifax.

Probably the most outstanding of the colonial printers was a
man who is most remembered for his other occupations. Benjamin
Franklin was a statesman, philosopher, inventor and scientist, as
well as journalist and printer. Printing was his first love and
throughout his long life he insisted that his vocation was printer.
Franklin was born in Boston and at an early age he was apprenticed
to an older brother to learn the art of printing. He worked in London as a printer for nearly two years before setting up his shop in
Philadelphia. This work was good experience, for the materials
and workmanship in the London establishments were superior to
those with which he had been acquainted in America.

At first Franklin worked for other printers, including William Bradford, but later he entered into a partnership with Hugh
Meredith. In 1730, while Franklin was still only 23, his partnership was ended and he set out alone as "B. Franklin, Printer."
In the next forty years or so of the operation of this press more
than 700 titles were issued from it, exclusive of paper money,
broadsides and newspapers. In 1729, while still in partnership
with Meredith, Franklin began publishing the Pennsylvania Gazette,
the second weekly newspaper to be established in Philadelphia.
The newspaper proved fairly successful and led Franklin to begin
his second major publication, Poor Richard's Almanac. The almanac was the colonial printer's main stock in trade, and Franklin improved his by writing most of it himself. His witty sayings
and sensible advice made Poor Richard a household word for many
generations.

The product of the American colonial printer was varied.
After about 1725, the average printer published a newspaper, sometimes doubling as editor, writer, reporter, pressman and circula-

tion manager. Eventually he came to the point where he became
editor only, while journeymen printers did the press work. Along
with the newspaper, the printer sometimes published an annual almanac, a type of reading matter that was second only to the Bible
in the average colonial home. The almanac contained the calendar
for the year, often with elementary astronomical information and
the astrological signs. Along with this, it contained witty sayings,
home remedies, and general advice on home and farm problems.
In addition, each almanac usually gave the names of the officials
of the province, and sometimes reprinted the local tax laws. Depending upon the wit and ability of the editor the almanac flourished or failed; some lasting only an issue or two while others survived a half-century or more. In the case of Franklin's Poor
Richard, annual sales sometimes reached 10,000 copies or more,
but most of the almanacs were far less popular. In the latter colonial period, the almanac was joined by the provincial register,
similar in some respects, but containing more political and statistical information about the individual provinces.

Official government publications were important elements in
most of the colonial printers' output. In fact, in several instances
the early printers were induced to come to the colonies in order
to perform the public printing, and in at least one case, South Carolina, a bonus was offered by the legislature to the first printer
who would locate in the colony. The publications of the provincial
governments included laws, particularly tax laws, law codes, legislative journals, and the various legal forms needed for the trans-
action of official business. On the other hand, early colonial
printers were quite often severely restricted by the provincial governments and their Royal governors, and the items printed were
sometimes censored. Official favoritism too sometimes played a
part and where there were two or more printers in one colony, one
might be favored for political reasons, or might win political approval by his good work, as Franklin did once early in his printing
career. Official printers in each colony were not only favored with
government printing but were often allowed more license in what
they did print. A celebrated case in colonial legal history was that

of Peter Zenger, who in 1734 published some attacks against the
local governor in his newspaper, the New York Weekly Journal.
For this he was imprisoned under a charge of libel but when he
finally came to trial he was acquitted. His lawyer, Andrew Hamilton, argued that if the jury found the facts as published to be true,
then there could be no libel. The case established a legal precedent in similar cases of libel, providing that the jury should be the
judges of both the law and the facts in a particular case. The Zenger case is considered a forward step in the development of freedom of the press and of public means of mass communication in
general.

        The colonial printer, when not engaged with newspapers, al-
manacs and governmental publications, turned out a wide variety of
broadsides, pamphlets and books. The numerous broadsides were
usually little more than circulars announcing new laws or giving
the results of court cases or proposing some change in governmental procedures. They were printed on one side of a sheet only, and were designed to be posted in public places where they
could be easily seen by a large number of people. In effect they
were supplements to the newspapers and sometimes they were actually called "extras." The pamphlets were usually political or religious, and the number published by all the colonial printers undoubtedly ran into the thousands. They were usually hastily printed,
poorly sewn, and often quickly read and forgotten but their numbers
indicate that they served a communication need and many of them
were so popular that, despite several known printings, no copies
have survived. Indeed, one historian estimates that for every colonial publication of which a copy has survived at least four other
publications have been lost completely. The reason for this, aside
from the poor physical condition of the publications was the fact
that in most cases only a hundred or so of each item was printed.

        In subject matter, religion led the list of publications for
most colonial printers, amounting to almost two-fifths of all the
known colonial printing. Collected sermons were especially popular in New England, but they were widely printed and reprinted in
all the colonies. Law codes, legal form books, legislative journals

and official manuals accounted for another fifth of the printing,
while literature in all its forms was almost as extensive. Most of
the literary works published were editions of the classics, with a
few contemporary European and English authors, and a very few
American items. The relatively small percentage of literary publications was probably due to the fact that such items could be purchased in English editions cheaper than they could be reprinted in
America. This was also true of the Bible, of which there were
few editions published by colonial printers. The social sciences,
including history, economics, education and political science, accounted for the final fifth of the known publications except for about
three per cent made up of publications in the sciences and the arts.
Among the histories were several volumes on the development of
the individual colonies and many more on early relations with the
Indians. Some books went through many editions, as for example,
the New England Primer, which was printed in more than thirty
editions and thousands of copies between 1690 and 1830. The Office
and Authority of the Justice of the Peace, a legal handbook, went
through forty editions between 1710 and 1800. All told, at least
18,300 different publications are known to have been issued by colonial American printers, counting a full year of a newspaper as
one item, and some estimates place the actual figure, including
items no longer in existence, as high as 80,000 separate publications.

        The earliest newspaper printed in the English colonies was
an issue of Public Occurences both Foreign and Domestick, published by Benjamin Harris in Boston on September 25, 1690. The
provincial government objected to the contents of this first issue,
and banned further publications. Earlier there had occasionally
been published some antecedants of the newspaper in the form of
news broadsides, such as one published in Boston in 1689 by Samuel Green, and entitled The Present State of the New-English Affairs, Published to Prevent False Reports. After Harris' unsuccessful venture it was fourteen years until another printer dared to
issue a newspaper, and this time it was done only with the approval and authority of the government. The publisher was John Camp-

bell, the title was, appropriately enough, The Boston News-Letter, and the first issue was dated April 24, 1704. In size, the News-Letter was only a single sheet, about 7 by 11.5 inches, and in contents it consisted mainly of news borrowed from London newspapers. Some local news and news from the other colonies was carried in later issues, along with notices and announcements of both the Massachusetts government and the British government in London. It came out weekly or sometimes every two weeks and it managed not only to meet the approval of the authorities, but actually secured a subsidy on one or two occasions. It never became financially successful and as late as 1719 the publisher complained that he had less than 300 paying customers. Other early newspapers were the Boston Gazette (1719); the New England Courant (1721); also of Boston; the American Weekly Mercury (1719), and Franklin's Pennsylvania Gazette (1729), both of Philadelphia. New York's first newspaper was the New-York Gazette, founded in 1725, while the Maryland Gazette began in Annapolis in 1727 and the South-Carolina Gazette at Charleston in 1732. The Virginia Gazette, at Williamsburg, was published as early as 1736 and the North-Carolina Gazette, at New Bern, in 1751. In all, more than a hundred different newspapers, most of them short-lived, were published in the thirteen colonies before the Revolution.

The contents of the average colonial newspaper ran strongly to political tracts, with literary works in serial form being also fairly common. News as such was usually weeks or months old, often copied from English newspapers brought over by the mail ships or "packets." Public laws and official decrees sometimes made up most of a single issue, particularly when the provincial legislature was in session. Later in the eighteenth century advertising developed and contributed to the financial stability of the newspaper. Most of the advertisements were of the classified type, short and to the point, calling attention to goods for sale, a runaway slave, or a delinquent wife who had left the advertiser's bed and board. In the late colonial period, the larger merchants would sometimes take a half or full column to list their choice wares, item by item, and all "just arrived from England." Although edi-

torials themselves were scarce, the editor's policies were often
strong, and well known to his readers.   Rival editors often used
vicious language in attacking each other, usually over fictitious
names.   Readers contributed their ideas and opinions in long letters to the editors, often signed by pseudonyms, such as "Publius"
or "Pro Bono Publico."   No daily papers were published prior to
the Revolution, but exciting news appearing between issues was
sometimes made public in the form of "extras."   Lists of ships ar-
riving and departing, schedules of stage-coaches, and similar bits
of public information were usually included, often on the front page.
In format, the colonial newspaper was usually only two to four
pages, with the pages themselves being about half the size of the
modern newspaper.

The first American magazine, published for about three
months in 1741 by Andrew Bradford of Philadelphia, was appropriately enough entitled the American Magazine but its subtitle was
more descriptive: A Monthly View of the Political State of the Colonies.   Benjamin Franklin followed with his General Magazine and
Historical Chronicle only a few days later, and this periodical
lasted six months.   Both were really little more than supplements
to their publishers' newspapers, and as such carried little appeal.
In 1743, the American Magazine and Historical Chronicle began in
Boston under the editorship of Jeremiah Gridley, and survived for
about three years.   Even at that it was one of the most successful
of the colonial magazines.   Between 1741 and 1775 no less than
seventeen different magazines were started in the colonies, but
most lasted only a short time, and none survived the Revolution.
The American colonial magazines lacked one prime ingredient --
writers.   They could not compete with the several good British
periodicals in content and since timeliness was of little importance
the American magazine did not attract an audience.

Throughout the colonial period the printing press in use was
little changed from that developed by Gutenberg two centuries earlier.   Most presses or their component parts were bought in England but Christopher Sauer, a noted printer of Germantown, Pennsylvania, built his own press, and possibly a few other printers

did so in the later colonial period. The type that was used came
from England or Germany until about 1770 when the Sauers and
Abel Buell of Connecticut began to cast their own type. Jacob Bay,
a native of Switzerland, set up the first type-founding business in
America at Philadelphia in 1773. Paper was made in the colonies
as early as 1690 when William Rittenhouse, a German, built a paper mill for William Bradford near Philadelphia. The colonial paper industry grew slowly, and the quality remained poor but by
1775 much of the paper used in the colonies was made here, especially in Pennsylvania. Benjamin Franklin was very much interested in the manufacture of paper, and is supposed to have aided in
the establishment of no less than eighteen papermaking factories
from Virginia to New York. This early American paper, like that
of Europe down to the nineteenth century, was made of cotton and
linen rags. The ink used was made of linseed oil and lampblack,
and although both these ingredients were available in the later colonial period, it seems that most printers preferred to buy their
inks from England. Franklin and Bradford, among a few other
printers, did at times make their own printing ink but they too purchased much from England as surviving records show. In the early
days the printer's working staff consisted largely of his wife and
children but as his business grew he took on apprentices and sometimes hired extra journeymen. Most printing establishments had
only one press and the largest probably had no more than three or
four, with a force of ten or twelve typesetters and pressmen.
Wages paid to skilled printers were comparatively high, and they
were considered to be among the most important of the "mechanicks"
or craftsmen of the colonial period.

The position of the printer in colonial society was an interesting one. He was quite often an influential citizen of the colony
in which he lived, and sometimes he grew into relative economic
wealth as well. Benjamin Franklin was, of course, no ordinary
printer. Justus Fox of Philadelphia, besides being a printer, practiced the professions of engraver, type-molder, physician, apothe-
cary and surgeon. William Bradford of Pennsylvania, Samuel
Green of Massachusetts, Lewis Timothy of South Carolina, and a

score or more other printers were important leaders in their respective towns and provinces.   Part of this was due to their newspapers which, despite occasional control and censorship, exercised
considerable influence in colonial politics.   The printer was often
a self-educated man who took a place of leadership in his comunity.
A book-store was often attached to the printing shop.   This attracted the more educated citizens and often became a focal point
for the local leaders, whether literary, social or political.

An interesting sidelight on colonial printing is the number of
women who took an active part in the printing business.   Franklin
freely acknowledged the help of his wife in the print-shop during
the early days of their marriage and in Charleston, Anne Timothy
took over and operated the press several years after the death of
her husband, Lewis Timothy, before her son, Peter Timothy, was
old enough to handle the business.   Dinah Nuthead, the widow of
William Nuthead, operated a printing house in Annapolis, Maryland,
for a few years after 1695 and Ann Franklin, sister-in-law of Benjamin, operated a press in Newport, Rhode Island, after 1758.
Several families included printers in several generations and the
descendants of Samuel Green of Massachusetts were printers and
publishers for nearly two centuries.

As the American Revolution got under way, the colonial
printer soon became an important part of it.   The Stamp Act of
1765 directly involved the publications and printed forms produced
by the printer and, as the differences between the colonies and
England became more pronounced, it was the printer who kept the
people informed of developments through his newspapers and broadsides.   The actions of the Continental Congress, and the retalia-
tory actions of the British Parliament were hot news events that
were published from Maine to Georgia.   The Revolutionary Committees of Correspondence made full use of the printing press in
distributing their news from colony to colony.   Particularly important was the political pamphlet.   One pamphlet in particular,
Thomas Paine's Common Sense, coming as it did in January, 1776
and selling many thousand copies, did much to change an economic
dispute into a war for independence simply by pointing out to the

Americans that independence was possible and that the dawn of an
American empire could be at hand. It is indeed hard to imagine a
successful American Revolution without the aid of the provincial
printing presses. And the colonial printer, taking sides as he did
with America or England -- for several of them did remain loyal
to the King -- was worth at least a regiment to the cause he favored. Printers on both sides suffered during the war through destruction or seizure of their presses and from shortages of paper,
ink and labor. But in the end, the importance of the printer and
his product was fully appreciated, and when, in 1789, the first ten
Amendments to the new United States Constitution were submitted,
prominently placed in Article I was the firm guarantee of freedom
of the press.

Table II
Notable Early American Printers*

Date	Printer	Location
1639	Matthew Day	Cambridge, Massachusetts
1649	Samuel Green	Cambridge, Massachusetts
1675	John Foster	Boston, Massachusetts
1685	William Bradford	Philadelphia, Pennsylvania
1689	William Nuthead	St. Mary's City, Maryland
1693	William Bradford	New York, New York
1709	Thomas Short	New London, Connecticut
1723	William Bradford	Perth Amboy, New Jersey
1727	James Franklin	Newport, Rhode Island
1728	Benjamin Franklin	Philadelphia, Pennsylvania
1730	William Parks	Williamsburg, Va.
1731	George Webb	Charleston, South Carolina
1733	Lewis Timothy	Charleston, South Carolina
1738	Christopher Sauer	Germantown, Pennsylvania
1749	James Davis	Newbern, North Carolina
1751	James Parker	Woodbridge, New Jersey
1756	Daniel Fowle	Portsmouth, New Hampshire
1761	James Adams	Wilmington, Delaware
1763	James Johnston	Savannah, Georgia
1764	Denis Braud	New Orleans, Louisiana
1783	William C. Wells	St. Augustine, Florida
1787	John Bradford	Lexington, Kentucky
1791	George Roulstone	Rogersville, Tennessee
1793	William Maxwell	Cincinnati, Ohio
1797	John McCall	Detroit, Michigan
1799	Andrew Marschalk	Natchez, Mississippi

* This list includes only the first printers in the various colonies
  or states before 1800, and a few of the other more important colonial printers.

130 Communication

Bibliography

Books

Green, Samuel A. : John Foster, the earliest American engraver
and the first Boston printer. Boston, 1909. 149 p.

Gundy, H. P. : Early printers and printing in the Canadas. Toronto, 1957. 54 p.

Hildeburn, Charles R. : Sketches of printers and printing in colonial New York. New York, 1895. 189 p.

Kimber, Sydney A. : The story of an old press: an account of
the ... Stephen Day Press. Cambridge, Mass. , 1937.
43 p.

Klapper, August: The printer in eighteenth-century Williamsburg.
Williamsburg, Va. , 1955. 30 p.

Lehmann-Haupt, Hellmut: The book in America. New York, 1939.
453 p.

Leonard, Irving A. : Books of the brave. New York, 1949. 381 p.
(On the use of books in colonial Latin America.)

McMurtrie, Douglas C. : The beginnings of the American newspaper. Chicago, 1935. 36 p.

McMurtrie, Douglas C. : The book: the story of printing and
bookmaking. New York, 1943. 676 p.

McMurtrie, Douglas C. : A history of printing in the United
States: middle and South Atlantic states. New York, 1936.
462 p.

Mott, Frank L. : A history of American magazines, 1741-1850.
New York, 1930. 848 p.

Orcutt, W. D. : The magic of the book. Boston, 1930. 315 p.
(See pp. 17-62 on early New England printing.)

Oswald, John C. : Benjamin Franklin, printer. Garden City,
N. Y. , 1917. 244 p.

Oswald, John C. : Printing in the Americas. New York, 1937.
565 p.

Richardson, L. N. : A history of early American magazines, 1741-
1789. New York, 1931. 414 p.

Roden, Robert F. : The Cambridge press, 1638-1692. New York,
1905. 193 p.

Stillwell, Margaret B. :   Incunabula and Americana.   New York,
    1931.   483 p.

Thomas, Isaiah: History of printing in America.   Albany, N. Y. ,
    1874.   2 v. (Reprinted, N. Y. , 1964. 2 v.)

Thompson, L. S. :   Printing in colonial Spanish America.   Hamden,
    Conn. , 1962.   108 p.

Weeks, Lyman H. :   A history of paper manufacturing in the United
    States, 1690-1916.   New York, 1916. 352 p.

Winterich, John T. :   Early American books and printing.   Boston,
    1935.   256 p.

Wroth, Lawrence C. :   The colonial printer.   Portland, Maine,
    1938.   368 p. (Reprinted, Charlottesville, Va. , 1964.)

Periodical Articles

Harlan, Robert D. :   'William Strahan's American book trade,
    1744-1776," Library Quarterly, XXXI, (1961), 235-244.

McMurtrie, Douglas C. :   'The first typefounding in Mexico," The
    Library, 4th series, VIII, (1928), 119-122.

Silver, Rollo: "Government printing in Massachusetts, 1751-1801,"
    Studies in Bibliography, XVI, (1963), 161-200.

Wagner, Henry R. :   'Sixteenth century Mexican imprints," in Bib-
    liographical Essays, a Tribute to Wilberforce Eames. (Cam-
    bridge, Mass. , 1924), 249-268.

Winship, George P. :   'Spanish America," in R. A. Peddie, ed. :
    Printing, a short history. (London, 1927), 306-318.

Wroth, Lawrence C. :   'The origins of typefounding in North and
    South America," Ars Typographica, II, (1926), 273-307.

IX
Libraries in Colonial America

The American colonists were largely engaged in making a
living, with religious and political interests taking up most of their
free time, but a few of them were interested enough in books and
learning to form libraries -- college, semi-public and private.
None of these colonial libraries reached a large size, and the influence of any one of them may have been limited but the sum total of
them indicates a relatively high degree of culture.   Considering the
time and place, their very existence is noteworthy, and in them we
see the beginnings of American library history.   Although books
were scarce items for the frontiersman and the small farmer and
almost completely unknown to the slave, they were available to the
citizens of most towns by 1750, and were available in private and
academic collections throughout the colonial period.

It is interesting to note that a college and a college library
were planned for the infant colony of Virginia along with a school
for the education of the Indians.   The Indian attacks of 1622 put an
end to these philanthropic and educational designs.   Instead, Virginia had to wait another seventy years for the founding of its first
college, William and Mary, and even longer for its first college
library.   In Massachusetts, however, Harvard College had a library
almost before it was founded.   In fact, the college name comes
from John Harvard, who in 1638 gave the college some 380 books
and a small cash endowment.   Other gifts followed, including one
of forty books from Governor John Winthrop in 1642, but Harvard's
library grew only slowly in the seventeenth century.   Its holdings
were largely theological, since the college of that day was mainly
a training school for Puritan ministers.   In 1764, with the college
more than a century and a quarter old, the library still contained
less than 5000 volumes.   In that year it was burned with almost a
total loss of its book collection.   After this tragedy, friends of the

college came to its aid, and the Massachusetts legislature voted
L2,000 to replace the burned Harvard Hall. In addition, a popular
subscription raised almost another L1,000. Many other gifts of
books and money were received so that rapid growth was experienced for a few years and by 1775 the library was back to its former size. According to its catalog of 1790, the Harvard Library
was still largely theological but it contained a variety of historical,
scientific and literary works as well. In literature the English authors were fairly well represented, including Shakespeare, Milton,
Spenser, Chaucer, Pope and Dryden. European works were represented by Boccaccio, Voltaire, La Fontaine, and Rabelais,
among others. Needless to say, the classics were present and
most of them were in Greek or Latin rather than in translations.

Yale College also began with a collection of books. The
eleven ministers who, in 1700, organized a society for the formation of a college in New Haven each made a donation of books and
in the next decade other donations increased the collection to several hundred volumes. In 1714, a group of English gentlemen, including Sir Isaac Newton, made a donation of 800 volumes to Yale
through the good offices of Jeremiah Dummer, then the agent of
Connecticut in London. In 1717, Rev. Elihu Yale, for whom the
college was named, gave 300 books and in 1733, the Rev. Dr.
George Berkeley of London sent a gift of a thousand volumes, including many valuable folios. By 1765, Yale had a library of
about 4,000 volumes including, besides theological works, large collections of history, classics, philosophy and mathematics. The
President of the College noted in that year that the collection contained "not many authors who have wrote within these thirty years."

William and Mary College, in Virginia, was the second oldest in the colonies, having been founded in 1693, but its library
grew slowly in the eighteenth century. Aid for the college library
was received from time to time from the Virginia legislature but
this was usually small. Several gifts and bequests of books added
to the William and Mary collection. Of these only the library of
James Blair, a president of the college, was of notable size. It is
doubtful whether the William and Mary Library numbered more than

2,000 volumes in 1775.

Among other colonial colleges, the library of King's College (later Columbia University) in New York, was formed in 1757,
largely on the basis of a gift from the Rev. Dr. Bristowe of London.   Oxford University Library sent a gift of duplicates from its
collection and several British noblemen made gifts of books to the
college library.   During the Revolution this collection was destroyed
by British soldiers who used its quarters as a military hospital.
In 1764, the library of the College of New Jersey (later Princeton
University) contained about 1,200 books, all of which were gifts.
The Library of the College of Rhode Island (later Brown University),
contained only 250 volumes in 1772, while that of Dartmouth College was also insignificant before the Revolution.   The only other
college library dating from before the Revolution was at the academy in Philadelphia which later became the University of Pennsylvania.   Here the library was small, but it did survive the Revolution and was even enlarged by a gift from the King of France.   His
contribution consisted mostly of scientific and mathematical works
from the Royal printing office.

In all the colonial colleges the libraries were largely reference collections and were for the use of the faculty rather than for
students.   In fact, students were expected, especially during their
first two years in college, to study only their textbooks and to own
those.   Since the book collections were small, arrangement was not
much of a problem and the only keys to them were manuscript accession lists and a few printed catalogs.   The librarians were usually younger faculty members who were detailed to keep the library
room open for a few hours each week.   Generally speaking, the colonial college library was an uninviting place, more of a museum
than a library in the modern sense of the word.

Probably the first attempt at a public library in the colonies
came in 1656 when Capt. Robert Keayne of Boston willed his library to the city for public use.   In order to house the library,
and also to provide a town hall and meeting place, Keayne provided
funds for a building, and this was erected and in use by 1658.
This first "Boston Public Library" remained small, and just how

much it was used is uncertain.   But it was public property, and
on several occasions the town fathers of Boston took notice of its
presence.   For example, in 1702, they requested John Barnard,
Jr. , to prepare a catalog of its contents.   In 1711, the town hall
was burned, but most of the books were saved.   Another fire in
1747, however, completely destroyed it and only one book, Samuel
Mather's A Testimony from the Scripture Against Idolatry and Superstition, is known to have survived.   Many New England churches,
especially in the eighteenth century, established small libraries for
public use, such as the First Church Library in Milford, Connecticut, established in 1745, and the King's Chapel Library in Boston,
reportedly founded on a gift of books from the Bishop of London in
1698.   These church libraries were of course almost entirely theological in content, and just how much they were used is a matter
of question.

        Rev. Thomas Bray, the English religious leader who had
sponsored parish libraries in England, also encouraged and promoted the establishment of semi-public church libraries in the
American colonies.   This was done through the Society for the
Propagation of the Gospel in Foreign Parts, an English missionary
organization.   Libraries were established around 1700 in Anglican
churches from Charleston, South Carolina, to Boston.   Usually
these parish libraries were small collections of books, religious in
nature, placed in the care of the parish vestry for the use of ministers.   There were also collections of books called "laymen's libraries" for the general public.   The province of Maryland received a large portion of these parish libraries and in the course of
a decade some thirty parishes there obtained collections of books
varying in size from about a dozen books to three hundred or more.
At Annapolis there was a provincial library, not connected with the
parish libraries, but still a public collection.   It had begun with a
gift from Princess Anne, for whom the town was named, and was
added to by gifts and aid from the Maryland legislature.   In 1700
this library numbered about 1,100 books, and a number of them
have survived to the present as a part of the St. John's College
Library.

Other parish libraries, stemming from the activities of Bray and the Society, were formed in New York, Pennsylvania, North Carolina and South Carolina. A collection of books sent to Bath, North Carolina in 1700, numbered 166 bound volumes for the use of ministers, and some 800 books and pamphlets for the use of the general public. Oddly enough, the ministerial books were more general in nature, including history, philosophy and travel, while those for the general public were almost entirely theological or inspirational in nature. A Bray library sent to Charleston, South Carolina, led to the passage of a legislative act in 1700, possibly the first library law passed in the English colonies. This act placed the minister in charge of the library and gave detailed instructions as to its use. It did open the use of the books to "any inhabitant" of the colony. A similar act "for Securing the Parochial Libraries of this Province" was passed in Maryland in 1704. With such an auspicious beginning it would have seemed logical for the Parish libraries to grow and eventually to become active public services but such was not the case. No provisions were made for adding new books and after the death of the Rev. Bray interest in the parish libraries subsided. Most of the books eventually disappeared but a few have survived as a part of public or church collections, a reminder of a library venture that came almost two centuries before the public was ready for it.

The first successful attempt at making books available for general public use came through the establishment of the subscription libraries in the eighteenth century. Benjamin Franklin is usually given credit for beginning the first American subscription library in Philadelphia in 1731 and it followed, in general, the pattern already in operation in England. He and a small group of friends formed the Philadelphia Library Company and some fifty members paid Ł2 each for membership, with 10 shillings per year dues. Franklin sent to England for books and on his later visits to Europe he personally selected and sent back many volumes for the library. At first the books were kept in the home of one of the members, Robert Grace, but in 1740 they were removed to a room in the State House, a public building now known as Independence Hall. This room was opened a few hours weekly for public use but only members could remove books. Following the success of this subscription library, others were formed in Philadelphia but by 1773 at least three of them had joined the original one and the resulting collection, still known as the Philadelphia Library Company, was moved to the second floor of the Carpenter's Hall. There during the Revolution and the later Constitutional Convention, it served the founding fathers of the United States as virtually the only library available. In 1789 it moved into a building of its own and it has survived to the present as an important part of the Philadelphia public library system.

Other colonial towns soon followed the lead of Philadelphia in establishing subscription libraries. There were four in Connecticut before 1740 and about fifty in New England before 1780. Some of them were merely voluntary associations, but generally they involved some form of legal contract, either between individuals or in the form of a corporation chartered by the provincial government. The Redwood Library, in Newport, Rhode Island, was one of the more fortunate of these early libraries. It was operated by the Redwood Library Company, chartered by the provincial assembly in 1747 and named for Abraham Redwood, one of its early organizers and benefactors. In 1750 it moved into its own quarters, probably the first public library building erected in the American colonies. This library was fortunate in having a librarian from 1755 to 1775 in the person of Dr. Ezra Stiles, a minister in Newport who devoted a few hours of his time each week in return for the privilege of using the books. In 1748, the Charleston Library Society was formed in that South Carolina port city, and it received its official charter in 1755. Despite wars and fires this collection has survived, and throughout its long existence it has served its city as a valuable and valued cultural asset. Another surviving colonial library is that of the New York Society, founded in 1754. Several small collections of publicly owned volumes, including some sent by the Society for the Propagation of the Gospel, were later added to the New York Society Library. By 1773 it contained over 1500 books, but it was largely destroyed during the Revolution, and reorganized as a subscription library in 1788.

Strictly speaking, the subscription library was a private organization but it was a public library facility in the sense that it
was available to any interested reader who could afford the relatively small membership fee.   It was sometimes available, as was
the Philadelphia Library Company, to any reader during its brief
open hours.   It usually contained local and other provincial newspapers, as well as a few magazines from England and possibly other European countries.   Its bookstock consisted of the books that
its members wanted to read; sometimes the reading matter was
heavily theological or classical, but in other cases it consisted of
contemporary literature and political and economic works, depending upon the tastes of the readers.   Franklin's library, for example, contained a number of works on philosophy, history and science, while that of the Charleston Library Society contained more
literature, both classical and contemporary.   Ordinarily the collection was in charge of some member who devoted a small amount of
time to it, or perhaps of an interested non-member who received
the use of the collection for keeping it open a few hours each week.
Only rarely was there a paid librarian but usually there was a
strong core of members who were interested in building up the library.   All things considered, the subscription library was the
nearest thing to public library service that was available in the colonial period.

Private libraries were almost as scarce in the colonial period as public collections but there were a few notable examples of
book collecting among the early leaders in the colonies.   In New
England some of the best private libraries were gathered by ministers whereas in the southern colonies it was usually the wealthy
planter who had the time and means to become a bibliophile.   Government officials in all the colonies at times had libraries of some
size, but these collections usually returned to England with their
owners.   It is interesting to note that the earliest settlers of Massachusetts brought books with them.   Several of the Pilgrim settlers at Plymouth, including Governor William Bradford, owned
small collections of books, while Governor John Winthrop of Massa-

chusetts also brought books with him. John Winthrop, Jr., later
governor of Connecticut, left a library of over a thousand volumes
at his death in 1676. Increase Mather, the noted seventeenth century minister, collected a library of some 3,000 volumes, while
his son, Cotton Mather, who inherited only a part of his father's
library, built his own to more than 4,000 volumes. Most of the
books in both of these libraries were theological, including Bible
commentaries, sermons, and works of the Latin theologians, but
there were also works of history, geography and philosophy, with a
few books of science. Works of fiction, poetry and drama were
conspicuous by their absence, but included in the son's collection
was one intriguing title: The Woman's Advocate, or, Fifteen Real
Comforts of Matrimony. Cotton Mather wrote and published more
than 400 books and pamphlets on religious and historical subjects,
making him one of the most prolific writers America has ever produced. Thomas Prince, a minister of Boston, formed an important
library of books and manuscripts relating for the most part to New
England history, and deposited them in the Old South Church in
Boston before his death in 1758. These works later became the
property of Boston Public Library. Samuel Sewall, a contemporary
of Cotton Mather, made frequent references in his journal to buying and reading books. Just how many books he possessed at any
one time is uncertain as he was noted for his generosity in giving
and lending books.

In the Middle Colonies, John Sharp of New York built up a
large collection of books and in 1713 gave it to the city for public
use. It was largely theological, and there is little record of its
use until it became a part of the New York Society's Library in
1754. Rev. Alexander Innes left a sizeable collection of books at
his death in 1713, and these were donated to the Anglican churches
of New Jersey and New York. Samuel Johnson, early president of
King's College in New York built his library around English literature, the classics and history, while the library of James Logan of
Philadelphia was strong in the sciences and mathematics. Logan
had served as chief justice and as lieutenant governor of Pennsylvania and collected over 3,000 volumes before his death. A build-

ing was erected to house the Loganian library, and it was opened
for public use, with books circulating outside the building only "under certain circumstances." This collection eventually became a
part of the Philadelphia Library Company, and added considerably
to the value of that institution. Benjamin Franklin, in addition to
starting the circulating library, also gathered a personal library of
several thousand volumes, some of which he bequeathed to the
Philadelphia Library Company and to the library of the American
Philosophical Society. Thomas Chalkley, also of Philadelphia,
gathered a small library on the history and doctrines of the Qua-
kers, and in 1742 gave it to form the beginning of the Friends' Library which was to become the most important library of that religious group in America.

In the South the most important private library of the colonial period was that of William Byrd of Westover, Virginia. His
father had built up a large estate, and had started to collect books,
but it was the son who, before his death in 1740, enlarged the library to more than 4,000 volumes. The Byrd Library is interesting because of the nature of its contents and its contrast with the
New England ministerial libraries. Byrd was a planter, lawyer
and public official, as well as a writer, and his library reflected
the cultural level and interests of the Virginia planter. Almost a
fourth of the collection was made up of works of history, with another fourth in classical literature, and about ten per cent each in
English literature, law and science. There were a number of volumes in French and Latin, but theology was represented only by a
few works of the church fathers, and some volumes on the Church
of England. The remainder of the collection was made up of philosophy, travel, and practical handbooks of value to the planter and
his family. The Byrd Library had probably the best collection of
literature in the colonies. Several other Virginia planters had libraries numbering in the hundreds of volumes. As early as 1698
William Fitzhugh of Stafford County had a large library which he
kept in a room called his "Study of Books," and his annual order
for supplies from London always included additional books for his
collection. Ralph Wormesley of Rosegill, who died in 1701, left a

library of some 400 volumes including much English literature.
Colonel Robert Carter, later in the eighteenth century, had a library of some 700 volumes, well selected and including the classics, law, history, travel, science and philosophy.   His library
was also notable for literature, including the latest plays, poetry
and fiction from England.   Other examples of early Virginia libraries are not difficult to find, and lists of contents of a number of
them have survived.   In addition to the small professional collections of the lawyers and doctors, many other gentlemen had volumes on such practical subjects as farming, surveying, and architecture, as well as books on etiquette and gentlemanly conduct.

In both North and South Carolina there were several private
libraries of note, though none quite equalled those of William Byrd
or Cotton Mather.   Gabriel Johnston, governor of North Carolina
from 1734 to 1752, had a distinguished library, particularly strong
in biography, travel and history but including books on medicine,
economics, literature and law as well.   This library passed to his
newphew, Samuel Johnston, also a later governor of the state, and
under his attention it grew considerably.   It remained in the family
well into the nineteenth century, and at the end of the Civil War it
was estimated to contain about 4500 volumes.   Edward Mosely, Col.
James Innes, John Hodgson, and James Iredell were other colonial
North Carolinians with relatively large private libraries.   In South
Carolina, plantation libraries were customary but were not usually
very large.   John M'Kenzie, a Charleston lawyer and planter, bequeathed in 1771 a "valuable library" to the Charleston Library Society in the hope that a college could be developed around it.   Henry Laurens, merchant and planter, developed a large family library
which he augmented with books personally selected on his business
trips to Europe.   Governor James Glen, in office from 1743 to
1756, made a collection of works on history, particularly those per-
taining to South Carolina, and used them as a basis for his short
history of the colony which he published on his return to England.
A little later a Presbyterian minister, Alexander Hewat, did much
the same thing, but both carried their collections of books back to
England with them.   Other South Carolina planters and ministers,

including especially the Izards, Middletons and Rutledges had notable libraries which remained in the same family for several generations.

Most of the colonial leaders, whether in business, church or
government, had at least small collections of books in their homes,
and the men who lead the colonies into the Revolution were obviously well-read.   Their speeches and writings abound with allusions to
authors both classical and contemporary and most of these works
were undoubtedly in their own private libraries.   Among those
leaders known to have had sizeable private book collections were
John Hancock and John Adams of Massachusetts, the Livingstones
of New York, the Pinkneys and Carrolls of Maryland, Jefferson and
Madison in Virginia, John Rutledge and the Pinckneys of South Carolina and many others.   Jefferson's first library was burned in
1770, and although he mourned its loss, he noted that it had consisted of largely replaceable law and text-books.   He immediately
began to rebuild it and by 1783 his library totalled over 2500 volumes.   George Washington was also a book collector and he de-
lighted in fine bindings, having many books bound to his own design
by a Philadelphia binder.   His library is noteworthy because of his
interest in essays, drama and fiction, as well as in the more serious works so common in his day.   After his marriage to Martha
Custis his purchases of books from London contain works that were
obviously selected for his wife and step-children.

Rental or circulating libraries associated with printshops
and bookstores developed in the late colonial period.   Particularly
after about 1760, it became possible in most colonial towns to rent
books from the booksellers for a small fee.   Rentals were for individual books or for the use of a number of books over a given period of time and the rates for the most part were low.   Possibly the
first of these circulating libraries was opened by William Rind, of
Annapolis, Maryland, in 1762.   He proposed to allow his customers
the use of two books at a time for an annual fee of 27 shillings.
His venture was unsuccessful and was discontinued in 1764.   Boston, Philadelphia, New York and Charleston had similar ventures
in or shortly after 1765, with varying degrees of success.   One in

Boston, operated by John Mein, was particularly ambitious. He
published a catalog of some 1200 volumes available for rent at the
rate of 28 shillings per year for all that one could read, one volume at a time. Mein was a Loyalist and as the Revolution approached he was forced to leave the city. In New York, Samuel
Loudon's circulating library offered some 2,000 volumes to dis-
criminating readers in the early 1770's, and some of his most popular volumes were poetry. The circulating library achieved its
greatest success in the years after the Revolution, but it did have
its beginning in the colonial era and added in small degree to the
reading matter available.

The main business of the bookstore was, of course, the
selling of books. From the earliest days the printer had sold his
own wares but he soon began to carry other books in general demand. In the later colonial period regular bookstores began to appear, sometimes in conjunction with a printing office, sometimes
separately. The general merchant also carried some books at
times and many of the wealthier book collectors ordered their
books directly from England. As the regular bookstores emerged
their stocks varied considerably from colony to colony. The basic
bookstock included primers, textbooks, prayer books and dictionaries, with the local laws and almanacs being regular standbys.
Aside from this, the New England bookseller would find religious
books, particularly sermons, always in demand, whereas the New
York or Charleston merchant would find that more mundane works
would meet the usual requests of his customers. Practical handbooks on all subjects were in vogue in the later colonial period,
and fiction also made its appearance then. In the larger towns
books were obtainable in Greek, Latin, French and German, as
well as English, and subscriptions could be placed for both English
and American periodicals. Book auctions were by no means unknown, especially as a means of selling private collections, or the
book stocks of bankrupt merchants. When Michael Perry, bookseller of Boston, died in 1700, he left a bookstock of over 6,000
volumes, but including only 213 titles. About one-fifth of the total
was made up of primers and catechisms, indicating the interest in

educating and indoctrinating the youth of the city. Other "best-
sellers" in his store included Pilgrim's Progress, Cotton Mather's
Folly of Sinning and Aesop's Fables. Some 70 years later, John
Mein's bookstore in the same city had a total stock of 10,000 volumes, with over 1200 titles. The selection was broader, but the
emphasis was still religious.

In general, the average colonial American was not a literary
man, but the men who emerged as his leaders generally were. The
ministers, public officials, lawyers and college teachers were well
educated. Moreover, the leading planters and merchants were often ardent readers and pursued their literary tastes with both their
minds and their pocket books. From their own private libraries,
and from the book stores and circulating libraries, they had access
to most books available in England at that time. That they made
effective use of them is evidenced in the Declaration of Independence, the Constitution of the United States, and the numerous journals, diaries and books that have come down to us from the colonial era.

Bibliography

Books

Bolton, C.K.: American library history. Chicago, 1911. 13 p.

Bolton, C.K.: Proprietary and subscription libraries. Chicago,
    1912. 10 p.

Cannon, Carl L.: American book collectors and collecting from
    colonial times to the present. New York, 1941. 391 p.

Clough, Wilson O., ed.: Our long heritage: pages from the books
    our founding fathers read. Minneapolis, 1955. 297 p.

Conner, Martha: Outline of the history of the development of the
    American public library. Chicago, 1931. 179 p.

Eaton, F. Thelma: Contributions to American library history.
    Champaign, Ill., 1961. 277 p.

Gray, Austin K.: Benjamin Franklin's library. New York, 1936.
    80 p.

Keep, Austin B.: History of the New York Society Library, with
    and introductory chapter on libraries in colonial New York.
    New York, 1908. 607 p.

Lehmann-Haupt, Hellmut: The book in America: a history of
    the making and selling of books in the United States. New
    York, 1939.   453 p.   (This edition has a chapter on early
    American libraries.)

Morison, Samuel E. :   The Puritan Pronaos: studies in the intel-
    lectual life of New England in the seventeenth century.   New
    York, 1936.   288 p. (See especially pp. 110-147.)

Pennington, Edgar L. :   The beginnings of the library in Charles
    Town, South Carolina.   Worcester, Mass. , 1935. 31 p.

Potter, A. C. :   The library of Harvard University.   Cambridge,
    Mass. , 1934.   4th ed. ·186 p.

Predeek, Albert: A history of libraries in Great Britain and North
    America.   Chicago, 1947. 177 p.

Roberts, A. S. :   Two centuries of the Redwood Library and Athen-
    aeum, 1747-1947.   Newport, R. I. , 1948. 58 p.

Shera, Jesse H. :   Foundations of the public library.   Chicago,
    1949.   308 p.

Shores, Louis: Origins of the American college library, 1638-
    1800.   New York, 1935.   290 p.

Steiner, Bernard C. :   Rev. Thomas Bray: his life and selected
    works relating to Maryland.   Baltimore, 1901. 252 p.

Thompson, C. Seymour: Evolution of the American public library,
    1653-1876.   Washington, 1952.   287 p.

Tolles, Frederick B. :   James Logan and the culture of provincial
    America.   Boston, 1957.   228 p.

Tuttle, Julius H. :   The libraries of the Mathers.   Worcester,
    Mass. , 1910.   90 p.

U. S. Bureau of Education: Public libraries in the United States of
    America, their history, condition and management.   Wash-
    ington, 1876.   1187 p.

Whitney, Henry M. :   The development of public libraries within the
    bounds of the Old New Haven Colony.   New Haven, Conn. ,
    1904.   16 p.

Wright, Thomas G. :   Literary culture in early New England, 1620-
    1730.   New Haven, Conn. , 1920.   322 p.

Periodical Articles

Borden, A. K. : "Seventeenth century American libraries," Library
        Quarterly, II, (1932), 137-147.

Bruce, Philip A. : "Libraries," in pp. 402-441 of his Institutional
        History of Virginia in the 17th Century. (New York, 1910.)

'The Byrd Library at Westover," Virginia Magazine of History and
        Biography, XII, (1904), 205-207.

Canavan, Michael J. : 'The Old Boston Public Library, 1656-1747,"
        Proceedings of the Colonial Society of Massachusetts, XII,
        (March, 1908), 116-133.

Fletcher, Charlotte: 'The Reverend Thomas Bray, M. Alexandre
        Vattemore, and library science," Library Quarterly,
        XXVII, (1957), 95-99.

Houlette, William D. : "Parish libraries and the work of Rev.
        Thomas Bray," Library Quarterly, IV, (1934), 588-609.

Keys, Thomas E. : 'The colonial library and the development of
        sectional differences," Library Quarterly, VII, (1938), 375-
        390.

Kraus, J.W. : 'Harvard undergraduate library of 1773," College
        and Research Libraries, XXII, (1961), 247-262.

Spain, Frances L. : "Libraries of South Carolina, their origins
        and early history," Library Quarterly, XVII, (1947), 28-42.

Weeks, Stephen B. : "Libraries and literature of North Carolina in
        the eighteenth century," A. H. A. Annual Report, (1895), 171-
        269.

X
American Libraries, 1775-1850

The Revolution had a disastrous effect on many of the early American libraries and the cultural development of the United States in general was set back almost a generation. From Boston to Savannah, libraries were scattered, destroyed or stolen, and only a few managed to escape undamaged. Aside from loss by military action, the libraries also lacked attention and for more than a decade there was no concerted effort to rebuild or improve them. Many private libraries belonging to Loyalists were confiscated or sold at auction and the breaking up of families saw other collections divided and sold. Following the Peace of Paris in 1783 there was some progress, but it was not until after 1790 that books, newspapers, magazines and libraries returned to their pre-war levels and finally began to forge ahead.

Though forced to move from Cambridge to Concord during the early part of the war, Harvard College saved its library, and even added to it with funds allocated by the state legislature and with books confiscated from Loyalists. Yale College also had its library moved for safe-keeping, but many volumes were lost in the process. In 1791, Yale owned only 2,700 volumes, and it was not until 1805 that it again reached its pre-Revolutionary size. Princeton's Nassau Hall, which housed the college library, was occupied by both British and American troops at different times, and served successively as barracks, prison, hospital and stable. After the war, the state of New Jersey voted a sum of money to aid in restoring the war-damaged buildings, and the college began levying an annual library fee for the purchase of books. In New York, King's College had most of its books stolen or destroyed during the British occupation, but a few of them were returned by order of the British commander. The New York Society Library was burned during the fighting in 1776, and so were two subscription libraries,

the Union Library and the Corporation Library.   In Providence, the
College of Rhode Island had its library moved to the country for
safekeeping, and when it was returned only about 500 volumes were
found to be usable.   Fortunately, in 1784, John Brown made a gift
of 1400 volumes to the college library, and in 1792 Nicholas Brown
donated funds for the purchase of a law library.   For this and other important gifts, the college was renamed Brown University.   In
the south, particularly in coastal Virginia and South Carolina, many
plantation homes were burned or ransacked by raiding British
troops and their libraries were destroyed.   Bookstores and circulating libraries also suffered during the war years, and few of the
subscription libraries survived.   The coming of peace and independence, however, gave new impetus to all types of library and
literary activities, and new activities were begun on a larger scale
than ever before.

Harvard's library was one of the first to revive and it soon
achieved and maintained a position of pre-eminence among libraries
in the nation.   By 1790, it contained some 12,000 volumes, and its
printed catalog of that year indicates that more than half of its contents were still theological.   However, there was a good collection
of English literature and the classics, and a few titles by recent
European authors.   History and travel were present, but titles in
the sciences were scarce and periodicals, with the exception of the
Gentleman's Magazine, were almost entirely absent.   By 1827 there
were 25,000 volumes in the Harvard Library, and by 1840, when it
was moved into a building of its own, the book stock had reached
40,000 volumes exclusive of pamphlets.   Yale's library grew much
more slowly at first, but it had reached 6,500 volumes by 1823,
and 21,000 by 1850.   Among the other surviving colonial colleges,
Princeton suffered another disastrous fire in its library in 1802,
but by 1812 its collection, thanks to numerous donors, had again
reached 4,000 volumes.   Columbia College, which grew out of the
ruins of the pre-Revolutionary King's College, also had a slow
growth and possessed only a few more than 10,000 volumes by the
mid-nineteenth century.   Brown University was about the same size,
and in the south, William and Mary had grown even slower, having

less than 5,000 volumes as late as 1850. For all of the colleges, acquisitions were largely in the form of gifts, but fortunately these were relatively plentiful. Harvard alone listed more than 1,000 donors in the period from 1780 to 1840. Funds from other sources were scarce and student library fees made up most of the amount available for book purchases.

Along with the older colleges, the early nineteenth century saw the founding of many new ones, both public and private. In almost every case, a library was begun as soon as the college doors were opened to students, and sometimes even before. Bowdoin College in Maine began with a small collection of books in 1802, but in 1811 it received a gift of 4,000 volumes from James Bowdoin, its prime benefactor. Amherst College, in Massachusetts, began in 1821 with a single case of books, but by 1832, after a drive for donations, its library reached 3,000 volumes, suitably housed in a room in the chapel building. By 1855 it could boast 12,000 books and a building of its own. Wesleyan University, at Middletown, Connecticut, began with a ready-made library of 2,000 volumes purchased from Thomas Chapman of New Jersey. Hamilton College, in Clinton, New York, was founded in 1812, and inherited a small library from an earlier academy. A campaign for donations of books and funds was not too successful, and the library numbered only 1,600 volumes in 1826. Another small college library, that of Dickinson College in Pennsylvania, began in 1783, but with insufficient funds and no large donations, it grew so slowly that in 1850 it still numbered only about 5,000 volumes.

Before 1850 publicly owned colleges took the form of state universities, and these were established in almost every state. The University of Pennsylvania grew out of an academy which had been established before the Revolution, while several other states provided for universities in their first constitutions. North Carolina's University Library began in 1795 with a small collection including fourteen volumes donated by the governor of the state, William R. Davie. Other donations followed, and in the 1820's, the president of the University sent to England to purchase almost a thousand volumes for the college library. In 1850, the library was moved

into a separate building, and at that time it numbered a few less
than 7,000 volumes. South Carolina's University Library opened
in 1805, with an appropriation of $3,000 from the state legislature
for books. It continued to receive support from the state, moved
into its own building in 1841, and by mid-century it contained some
12,000 volumes, forming the largest and most important library
south of Virginia. Not only was it impressive in numbers, but
many of its works were rare and valuable. The University of Virginia, opening in 1825, had the benefit of the advice of ex-President Thomas Jefferson in selecting and organizing its library. Although Jefferson's own library had been purchased by the Library of
Congress, President James Madison donated his library of 2,500
volumes to the University of Virginia along with a gift of $1,500.
Many other gifts came from Virginia's planter families, and by
1850, its university library contained more than 30,000 volumes,
making it one of the best in the nation. The University of Georgia,
opening in 1800, had a small collection of books in the New College
building which was destroyed by fire in 1830. A serious effort to
provide a useful college library began after this date, and by 1840
Georgia had the third largest college library in the South. Other
state universities with libraries founded before 1850 included Vermont (1800), Tennessee (1807), Indiana (1828), Alabama (1831),
Missouri (1840), Michigan (1841), Mississippi (1848), and Wisconsin (1849).

Although Harvard, Yale and possibly one or two other college libraries reached a point where assistant librarians were employed, most of them had only one staff member. As in the colonial days, these "librarians" were usually either junior members of
the faculty, or retired teachers. Organization of the collection was
for the most part limited to location symbols, such as "Alcove 5,
Shelf B, Book 2," although there was usually a broad subject or
language division by alcoves or sections. Catalogs were either in
manuscript or printed lists, arranged alphabetically or by accession. Hours of opening were limited, sometimes to an hour or so
per day, and circulation rules were quite strict. In some cases,
only faculty or upper classmen could remove books from the li-

brary, and in other cases students could use the library only on
the recommendation of a faculty member. The library was usually
housed in a room or wing of a building, but by 1850 the larger colleges were moving their book collections into separate buildings.
Generally speaking, the college library was still a reference library,
with its basic purpose that of preserving books rather than using
them and the person in charge was more of a "book keeper" than a
librarian.

In addition to the regular college library, there was often
another type of library on the average college campus. This was
the literary society collection. It became the custom in the nineteenth century for each campus to have one or mor societies, usually two, with their own meeting halls, and their own libraries.
With such names as the Cliosophic or the Athenaen or the Callio-
pean, these groups combined debating or declaiming with library
service and with small subscriptions collected from members they
built up serviceable book collections designed to meet the immediate needs of the students. In time, many of these literary society
libraries grew to be almost as large as the college libraries and
with valuable gifts from their loyal alumni they became important
scholarly collections. They had student librarians and were strictly for student use; meeting their library needs much more effectively than the main college library. In the later nineteenth century, however, most of these society libraries merged with the college libraries. In a few cases, particularly at Harvard, departmental libraries also had their beginnings before 1850. Harvard
had separate libraries at the Medical School, the Divinity School,
and the Philips Observatory, while Yale had collections for its Law
School and its Medical School before 1850.

Somewhat akin to the college library and even more important from the reference point of view were the scientific society libraries that developed in the larger cities during the early nineteenth century. The oldest of these was the American Philosophical Society Library, founded in Philadelphia in 1743 and which by
1850 contained over 15,000 books and nearly as many pamphlets.
Franklin Institute, also in Philadelphia, was founded in 1824 as a

scientific society particularly interested in the physical sciences
and its library was nearly as large as that of the Philosophical Society.   In Boston, the American Academy of Arts and Sciences
(1780) and the Boston Society of Natural History (1831) each had libraries of more than 10,000 volumes, while the Massachusetts Horticultural Society library (1829) had about 2,500 at mid-century.
The New York Academy of Sciences (1818) and the Albany Institute
of Science (1824) each had respectable libraries of their own and
throughout New England, the Middle Atlantic and Middle Western
states, the major cities usually supported one or more scientific
societies by 1850.   Historical societies were also plentiful, with
those of New England, and the eastern states having the better libraries.   Massachusetts Historical Society (1791), the American
Antiquarian Society of Worcester, Massachusetts (1812), and the
Historical Society of Pennsylvania (1824) were among the largest
and most important as far as their libraries were concerned.   Almost in a class by itself was the Boston Athenaeum Library,
founded as a subscription library in 1807.   Through wise purchases,
valuable gifts, and the deposit of several important collections, the
Athenaeum rapidly became one of the most important libraries in
the nation.   By 1814 it contained over 8,000 volumes, and by 1827
more than 21,000.   Moving into a new building in 1849, it had
passed the 50,000 mark and ranked along with Harvard and the Library of Congress as the largest libraries in the United States.
Strictly speaking, these scientific and historical society libraries
were only for the use of members, but in general practice a serious applicant could usually obtain access to them.

       The period after the Revolution and down to 1850 saw rapid
development of the social library in all its phases.   In its simplest
form, the social library was a subscription library, containing popular reading available to all who cared to pay a small fee, and as
such it had been known long before the Revolution.   But after 1800,
the social library took on other forms, with book collections built
along specific lines and serving specific groups of readers.   Some
of these forms were lyceum libraries, mechanics' libraries, mercantile libraries, apprentices' libraries, young men's association

libraries, and even factory workers' libraries. Best known in New
England and the middle states, they spread gradually into the Middle West and even to the larger towns in the southern states. In
New England alone, more than 1,000 social libraries were established between the Revolution and 1850 and many of them survived
for long periods. Almost every village had at least one collection
of books available on some terms and the larger towns often had
several. A few of them were connected with local societies and
hence directed their collections along subject lines such as theology, history, agriculture or medicine. Most of them were general
in nature, however, and were designed to meet or improve the
reading interests of members. In book stock, the libraries ranged
from less than a hundred volumes, up to 10,000 or so and in a
few cases they were even larger. Some completely excluded fiction while others included much of the book stock in this increasingly popular form of reading. Science, economics, agriculture, sociology and law made up only a small percentage of the titles in
most social libraries but literature, travel, history and religion
were well represented. Many added to their holdings of books and
pamphlets by supplying the latest English and American periodicals.

The organization of social libraries was usually very simple.
In the smaller ones there was little or no attempt at arrangement
or classification, but in the larger collections books were usually
divided by larger subjects, or even by locally invented systems of
classification. Catalogs ranged from none through simple manuscript accession records to printed alphabetical or classed lists.
Housing might be in a public building, a member's home or business or, in the case of larger collections, in rented rooms or separate buildings. Hours of opening varied according to size and use,
but were usually few, and a voluntary or paid attendant charged
books and checked on their return. As early as 1793 a pamphlet
had been written to advise the book selectors for social libraries
on the best methods of obtaining books and the best books to be selected. This was entitled: The Selected Catalog of Some of the
Most Esteemed Publications in the English Language Proper to Form
a Social Library. Its author was Thaddeus Mason Harris, a young
man who had served for a short time as a librarian at Harvard.

His pamphlet was one of the earliest American works on book selection. He divided all books into three classes: memory, reason, and imagination. The first class included all phases of history,
biography and travel; the second, science, philosophy, and religion; and the third, poetry, drama, fiction and art. In all he
recommended only 81 titles. The smaller social libraries bought
only a few titles a year on the average, but collectively they made
up an important book market, so that book publishers and dealers
soon came to offer them special discounts in order to secure their
trade.

One popular type of social library was that designed for the
use of workers or apprentices. These were intended primarily for
the younger employees in the factories and trades, and though there
were a few factory libraries for the girls of the New England cotton mills, most of them were for men. They provided popular
reading, manuals on the various trades, text-books, and occasionally popular religious works. Educational materials were thus provided for the young people who could not attend school and they
were apparently fairly well used. In some cases the expenses of
the apprentices' library were born by the company or some community philanthropist but ordinarily they were paid for by small
subscriptions from the workers. Similar to the apprentices' libraries, but designed for the young men in the stores and business offices, were the mercantile libraries. These latter often grew to
considerable size and served management and owners as well as
workers, in time tending to become professional business libraries.
In New York, the Apprentices' Library was founded in 1820; its
services were free to apprentices but a subscription fee was charged
to other users. It grew rapidly and neared 50,000 volumes by
1850. In Philadelphia an Apprentices' Library Company was formed
in 1820 and a Mercantile Library in 1821. The idea spread rapidly and by mid-century most of the larger cities of the nation had
such libraries in one form or another. Being designed for popular
reading rather than research, they had liberal hours of opening and
went far toward meeting the library needs of their particular cli-
enteles.

Thus, until about the middle of the nineteenth century it can be safely said that the nearest approach to public library service was through the social libraries. Although privately owned, the membership fees were usually low enough for anyone who was likely to be seriously interested in reading. The quantity and quality of reading matter could be varied to suit the demands of the reading public, and was probably more in tune with popular reading tastes than a public library would have been. Fiction was most popular, closely followed by biography, travel, poetry and history in that order. The majority of the library users were men but women were becoming accustomed to use them also and they were even invited particularly in some cases. All in all, the social libraries served their purpose for more than a century and gave way only after regular public library service became widely available. About fifteen per cent of the social libraries founded in New England before 1850 survived into the twentieth century; some of them in their original form, some as public libraries and some as parts of other collections. They were not restricted to New England and the middle states by any means. They spread to the West, and to a lesser extent, to the southern states as well.

As the settlers from New England and the eastern states poured into the Middle West in the early nineteenth century they soon established the same type of towns and villages they had known back home. Schools and libraries came almost as soon as homes were built, and social libraries of one type or another soon followed. St. Louis had a subscription library as early as 1811, and there is reported to have been one in Vincennes, Indiana, in 1806. Cincinnati had an active circulating library in 1814, and Detroit in 1817. Chicago had a Sunday School library in 1832, a Lyceum library in 1834, and a Young Men's Association library in 1841, among others. If newspaper notices can be believed, there were a variety of "reading rooms" in almost every midwestern town, with St. Louis boasting, at different times, one in a hotel, one in a newspaper office, and a combined "Reading Room and Punch House" which must have been very popular. The New Harmony, Indiana, Working Men's Institute Library of 1847 consisted of about 1,000 volumes, includ-

ing 250 titles of history, 105 of science, 95 of fiction and 60 of
sociology but only twelve of poetry and seven of religion. In all
there were more than 160 social libraries chartered in Ohio before
1850 and though there were considerably fewer in Indiana, Illinois
and Michigan, the coverage in those states was fairly general for
the larger towns.

In the South the Charleston Library Society remained the
most successful of the subscription libraries, having about 4,500
volumes in 1808 and about 18,000 in 1850. It was not alone, however, since there were three other library societies in Charleston
and about 30 in other parts of South Carolina for longer or shorter
periods of time before 1850. One that is particularly worthy of
notice was the Georgetown Library Society, formed by a group of
planters in that coastal South Carolina town in 1800. It never grew
large in size, but it was well used and as a combination of a popular library and an agricultural collection it existed down until the
Civil War. It is interesting to note that the local printer was the
librarian for a time, and did much to insure the library's success.
New Orleans in 1820 contained a Library Society, a Law Library,
a subscription library with a public reading room and a "free library at the Presbyterian Church." The Library Society collection
was burned in 1828, but reopened later as a Commercial Library
which by 1837 contained over 5,000 volumes. Library fortunes in
the Crescent City were viable and by 1847 the scene there included
a State Library, a Merchants' Exchange Library, and a Young
Men's Society Library. Elsewhere in the South, there were subscription libraries in Natchez, Mississippi; Mobile, Alabama; Savannah and Augusta, Georgia; Knoxville, Tennessee; Lexington,
Kentucky; Wilmington and New Bern, North Carolina and in several towns in Virginia but few of them existed for any length of time.
Otherwise in the South the scarcity of large towns kept down the
number of opportunities for social libraries, and library development along with education in general was greatly retarded.

The purely commercial circulating library also increased in
numbers and popularity after the Revolution but its cultural importance was negligible when compared to the social libraries. It de-

pended upon a reading public slightly different from that of the social library; more on the casual reader than on the serious one.
It was usually small but in a few cases of old, established stores,
it sometimes reached several thousand volumes.   Caritat's Circulating Library in New York City, opened in 1797, had several thousand volumes in its catalog of 1804, including more than a thousand books of fiction.   Even more than the social library, the circulating library reflected popular reading tastes but unfortunately
there are few if any records of the bookstocks of these commercial
ventures much less any counts of actual circulation.   Suffice it to
say that they were less important than the social library in the ultimate creation of public libraries but that they did provide a needed
public service.   They may be considered as the ancestor of the
public library pay collection rather than of the present day drug-
store rental shelf.

If we define the public library as being a book collection
that is publicly supported, publicly controlled and for general public use, then there were very few public libraries in the United
States before 1850.   However, those few were important and de-
serve recognition.   In Salisbury, Connecticut, a collection of books
donated in 1803 by Caleb Bingham was preserved and made available by the town as the Bingham Library for Youth.   It survived
to become a part of the present Scoville Memorial Library.   In
Lexington, Massachusetts, in 1827, the town meeting voted to purchase a library for the youth of the town and to employ a librarian
to manage it.   The collection was deposited in the town church,
but so small was the public support that it went out of existence in
1839.   Other examples of small public collections such as these
might be found, but the town usually considered to be the pioneer
in permanent public library service in the United States was Peterborough, New Hampshire.   There, in 1833, it was decided by the
town meeting that a part of the State Literary Fund, usually applied
to the support of schools, should be used for the purchase of books
for a free public library.   Other donations added to the size of the
book collection, and it was kept for public use in the store that
housed the local post-office, with the postmaster acting as librari-

an. By 1837, the collection numbered 465 titles, made up largely
of religion, history and biography. The Peterborough Public Library provided a prototype for the future public libraries of the
nation. Only in the late 1840's was there a definite movement toward public libraries, and this came in the passage of laws in
Massachusetts and other New England states allowing for the levying of taxes to support them.

At least one type of library was publicly supported and controlled before 1850, and that was the school district library. This
type of book collection apparently originated in New York, but it
spread rapidly throughout New England and the Middle West. New
York's legislature passed an act in 1835 which made it permissable
for school districts to levy taxes for local school libraries. This
law brought little response but a second one in 1838, which provided state funds to match local levies for books, was more successful and in three years more than 400,000 books were placed in
the schools of New York state. This idea grew until by 1850 there
were nearly a million and a half volumes in the state's school libraries. Without staff or proper quarters, however, many books
were lost or allowed to deteriorate for lack of care. The interest
in the libraries declined, and state laws were passed allowing the
library funds to be spent for school equipment and even for teachers' salaries. The school library plan was popular at first, and
other states followed the example set by New York. In Massachusetts, a school library law was passed in 1837, and 2,084 libraries were reported in that state by 1850, but in all they had purchased only about 100,000 volumes or about fifty books apiece.
Here again the movement was more or less a failure. Connecticut
followed Massachusetts in 1839, and Rhode Island in 1840. In these
two states the school library program was slower in getting under
way but a little more successful in the long run. Several Middle
Western states, including Michigan, Indiana and Ohio, made ar-
rangements for school district libraries before 1850, but in general they were not too successful.

The school district libraries were apparently intended more
for the teachers and parents than for the children. Their contents

usually consisted of text-books, general works, and a smattering of inspirational books, of which the majority were above the reading level of all but the older children. Several publishing firms took advantage of the school district library laws and hastily compiled sets of works, poorly selected, printed and bound, but sold through local representatives. These sets often took up most of the funds available, and their drab appearance and dry content did little to promote the school library movement. For lack of quarters in the schools themselves, the library books were often stored in the homes of teachers or school board members and an investigation of the New York school district libraries in the 1850's found many of the books molding in closets, cellars and attics. The school district library movement was premature and unsuccessful but it did serve to establish the precedent of public support for library service, and in this respect to pave the way for genuine public libraries in a later era.

Probably the most numerous and least known of all libraries of the ante bellum period were the Sunday school libraries. Practically every church, particularly in the North and West, had a small collection of books, designated as the "Sunday School Library." Sometimes they were rather general in content, but usually they contained religious and inspirational works. Where other sources of reading matter were not available, they were probably well-used, but in time many of them came to include works of such maudlin sentimentality that their use declined. The term "Sunday school book" came to be used almost as a term of derision when other types of literature became available. In the larger cities, several churches of the same denomination were sometimes able to combine their efforts and provide a larger collection of books, complete with a library room and the services of at least a part-time librarian, but these libraries were more for the use of the ministers and church workers than for the average member or his children.

Much of the secondary education before the Civil War was in the hands of private schools and academies. Their libraries were usually poor but in some cases they approached the level of

the smaller college libraries. They often consisted of gift books
rather than purchases and their contents were not well selected.
Private libraries of the teachers were usually available to augment
the school-owned collection and often there were literary societies
with libraries even in the academies. In the smaller towns of the
South and West the academy library was often the best available,
and the only one that the average student ever knew.

Along with the other types of libraries that were progressing with difficulty in the early nineteenth century, several important
government libraries were established.   Of these, the one destined
to become the greatest in the western hemisphere was the national
library in Washington, D. C. , the Library of Congress.   The government of the United States, in its earliest formative period,
made use of several book collections in Philadelphia and New York
but it was not until after the seat of government had been moved to
Washington that a move was made to create a library especially for
the use of the national officials. In 1800, Congress appropriated
the first money for the purchase of books and in 1802 a room for
the library was set aside in the new Capitol building.   President
Thomas Jefferson appointed the first librarian who also served as
Clerk of the House of Representatives. In its early days the Library of Congress was almost wholly a legal reference collection
for the use of members of Congress, and by 1814, it had only
about 3,000 volumes. In that year, while the United States was at
war with Great Britain, the Capitol was burned by the invading
army and the library was lost. After the war, ex-President Jefferson offered to sell his magnificent library at cost to the government to replace the destroyed one and after much debate in Congress, the offer was accepted. In 1815, a total of 6,700 books
were purchased from Jefferson for $23,950 and this collection made
up a library actually superior to the one that was lost.   George
Watterson was appointed librarian and temporary quarters for the
new library were found in the Post Office Building until 1824 when
it was removed to the new Capitol building. By that time Congress
was appropriating $5,000 per year for the national library, and it
was growing rapidly. At mid-century, the Library of Congress had

reached 50,000 volumes, but it was still largely a legislative reference library and could boast but one librarian and one assistant
as its total staff.   In 1832, part of the legal works in the library
had been removed to a room for the use of the Supreme Court but
it was still under the jurisdiction of the librarian of Congress.   In
addition, both the House and Senate had libraries or at least collections of official documents for their own use.

        The various government departments also developed libraries
of their own almost from the time they were founded.   The State
Department, for example, was instructed by law to collect the laws
of the various states from 1789 on, and these together with the publications of the Federal government formed the beginning of the
State Department Library.   By 1825, the Department had added to
this core the legal publications of other major countries plus books
on history, international law, and diplomacy, to a total of more
than 3,000 volumes.   Newspapers, both American and foreign, were
also collected in the State Department Library and by 1850 the number of volumes totalled over 15,000.   The Treasury Department Library was begun in 1803 but it was not of significant size until after the Civil War.   This was also true of the collection in the War
Department although some of the military agencies of the nation,
such as the Military Academy at West Point, had important libraries.   The Academy Library began in 1812 and had some 20,000
volumes by 1850.   The U.S. Naval Academy at Annapolis was organized in 1845, and its library had reached only about 3,000 volumes by the mid-century.   The Bureau of Ordnance Library was
begun in 1838, and the Artillery School Library at Fortress Monroe, Virginia, was formed in 1824.   Each of these libraries had
about 2,000 volumes in 1850.   In the other government libraries
there were only small collections of legal works and government
publications except in the Patent Office Library which contained
some 20,000 volumes of scientific, historical and legal works.

        In addition to the libraries of the Federal government, most
of the states also had libraries in their capitols.   Even before the
Revolution there were usually collections of legal works available
in most of the provincial legislative halls.   Virginia had a small

library as early as 1661 and a few of the books from this era have
survived.   Pennsylvania had an active collection of reference books
in its capitol building in Philadelphia in the late colonial period and
New Hampshire also had a pre-Revolutionary legislative library.
However, it was not until after 1800 that most of the states established state libraries by law and made provisions for their maintenance and growth.   South Carolina had a state library as early as
1814, Pennsylvania by 1816, New York and New Hampshire by 1818
and other states shortly after.   These state libraries were mainly
legal and historical.   Their acquisitions came largely from exchange of state publications with other libraries and through re-
ceipt of Federal documents through acts of Congress.   Gradually
the legal works came to be maintained separately from the historical ones or separate state law libraries or supreme court libraries
were established.   The state libraries themselves tended to become historical and general reference libraries, designed for the
use of state officials and legislators but open to the general public
for reference use.   On the other hand, where historical libraries
were already available in the state capital, in the form of an historical society library or a university library, then the state library usually remained a strictly legal collection.   In either case,
growth of the state libraries was slow before 1850 and by that date
the total of volumes in all of them was scarcely 200,000.   Closely
related to the state libraries were the territorial libraries established by the Federal government in several of the western terri-
tories before they became states.

        The period between the Revolution and the Civil War saw the
development of many important private book collections.   It was a
period when a few major fortunes were being made and a larger
number of business and professional men were wealthy enough to
afford libraries.   The book collections of Presidents Washington,
Jefferson and Madison have already been mentioned but most of the
other early Presidents had notable libraries as well.   John Adams
had one of the largest private libraries in the nation and it was a
fairly well-rounded collection.   It was weak in literature and science, but strong in theology, the classics and history, particularly

Americana. In the 1820's he gave most of it, some 2,750 books
in all, to the town of Quincy, Massachusetts. John Quincy Adams
gave away many of his books during his lifetime, and still left a
library of about 8,000 volumes at his death. President Monroe
left a small private library as did President Jackson, although the
latter lost many of his books in a fire that destroyed his home in
1834. President Van Buren's library was largely that of a prosperous lawyer but President Tyler had an extensive library at his
home in Virginia, particularly strong in the classics and English
literature.

When Benjamin Franklin died in 1790 he left a library of
over 4,000 volumes consisting of books on a wide range of subjects. It was rather weak in literature, but strong in science and
included a few finely printed books as evidence of his lifelong interest in typography. Peter Force, the editor and historian, began collecting books in the 1820's and became such an avid collector that he often borrowed money on his home in order to add
more volumes to his library. Centering his interest on American
history he collected books, pamphlets, newspapers, periodicals and
manuscripts until he owned more than 60,000 items in all. In
1867 his heirs sold this collection to the Library of Congress,
thereby doubling that Library's holdings in American history.
George Ticknor of Boston collected more than 3,000 volumes of
Spanish history and literature which, after his death in 1871, went
to the Boston Public Library. John Carter Brown of Rhode Island
was also a great collector of Americana and in the first half of the
nineteenth century he began the accumulation of literary treasures
that was to eventually become the John Carter Brown Library on
the campus of Brown University. In Philadelphia, Stephen Colwell,
lawyer and economist, bequeathed his library of some 6,000 books
and pamphlets on politics and economics to the University of Pennsylvania Library. In Cincinnati, W.H. Mussey gave his collection
of history and classics to the Public Library. Even in relatively
out of the way places, leading citizens often had private libraries
of several hundred volumes. For example, Zebulon Baird Vance,
growing up in western North Carolina in the 1830's had the advan-

tage of using a library collected by his uncle Robert Vance.   Also,
David Caldwell, Presbyterian minister and teacher of Piedmont
North Carolina, had a library that was renowned among his students and neighbors.   Elsewhere in the nation, North or South,
East or West, ministers, educators, merchants and planters acquired useable private libraries while the average lawyer or doctor
had at least a workable professional library.   Most of these small
libraries were scattered on the death of their owners but some remained in the same families for several generations and a few of
the more important collections ended up as prized possessions of
public and university libraries.

In the Constitution of the United States, Congress was given
the power to pass copyright laws.   Such a law was passed in 1790,
giving any author who was a citizen of the United States the sole
right to print or sell his copyrighted work for a period of fourteen
years, renewable for an additional fourteen year period.   In 1831,
this act was replaced by one extending the copyright period to
twenty-eight years, renewable for fourteen years.   In 1846, a deposit law was passed, requiring that one copy of each copyrighted
work should be placed in the Library of Congress and one copy in
the newly established Smithsonian Institution Library.   The combination of copyright and depository laws promoted the growth of government libraries while, at the same time, encouraging the writing
and publishing of books.

Another series of laws designed to help the growth of libraries were those relating to the distribution of public documents. It
was understood, of course, that copies of all Federal documents
should be placed in the Library of Congress and also in all official
libraries requiring them but in 1813, Congress ordered that copies
of all Congressional journals and documents should be placed in the
libraries of all colleges, universities and historical societies in the
United States.   During the next quarter century almost every session of Congress directed that copies of public documents, including census reports and historical works published at government expense, should be distributed to institutional libraries.   This aided
considerably in building up the early libraries.   Where they have

been preserved they constitute valuable holdings today. In return, many of the states passed laws sending copies of their public documents to the Library of Congress and the State Department Library and made copies available for exchange with other states. The idea of exchange was even carried to the international level and in 1840 Congress directed that 50 copies of all Federal publications be set aside for international exchange.

Generally speaking, the period from 1775 to 1850 was not only one of growth and expansion in American libraries, but also one of experimentation. Various types of privately supported libraries were tried with lesser or greater degrees of success. Libraries in educational institutions lagged and a change in the philosophy and methods of teaching were necessary before much improvement could be made. Tentative steps were taken in the direction of public library service but definite progress in this respect was still in the future. A number of great private libraries were in the making but, public or private or school or college, all collections were comparatively small. 50,000 volumes was a major achievement, and only a half dozen libraries had reached this size while not more than 100 had even 5,000 volumes. But the seeds of progress were there and the foundations of most of the great libraries of the present-day had been laid. The nation was growing and with it the library as a means of communication was progressing. As of 1850 the dawn of the modern era in American library history was not far away.

Bibliography

Books

Bestor, Arthur E. , ed. : Three Presidents and their books: the reading of Jefferson, Lincoln and Franklin D. Roosevelt. Champaign, Ill. , 1955. 129 p.

Bidlack, Russell E. : The nucleus of a library: a study of the book collection of the University of Michigan... 1837-1845. Ann Arbor, Mich. , 1962. 106 p.

Boston. Athenaeum: The Athenaeum Centenary, the influence and history of the Boston Athenaeum from 1807 to 1907... Boston, 1907. 236 p.

Cole, George W. :   Early library development in New York state.
    New York, 1927.   19 p.

Conner, Martha: Outline of the history of the development of the
    American public library.   Chicago, 1931.   179 p.

Drury, Gertrude: The library and its organization.   New York,
    1924.   519 p.

Eaton, Thelma, ed. :   Contributions to mid-west library history.
    Champaign, Ill. , 1964.   180 p.

Edwards, Edward: A statistical view of the principal public li-
    braries of Europe and America.   London, 1849.   48 p.

Harris, Thaddeus M. :   A selected catalogue of some of the most
    esteemed publications in the English language proper to form
    a social library, with an introduction upon the choice of
    books.   Boston, 1793.

Jefferson, Thomas: Jefferson's idea on a university library.
    Charlottesville, Va., 1950.   49 p.

Jewett, Charles C. :   Notices of public libraries in the United
    States.   Washington, 1851.   207 p.

Joeckel, Carleton B. :   The government of the American public li-
    brary.   Chicago, 1939.   393 p.

Johnston, W.D. :   History of the Library of Congress.   Washing-
    ton, 1904.   535 p.

Keep, Austin B. :   History of the New York Society Library.   New
    York, 1908.   607 p.

Kruzas, Anthony T. :   Business and industrial libraries in the
    United States, 1820-1940.   New York, 1965.   144 p.

Lewis, John F. :   History of the Apprentices' Library of Philadel-
    phia, 1820-1920.   Philadelphia, 1924.

Quincy, Josiah: The history of the Boston Athenaeum.   Cam-
    bridge, Mass., 1851.   104 p.

Raddin, George G. :   An early New York library of fiction.   New
    York, 1940.   113 p.

Rhee, William J. :   A manual of public libraries, institutes and
    societies in the United States...   Philadelphia, 1859. 687 p.

Shera, Jesse H. : Foundations of the public library. Chicago,
    1949. 308 p.

Shores, Louis: Origins of the American college library, 1638-
    1800. New York, 1935. 290 p.

Thompson, C. S. : Evolution of the American public library, 1653-
    1876. Washington, 1952. 287 p.

U. S. Bureau of Education: Public libraries in the United States
    of America. Washington, 1876. 1187 p.

Periodical Articles

Bordon, Arnold K. : "Sociological beginnings of the library move-
    ment," Library Quarterly, I, (1930), 278-282.

Davis, Richard B. : "Jefferson as a collector of Virginiana,"
    Studies in Bibliography, XIV, (1961), 117-144.

Ditzion, Sidney: "The district school library, 1835-1855," Library
    Quarterly, X, (1940), 545-577.

Ditzion, Sidney: "Mechanics and mercantile libraries," Library
    Quarterly, X, (1940), 192-219.

Gilchrist, D. B. : "The evolution of college and university libra-
    ries," A. L. A. Bulletin, XX, (1926), 293-299.

Harding, Thomas S. : "College literary societies: their contribu-
    tion to the development of academic libraries, 1815-1870,"
    Library Quarterly, XXIX, (Jan. , 1959), 1-26.

Houlette, William D. : "Books of the Virginia dynasty," Library
    Quarterly, XXIV, (1954), 226-239.

Kaplan, Louis: "Peter Force, collector," Library Quarterly, XIV,
    (1944), 234-238.

Lowell, M. H. : "Indiana university libraries, 1829-1942," College
    and Research Libraries, XXII, (1961), 423-429.

McDermott, John F. : "Public libraries in St. Louis, 1811-1839,"
    Library Quarterly, XIV, (1944), 9-27.

Stewart, Nathaniel: "Sources for a study of American college li-
    brary history, 1800-1876," Library Quarterly, XIII, (1943),
    227-231.

Storie, Catherine P. : "The American college society library and
    the college library," College and Research Libraries, VI,
    (1945), 240-248.

Walter, Frank K. : "A poor but respectable relation--the Sunday
    School library," Library Quarterly, XII, (1942), 731-739.

Wellard, J. H. ; "Popular reading and the origins of the public li-
    brary in America," Library Journal, LX, (March 1, 1935),
    185-187.

XI
A Period of Library Progress, 1850-1900

Although the foundation of the American Library Association in 1876 is often considered the beginning of the modern library movement in the United States, its beginnings can be traced to the decade around 1850. In 1848, Massachusetts passed legislation allowing the city of Boston to establish a public library and to appropriate municipal funds for its support, thus making that city the first major municipality in the United States to have publicly supported free library service. Three years later this authorization was extended to other towns in the state by "An Act to authorize Cities and Towns to establish and maintain Public Libraries." New Hampshire had passed similar legislation in 1849, and Maine followed in 1854. It is interesting to note that the New Hampshire act saw the public library as more than a collection of books; it authorized the acquisition of maps, charts, periodicals and other publications as well as books. Eight other states had passed permissive legislation for public library service by 1875 and of these all were in New England or the Middle West except Texas. Of the eleven, however, only Massachusetts had made real progress in this early quarter century of development of public libraries and that state easily led the nation in 1875, both in number of public libraries and in number of books in them.

Another event that marked the beginning of the modern library era occurred with the first national meeting of librarians in 1853. This conference met in New York at the call of Charles Coffin Jewett, then the librarian of the Smithsonian Library and some 82 persons were in attendance. These "librarians" came largely from the Northeast, but there was one representative from New Orleans and another from San Francisco. Not all of them were active librarians but all were interested in the field and they met "for the purpose of conferring together upon the means for ad-

169

vancing the prosperity and usefulness of public libraries and for
the suggestion and discussion of topics of importance to book collectors and readers." Among those present were Seth Hastings
Grant, librarian of the New York Mercantile Library; Reuben Ald-
ridge Guild, library of Brown University Library; Lloyd Pearsall
Smith, librarian of the Philadelphia Library Company; and William
F. Poole, librarian of the Boston Mercantile Library. Almost all
of them were outstanding men, and at least a third of them are included in the Dictionary of American Biography. It is interesting
to note that most of the librarians present also had other professions in addition to their library interests and duties. They included ministers, college professors, historians and lawyers as
well as a physician or two and an astronomer.

The topics for discussion at the conference were mainly subjects familiar to the librarian of today. They included cataloging
and classification, public reading rooms, circulating books versus
reference books and the distribution of government documents. The
best methods of establishing popular libraries throughout the country were discussed and the need for strong public support for them
was emphasized. A central national library, preferably built
around the Smithsonian Institution Library, was proposed and some
form of national cumulative bibliography was encouraged. Charles
Folsom, librarian of the Boston Athenaeum, presented a scheme
for arranging punched cards on a string that sounds remarkably
like a card catalog, but his cards were really slips of paper nine
inches long and two inches wide, and they were merely steps in
preparation for a printed library catalog. Before adjourning, the
members resolved "that this Convention be regarded as preliminary
to the formation of a permanent Librarians' Association," but such
was not to be the case. The members of the Committee appointed
for that purpose soon had other interests and with the coming of
the Civil War and Reconstruction it was not until 1876 that a permanent national organization of librarians was finally achieved.

Although proprietary and subscription libraries continued to
thrive during the latter half of the nineteenth century, the general
trend was toward the development of free public libraries in their

stead. The value of public library services as a complement to
public education was rapidly being realized as was also the general
cultural and social value of having good reading matter readily
available to persons in all walks of life. Several of the larger
Mercantile and Mechanics' Libraries grew larger and more important as the years passed but others, particularly the smaller ones,
were either dissolved or converted into free publicly supported institutions. The New York Mercantile Library, for example, with
over a quarter million volumes in its collection in 1900 was still
growing but this was the exception rather than the rule. Generally
speaking, only the endowed library could compete with the free public library after the latter was able to offer the same or similar
services at no charge to the borrower.

The growth of public libraries was slow but steady. New
England and the Middle West led the way, with Massachusetts
claiming 127 free public collections by 1875. Some of the Middle
Western states had library laws that permitted townships and counties to provide library service and steps were taken in this direction, particularly in Ohio and Indiana. Eleven county libraries
were reported in Indiana in 1875 but altogether they contained only
13,000 volumes and their use was apparently small. In 1892, New
York state instituted a system of traveling libraries which placed
small deposits of books in villages and rural areas wherever a responsible group would take charge of it. Van Wert County, Ohio,
went even further in 1897 and began what is usually considered to
be the first successful rural library service with a traveling book
van. Hamilton County, Ohio, and Washington County, Maryland, also established effective rural library service before 1900. Another
significant step in the promotion of general library service was the
establishment of state library commissions. The first of these was
established in Massachusetts in 1890 and by 1900 sixteen other
states had formed similar bodies for the aid and support of public
libraries. For the most part these agencies merely encouraged
the establishment of public libraries, advised their personnel, and
provided a central clearing house for library and book information.
In some states, particularly in Massachusetts, direct state aid to

public libraries was a part of the library laws and the disbursing
of such aid was directed by the library commission.

A good example of the foundation and growth of a large
municipal library can be found in Boston.   The Boston Public Library was authorized in 1848, supported by city ordinance in 1851
and 1852, and opened in 1854.   Various gifts   aided this new library in getting under way.   Mayor John P. Bigelow of Boston
gave $1,000, and Edward Everett gave a collection of over a thou-
sand books, including many valuable government publications. Joshua Bates gave an endowment of $50,000, the proceeds from which
could be used for the purchase of books.   In 1857, Charles Coffin
Jewett came from the Smithsonian Library to head the Boston Public and in 1858 it moved into its own new building.   Mr. Bates
later gave a large collection of reference works which, together
with other volumes, was opened to the public in 1861 as the main
reference room, or Upper Hall.   Under Jewett's direction, printed
catalogs of both the circulating library and the reference library
were issued, and the library grew rapidly in size and use.   By
1877 it contained nearly 300,000 volumes, was circulating over a
million volumes a year, had several branches in operation and was
easily the most important public library in the nation.   Numerous
gifts of money and books, including the Prince Library collected
before 1758, the Bowditch library of mathematics and science and
the George Ticknor collection of Spanish history and literature were
added to further the scholarly development of the library.

In contrast to Boston, New York City did not develop a free
public library until nearly the end of the nineteenth century.
Thanks to the generosity of the Astor family, it did have a most
valuable public reference collection.   In 1848, the will of John
Jacob Astor provided funds for a free reference library for the
city, including the cost of books, building and maintenance.   Later
his son and grandson added other gifts to form one of the most important libraries in the nation.   The Astor library was opened for
use in 1854 with 80,000 volumes, largely the results of buying expeditions made by the first librarian, Dr. Joseph C. Cogswell. By
1875, it contained over 150,000 works, none of which, according

to the librarian, could be classed as "light nor ephemeral." Another important private collection in New York City was the Lenox
Library, collected and endowed by James Lenox, and destined to
become a part of the New York Public Library. It was particularly strong in American history and Shakespearean literature. Although it lacked a public circulating library, New York was well
supplied with important private and semi-public collections including the New York Society Library, the New York Historical Society
Library, the Mercantile Library and the Apprentices' Library, to
name only a few. These together with numerous professional, society and commercial circulating libraries made it one of the book
centers of the nation.

Elsewhere in the nation, the Cincinnati Public Library was
established in 1833, but its early period of growth was a troubled
one and it was not firmly established until the 1870's. It moved
into a permanent building in 1870 and by 1875 it contained a well-
used 70,000 volumes. It was one of the first public libraries in
the nation to be opened for Sunday use, beginning this service in
1871. Chicago's Public Library was created by act of the state
legislature in 1873 and it opened a year later. Part of its first
collection was a group of books donated by English gentlemen in
sympathy for the city that had lost so much in the great fire of
1871. Chicago was fortunate in having William F. Poole as one of
its first librarians and under his wise guidance, the library soon
assumed a position second to that of Boston in size and importance.
In the South, many libraries were destroyed in the course of the
Civil War, particularly in Georgia, South Carolina and Virginia.
The Charleston Library Society building was ransacked in 1865, but
most of the valuable books had been removed earlier and were
saved. The Winyah Indigo Society Library in Georgetown, South
Carolina, was almost completely destroyed. In Virginia, the library of Washington College (later Washington and Lee) was also
destroyed or carried off by raiding soldiers as was the neighboring
library of Virginia Military Institute. Many other Southern private
libraries were destroyed, as for example that of ex-President Tyler. After the war, public library service was slow to develop in

the South and it was not until around the turn of the century that
much progress was made.   On the other hand, in the rapidly growing Pacific coast states of Washington, Oregon and California, library service followed close on the heels of the earliest settlements and the major cities had libraries of several types, including free public libraries, long before 1900.

The late nineteenth century was also a period of strong development of college and university libraries.   Many new colleges
were established after the Civil War, including colleges for Negroes
in the South, state and private institutions in the newly settled
West, and the state agricultural and engineering colleges established
with Federal aid under the Morrill "Land Grant" Act of 1862.
These new colleges all had to establish libraries and in many
cases the going was slow and funds were scarce.   Donations from
private benefactors often helped and in other cases whole libraries
were acquired from academies or societies by gift or purchase.
The older colleges also had problems, especially as student enrollments increased and as graduate work came to be offered.   Bookstocks had to be rapidly increased, departmental and specialized
libraries were formed, and trained or experienced librarians were
employed.   Most of the literary society libraries were amalgamated
with their main library collections and in a few cases training
classes were started for young librarians.   Harvard University
still had the largest college library and its growth and development
during this half century was to serve as an example of other larger
university libraries.   In 1866 Harvard had some 40,000 books and
30,000 pamphlets while in 1875 it had in its main and departmental
collections combined nearly a quarter of a million volumes.   By
1900 it had passed the half million mark, and included, besides the
main library still in Gore Hall, a number of special libraries in
various fields.   It was not until 1913 that the new Widener Library
was completed.

Among the other university libraries, Yale had some 78,000
volumes in 1875, with an additional 25,000 pamphlets, while at the
end of the century its collection reached nearly 300,000 volumes.
The two literary society libraries, totaling together about 20,000

volumes, were placed under the management of the college librarian
in 1871 but they continued to be shelved separately for many years.
Princeton University moved its library into a new building in 1873
and gave its total bookstock as 126,000 in 1900.   Columbia University Library reached 250,000 volumes by 1900 in all of its collections, while Brown University Library was about half as large.
Among the newer state and land-grant universities, some of the
larger were: University of Illinois, founded in 1867, with 42,000
volumes in 1900; University of Nebraska, 1859 and 47,000; University of Missouri, 1843 and 34,000; University of Michigan, 1841
and 145,000; University of Minnesota, 1868 and 65,000; and the
University of California, 1869 and 80,000.   Important new private
and endowed universities included Stanford University, founded in
1892 and with 35,000 volumes in its library in 1900; University of
Chicago, 1892 and 300,000; Vanderbilt University, 1875 and
32,000; and Cornell University, 1868 and 225,000.   The Southern
university libraries still lagged behind those of the remainder of
the nation despite steady growth.   By 1900, the University of Virginia Library bookstock was 49,000; the University of North Carolina, 31,000; South Carolina, 32,000; Georgia, 25,000; Louisiana,
21,500; and Texas, 34,000.

Although the school district libraries had preceded public libraries and spread throughout much of the nation except for the
South, they were fast losing their popularity before 1875.   Various
reasons were advanced for this failure but it seems that the major
causes were lack of experienced and interested personnel to handle
them and lack of adequate quarters to house them.   As public libraries were organized, many of the remaining school district
books came into their hands and the general trend was toward allowing the public librarian to take care of the reading needs of
school children and teachers as well.   There were exceptions, of
course, in some of the better secondary schools and in the larger
cities.   St. Louis, for example, was noted for its excellent system of school library service, as was Buffalo, New York.   In this
latter city, the school libraries were taken over in the 1890's by
the public library, which made deposits of selected books in the

various schools during the school terms. These deposits rotated
from classroom to classroom and in the summers they were returned to the public library for mending, sorting and general prepa-
rations for the coming year. Generally speaking, good school libraries, both elementary and secondary, had to wait for the twentieth century but steps were taken in that direction earlier in many
cases. Several states added school library supervisors to their
state departments of education and a number of public libraries
opened special rooms for children before 1900. Of course, one of
the reasons for lack of library service for children was the lack of
good literature written on the child's level. As more books became available and as more women entered the field of library
service the promotion of library work with children became an accepted part of the general library program. Both the National Education Association and the American Library Association became
interested in the problem of library service for children in the
1890's, and in 1896 a joint A. L. A. -N. E. A. committee was formed
to study the possibilities of getting books to children both in and
out of school. In that same year the N. E. A. formed its school library section, and in the next year, the A. L. A. devoted a special
conference in Atlantic City to a study of the relationship between
schools and libraries.

Among government libraries, the Library of Congress remained pre-eminent. By mid-century, it had passed the 50,000
volume mark, but on December 24, 1851, it suffered a disastrous
fire, and only 20,000 volumes were saved. These, however, were
among the more valuable in the collection and formed a nucleus
from which a new and more permanent library emerged. The library hall in the Capitol was rebuilt of fireproof materials and
$75,000 was appropriated by Congress for the replacement of books.
By the end of the Civil War the library had passed its original
high mark in size and was once more growing rapidly. For a
while there had actually been two national libraries. One of these
was the library of the Smithsonian Institution, donated to the government by the will of the British philanthropist, James Smithson,
in 1846. Charles Coffin Jewett became librarian of the Smithsoni-

an library in 1849, and proceeded to build it up into a collection
of more than 40,000 volumes, particularly strong in the scientific
fields.   He had plans of building it into a real national library,
which he felt the Library of Congress was not, and of making it into the bibliographical center of the United States, with a national
union catalog to reflect the holdings of all the nation's major libraries.   Congress did not agree with his plans and in 1866 the
Smithsonian Library was added to the Library of Congress, while
Jewett transferred his abilities to the new Boston Public Library.
In 1867, the Library of Congress added still another valuable library in its purchase of the Peter Force collection of early Americana, and by 1875, still housed in a wing of the Capitol, it was
overflowing its quarters with nearly 300,000 volumes.

       When Ainsworth R. Spofford became Librarian of Congress
in 1864, the library entered upon a long period of growth and progress, both in size and in service to the nation.   As early as 1871,
Dr. Spofford suggested the need for a library building designed
solely for the collection and in 1874 Congress appointed a committee to look into the possibilities for building a national library
structure.   The wheels of government grind slowly and the building
was begun in 1887 and was completed in 1897.   This new structure,
the present main building of the Library, was capable of holding
nearly three million volumes.   It was equipped with the latest in
library equipment from reading rooms and stacks to book con-
veyors and inter-office speaking tubes.   Though Spofford had begun
with a staff of five in 1864, this new building was manned by a
staff of 185 in 1900, with an additional 45 employees in the copyright office.   An immense re-classifying and re-cataloging project
was begun and this called for a large staff as did also the new and
notable services of printing and distributing catalog cards and providing book services for the nation's blind.   Though the Library of
Congress was still essentially what its name implied, a collection
of books designed to aid the Congress in the performance of its
duties, it had by 1900 come a long way toward becoming a truly
national library.

       The other government agencies in Washington continued to

develop their specialized departmental libraries. The Department
of Interior Library opened in 1850, that of the Attorney General's
Office in 1853, one in the Department of Agriculture in 1860, and
one in the Bureau of Education in 1868. These and other minor
governmental libraries remained rather small down to 1900, but
one of them in particular, the library of the Surgeon-General's Office did attain considerable prominence. Under the librarianship of
Dr. John Shaw Billings, an army officer, physician, bibliographer
and scholar, this collection grew from a miscellaneous group of
some 1,800 books in 1865 to a well-organized library of 50,000
volumes and more than 60,000 pamphlets in 1880. Dr. Billings
made it one of the best medical collections in the world, developed
a subject card catalog for it, began indexing medical journals, and
published a bibliography of medical literature. In addition to his
many other notable accomplishments, both in the library world and
in the fields of public health and hospital architecture, Dr. Billings
is remembered and honored by the library profession as one of the
first and best special librarians.

          There were many other specialized libraries that started or
improved during this period. The various state libraries, whether
historical or legal or both, continued to improve slowly, with their
acquisitions coming from small appropriations, gifts and exchanges
with other states. In size these collections varied from the New
York State Library with well over 100,000 volumes, down to some
of the smaller ones with less than 3,000 even as late as 1900.
The state historical society libraries gained in size and importance
as research centers, particularly in the North and West. The New
York State Historical Society Library had over 60,000 volumes in
1875, while that of Wisconsin had some 33,000. Wisconsin also
had the benefit of the collecting activities of the historian, Lyman
C. Draper, who gathered in print and manuscript one of the best
historical collections in the nation. It was strong in local history
materials for both the South and New England as well as for the
Middle West. Specialized medical libraries developed around the
medical schools and hospitals and in the headquarters of medical
societies. The New York City Hospital Library had about 10,000

volumes in 1875 while that of the Philadelphia College of Physicians was almost twice as large.   Scientific society libraries continued to expand in numbers and several of them reached considerable size.   The Academy of Natural Sciences in Philadelphia had
nearly 65,000 books and pamphlets in its library in 1875, while the
Essex Institute Library in Salem, Massachusetts, claimed over
100,000.   The older societies were joined by similar ones in the
western states and by newer groups devoted to agriculture and natural history.   In addition to these there were numerous smaller
legal, historical and scientific libraries, ranging from those of
county professional and patriotic societies to those of specialized
university departmental collections.

The growth of libraries set the stage for the development of
a library profession.   Although most of the outstanding librarians
of this period were members of other professions, they devoted a
large portion of their time to library service, developed special
skills in that field, and came to consider themselves professional
librarians.   A few of them were librarians only, including Ainsworth R. Spofford and Melvil Dewey and they, among others, began
the systematic training of assistants who in turn became professional librarians.   Along with the growth of the profession came
the organization of the American Library Association in 1876.   Its
first meeting was held in the hall of the Philadelphia Historical Society, with 104 persons present, including thirteen women.   Justin
Winsor, the librarian of Boston Public Library and a distinguished
historian, was elected the first president and Melvil Dewey, then
still a young man, became the first secretary.   A constitution was
drawn up in 1877 and the purposes of the association were given as
the promotion of public libraries; the encouragement of public interest in, and financial support of, libraries; and the elevation of
librarianship to an equal rank with other professions.   At the early
meetings of the association, papers were presented on very practical subjects: cataloging, indexing, bibliography, book sizes, copy-
rights, the qualifications of a librarian, and the reading interests
of the general public.   Growth in membership was slow, but the
A. L. A. ranked high professionally and its meetings called forth

speakers of the first rank in the educational field.   The needs of
different types of libraries were recognized and in 1889 a section
for College and Reference Librarians was formed, with another for
Library Trustees following in 1890.   By 1900 A. L. A. had nearly a
thousand members, with the proportion of women members steadily
increasing and the association was truly representative of all
phases of library work and all parts of the nation.

Closely associated with the growth of the A. L. A. and with
the library profession in general was the problem of training librarians.   Several of the larger public libraries began training
classes for their assistants in the late nineteenth century but with
the exception of the Astor Library in New York none of these assumed the form of a regular school.   In 1887, Melvil Dewey
started classes in "library economy" at Columbia University as a
regular part of the college curriculum.   Though students were not
lacking, the university administration was far from enthusiastic
about this new department and in 1889 Dewey took his school of library science with him when he moved to Albany as librarian of the
New York State Library.   There the school prospered and became
a model for succeeding schools.   In 1925 it returned to Columbia
as the School of Library Service.   Library training courses were
also developed before 1900 at Drexel Institute in Philadelphia and at
Pratt Institute in Brooklyn.   Some courses in library science were
also offered at the University of Illinois in the 1890's, and several
other universities offered courses in bibliography, while the teachers'
colleges offered training in a small way for school teacher-librarians.   For the most part early library training was very practical
and approached the subject from the point of view of method rather
than theory.   Dewey developed a curriculum at Albany which included book buying, cataloging, classification, card writing, book
lettering, library record keeping, and similar practical subjects.
He also strongly recommended for future librarians a sound knowledge of literature and a general education as well as training in library methods.   Rounding out the professional library field were
the state and local library associations which also had their beginnings in the 1890's.   New York State Library Association was the

first, being organized on July 11, 1890, and similar groups were
formed soon after in Iowa, New Hampshire, Massachusetts and
New Jersey. By 1900 state library organizations were quite general, and they were already being joined by library "clubs" in the
larger cities.

The growth of the library profession was closely paralleled
by the development of a professional library literature. In 1852,
Charles C. Jewett issued from the Smithsonian Library his plan
On the Construction of Catalogs for Libraries...with Rules and Examples. Jewett was mostly interested of course in printed catalogs, and in the possibility of a national union catalog but his rules
were useful to all catalogers. William Frederick Poole began indexing periodicals in 1848 while he was student librarian of the
Brothers in Unity Society Library at Yale. A second enlarged edition of his "Index to Periodical Literature" appeared in 1853 after
he became Librarian of the Athenaeum Library in Boston, and this,
with its supplements, is still a standard reference tool for nineteenth century periodical literature. The first American general
work on librarianship was Reuben A. Guild's Librarian's Manual,
issued in 1858, as one of the few concrete results to come from
the Librarians' Conference of 1853. In 1876, the U. S. Bureau of
Education published its compendium of the American library world,
entitled Public Libraries in the United States. This was at once a
history and a handbook of virtually all libraries in the United
States, and together with its second part, which was Charles A.
Cutter's Rules for the Printed Dictionary Catalog, it was a much-
needed library tool. Cutter's rules pointed the way toward the dictionary arrangement for library catalogs; as against generally used
method of classified subject or topical arrangement, with or without an author index. Previous to 1850, library catalogs had almost
always been printed in book form or kept in handwritten sheets or
note-books. After this date many of the major libraries still issued printed catalogs but more of them began to keep supplements
on slips or cards arranged in trays and eventually the card catalog
replaced the printed one for most libraries.

The first edition of Melvil Dewey's Decimal Classification

System appeared in 1876 and in the same year, the first professional library periodical, the Library Journal, was begun with Dewey as editor. Before the appearance of Dewey's classification every library had its own system, and these varied widely. The new system was simple and practical and although it did not meet immediate approval it was gradually adopted, particularly in the newer public and school libraries. Dewey was not the only librarian to be working on a classification system, however, for C. A. Cutter was also developing one, and before he died in 1903 the major part of his Expansive Classification System had been completed. Although it was not widely used in the United States, it did meet with some favor abroad and in a form greatly revised and adapted it became the basis for the Library of Congress Classification System which was developed after Herbert Putnam became Librarian of Congress in 1899. The need of a library materials supply house was felt by the members of the profession and for a time after 1876 a "Supply Department for the American Library Association" under Dewey's direction attempted to meet this demand. This venture was not successful and a private company, the Library Bureau, took over as a national vendor of special library supplies in 1888. Another library need, that for a national index of books in print was met in 1880 by Frederick Leypoldt with his American Catalog of Books in Print and for Sale. Begun in 1876 and issued in parts even before the first full edition appeared, this bibliographical masterpiece was continued down to 1910. One other outstanding service for libraries came just at the end of the century when the Library of Congress began printing its catalog cards and selling them to the libraries of the nation. Thus, in one form or another, most of the library services so well known to twentieth century librarians had begun by 1900.

Private book collectors were no rarity in nineteenth century America, and private libraries of considerable size were developed in all parts of the country. Many of these libraries were donated to public and college collections and others were endowed to become cultural monuments to their founders. More important, many wealthy men who themselves never found time to collect books, made up for this by leaving funds for use in building or enlarging libraries.   One of the first major library gifts was Enoch Pratt's endowment of the Free Library in Baltimore in 1886.   This library under his name but with later support by the city has become one of the outstanding public libraries of the nation.   In the 1890's, libraries and funds from the Astor, Tilden and Lenox families were used to form the basis of the New York Public Library.   A bequest from Walter L. Newberry formed the beginning of the Newberry Reference Library in Chicago in 1887.   John Crerar balanced this collection with the gift in 1895 of a scientific reference library for Chicago.   Harry Elkins Widener's library went to Harvard, while the Caleb Fiske Harris Collection of American poetry and drama went to Brown University in 1885.   Elsewhere over the nation other individuals gave collections of varying sizes to both college and public libraries but the greatest library benefactor of all was Andrew Carnegie.   This self-made millionaire of the steel industry was born in Scotland but made his wealth in the United States and repaid both his native and adopted countries with gifts of millions of dollars for the construction of library buildings.   He began as early as 1881 to encourage the construction of free public libraries and in forty years provided financial aid toward the construction of no less than 2,500 library buildings in the United States, Canada and Great Britain.   The Carnegie buildings were given with the understanding that the local governments were to provide books, staff and permanent maintenance and that the use of the libraries was to be free to all.   The Carnegie gifts provided a tremendous stimulus to the public library movement for several decades and it is difficult to imagine how American library history would have developed without them.

By the turn of the century there were 5,383 libraries in the United States containing over 300 volumes each and open to the public in one way or another.   According to the U.S. Bureau of Education reports, these libraries contained nearly 45,000,000 volumes but it is interesting to note that nearly half the libraries and over half of the books were in the nine North Atlantic states between Maine and Pennsylvania.   Another interesting fact is that as many

books were added to American libraries in the years between 1895
and 1900 as had been contained in all American libraries in 1875.
In the broad field of cultural communication, the library was taking
its rightful place in the United States, serving as a connecting link
between the knowledge of the past and the needs of the present. It
was still having growing pains as a social institution, but it had
passed its infancy and was well on the way to becoming a prominent and necessary part of the American scene.

Bibliography

Books

Adams, Herbert B.:   Public libraries and popular education.   Al-
    bany, N.Y., 1900.   49-271 p.

Apponyi, Flora H.:   The libraries of California.   San Francisco,
    1878.   304 p.

Bay, J. Christian: The John Crerar Library, 1895-1944:   an his-
    torical report.   Chicago, 1945.   188 p.

Borome, Joseph A.:   Charles Coffin Jewett.   Chicago, 1951. 173 p.

Clemons, Harry: The University of Virginia Library, 1825-1950.
    Charlottesville, Va., 1954.   231 p.

Columbia University: The School of Library Economy at Columbia
    College, 1887-1889.   New York, 1937.   272 p.

Conner, Martha: Outline of the history of the development of the
    American public library.   Chicago, 1931.   179 p.

Danton, Emily M., ed.:   Pioneering leaders in librarianship.
    Chicago, 1953.   202 p.

Ditzion, Sidney: Arsenals of a democratic culture; a social his-
    tory of the American public library movement in New Eng-
    land and the Middle States from 1850 to 1900.   Chicago,
    1947.   263 p.

Dunglison, Richard: History and condition of the medical libraries
    of Philadelphia.   Philadelphia, 1871. 46 p.

Eaton, Thelma, ed.:   Contributions to American library history.
    Champaign, Ill., 1961.   277 p.

Eaton, Thelma, ed.:   Contributions to mid-west library history.
    Champaign, Ill., 1964. 180 p.

Fletcher, W.I. : Public libraries in America. Boston, 1894. 160 p.

Flexner, Abraham: Daniel Coit Gilman. New York, 1946. 164 p.

Green, Samuel S. : The public library movement in the United
    States, 1853-1893. Boston, 1913. 336 p.

Hadley, Chalmers: John Cotton Dana. Chicago, 1943. 105 p.

Held, R. E. : Public libraries in California, 1849-1878. Berkeley,
    Calif. , 1963. 193 p.

Joeckel, Carleton B. : The government of the American public li-
    brary. Chicago, 1935. 393 p.

Johnston, W. D. : History of the Library of Congress. Washington,
    1904. 535 p.

Kilgour, Frederick G. : The library of the Medical Institution of
    Yale College and its catalogue of 1865. New Haven, 1960.
    74 p.

Lydenberg, Harry M. : John Shaw Billings. Chicago, 1924. 95 p.

Lydenberg, Harry M. : History of the New York Public Library.
    New York, 1923. 643 p.

Oliphant, J. O. : The library of Bucknell University. Lewisburg,
    Pa. , 1962. 154 p.

Ranz, Jim: The printed book catalogue in American libraries,
    1723-1900. Chicago, 1964. 144 p.

Rider, R.K. : Samuel Swett Green. Chicago, 1926. 92 p.

Shera, J. H. : Foundations of the public library. Chicago, 1949.
    308 p.

Spencer, Gwladys: The Chicago Public Library: origins and back-
    grounds. Chicago, 1943. 473 p.

Spofford, Ainsworth R. : A book for all readers... New York,
    1900. 509 p.

Thompson, C. S. : Evolution of the American public library, 1653-
    1876. Washington, 1952. 287 p.

U. S. Bureau of Education: Public libraries in the United States of
    America. Washington, 1876. 1187 p.

Utley, George B. : The librarians' conference of 1853. Chicago,
    1951. 189 p.

Wadlin, Horace G.: The public library of the city of Boston.
    Boston, 1911. 256 p.

Whitehill, Walter M.: Boston Public Library; a centennial history.
    Cambridge, Mass., 1956. 274 p.

Williamson, William A.: William Frederick Poole and the modern
    library movement. New York, 1963. 240 p.

Woodford, Frank Bury: Parnassus on Main Street: a history of
    the Detroit Public Library. Detroit, 1965. 487 p.

Periodical Articles

Bishop, W.W.: "A decade of library progress in America," Popu-
    lar Science, LXIV, (Dec., 1904), 131-138.

Briggs, F.A.: "The Sunday School library in the nineteenth century,"
    Library Quarterly, XXXI, (1961), 166-177.

Carnegie, Andrew: "The best fields for philanthropy," North Amer-
    ican Review, CXLIX, (1889), 682-698.

Ditzion, Sidney: "Social reform, education, and the library," Li-
    brary Quarterly, IX, (1939), 156-184.

Fletcher, William I.: "The public library movement," Cosmopoli-
    tan XVII, (1894), 99-106.

Harrison, J.L.: "The movement for public libraries in the United
    States," New England Magazine, X, (1894), 709-722.

Held, Ray E.: "The Odd Fellows' Library Associations of Cali-
    fornia," Library Quarterly, XXXII, (1962), 148-163.

Kilgour, Frederick G.: "Justin Winsor," College and Research Li-
    braries, III, (Dec., 1941), 64-66.

Lacy, Dan: "The Library of Congress: a sesquicentenary review,"
    Library Quarterly, XX, (1950), 157-179.

Leidecker, Kurt F.: "The debt of Melvil Dewey to William Torrey
    Harris," Library Quarterly, XV, (1945), 139-142.

Mead, Theodore H.: "A free lending library for New York," Scrib-
    ners' Monthly, XX, (1880), 929-935.

Norton, Frank H.: "The Astor Library," Galaxy, VII, (1869), 527-
    537.

Spofford, Ainsworth R.: "The public library of the United States,"
    Journal of Social Science, II, (1870), 92-114.

Thurber, Evangeline: "American agricultural college libraries, 1862-1900." College and Research Libraries, VI, (1945), 346-352.

Walter, Frank K.: "The Sunday school library," Library Quarterly, XII, (1942), 731-739.

Wright, Thomas: "Possible culture through libraries," Contemporary Review, XL, (1881), 25-44.

XII

Books and Printing Since 1775

From the days of Gutenberg until the late eighteenth century there were only minor improvements in the printing press, and in the processes of printing and binding books. There were improvements in typography and illustrations, but the printing process itself was relatively unchanged. The type was set in a wooden form, locked in and placed in the "bed" of the press. The type was then inked by hand, the press was raised by means of a turning screw, a sheet of paper was inserted over the type and then the press was lowered to make an impression from the inked type onto the paper. Each printed sheet meant a laborious raising and lowering of the screw press by hand, and the amount of printing that could be done in a day was very limited. On the other hand, with every step of the process under hand control, very fine work could be done by skilled and conscientious workers.

In 1798, Charles, Earl Stanhope, brought out an iron press in England that added the power of a lever to the screw process of raising and lowering the press and this speeded up printing considerably. The Columbian press, developed in the United States about 1810 by George Clymer, did away with the screw press and used levers and springs to provide the proper pressure. The Columbian press remained popular for more than a half century, and was probably the best of the Gutenberg-style flat-bed presses. In 1813, Friedrich Koenig, a German printer in London, produced the first press to make use of the cylinder. In his press the type bed remained flat, but the paper was pressed upon the type by means of a revolving cylinder moving from one end to the other. The London Times adopted the Koenig press and powered it with a steam engine in 1814, greatly increasing the speed of printing. Along with these improvements in the press came the use of stereotype plates. This process used movable types to make molds from which solid plates were cast.   These plates had the advantage of being easily handled and were so durable that thousands of impressions could be made from them.

To the cylinder press, stereotypes and steam power, the 1830's saw the addition of the assembly line method of printing, folding, stitching and binding, making possible the production of books and pamphlets at much higher speed.   In the 1840's, Richard M. Hoe developed the Hoe Rotary Press, which locked the type itself into a cylinder, and produced up to 8,000 impressions per hour. Some twenty years later, William A. Bullock further perfected this press by replacing the type with a stereotype cylinder (actually two half-cylinders locked onto a roller) and allowing for the continuous feeding of paper from a roll to the press.   This type of press met immediate approval by the producers of newspapers and magazines and it was continually enlarged and improved until the largest newspapers in the country could be printed and folded at the rate of many thousand per hour.   For the printing of books and pamphlets, however, the flat-bed presses continued to be used throughout the nineteenth century and in many cases down to the present.

A rival for the stereotype plate came after 1840 with the development of electrotype.   Whereas the stereotype plate was made from a papier-maché mold impressed by the original type, the electrotype plate was produced by taking an impression in wax from the original type, depositing a thin shell of copper on the wax by an electrolytic process, and then filling in the copper shell with type-metal alloy.   Both processes achieved the same result -- a stable plate capable of being continuously used for long runs -- but the electrotype plate gradually displaced the stereotype except for the production of newspapers.   The electrotype had the additional advantage of being able to reproduce pictures from woodcuts or engravings much better than could the stereotype.

Despite the improvement in printing methods, type-setting by hand continued throughout much of the nineteenth century.   In the 1820's, William Church, a native of Vermont then living in England, designed and constructed a machine for setting type mechanically from a hand-operated keyboard but the idea was slow to be adopted.

It was not until the 1850's that the John F. Trow printing office in
New York first put into operation a successful type-setting machine.
This machine, patented by William H. Mitchell, was a considerably
improved adaptation of the Church machine and it made type-setting
a comparatively easy task.   On top of this came the production of
type-casting machines for the quick and plentiful production of type,
both for hand-setting and machine-setting, and the printing trade
was rapidly approaching its modern form.   One more major printing development came in 1885 when Ottmar Mergenthaler built a
composing machine which was patented under the name of Linotype.
The New York Herald Tribune, in 1886, was the first newspaper to
apply this new process of type-setting.   It was operated from a keyboard similar to a typewriter keyboard and cast a complete line of
type in one piece, properly spaced and ready for printing or for
making of plates.   The Linotype soon took its place as standard
equipment in the larger newspaper and book publishing firms.

        The new high-speed processes required strong paper in the
form of rolls so that a continuous stream of paper could be fed into the rapidly rotating presses.   Moreover, as more and more
books, newspapers and magazines were published, paper had to be
plentiful as well as economical, strong and durable.   Up to about
1800, the paper-making process, which resulted in flat sheets of
good quality rag paper, had been little changed for three hundred
years.   In 1799, Henry and Sealy Fourdrinier, two brothers who
were stationers in London, patented a paper-making machine, and
about five years later they produced their first successful working
model.   This machine was built around a revolving wire band that
passed through a vat of paper pulp, picking up a layer of pulp which
was then removed from the wires and fed in a continuous stream
along a conveyor belt.   On this belt the pulp was carried through a
process of pressing and drying, producing rolls of paper in almost
any needed length.   This idea, with some changes, was put into effect in the United States in 1817 by the Gilpin brothers of Delaware.
They produced a paper-making machine capable of turning out a continuous sheet of paper, thirty inches wide, at the rate of sixty feet
per minute.   With many improvements, the Fourdrinier and Gilpin

machines remain the basis for most paper-making machinery in modern use.

The other great innovations in paper-making in the nineteenth century came in the discovery of new paper-making materials. Linen and cotton rags, the source of paper up through the eighteenth century, were too scarce and expensive for the production of the large quantities of paper needed for the nineteenth century presses. A new, cheaper source of paper was needed, and after much experimentation with various vegetable fibres a process was developed for making paper from wood pulp. At first the pulp was prepared by macerating wood chips by mechanical means but this was both slow and unsatisfactory, and it produced only a coarse paper. In the 1850's a method was developed for reducing the wood to pulp by chemical means, particularly sodas and sulphites which reduced the solid wood to a liquid, fibrous solution that could be handled in the paper-making machines. Since there was a seemingly endless supply of wood in the United States, these developments in the making of paper made America the center of the industry for the modern world. So important was the industry and so rapid its growth that by 1880 there were 742 paper mills in 29 states. In the twentieth century, the demand for paper rapidly caught up with the supply and several steps have been taken to insure a constant source of pulp materials. New forests of quick-growing soft woods are being continuously planted and experiments are being made with new paper sources such as rice straw and hulls, peanut hulls and the remains of sugar cane after the juice has been removed. Even so, much of the paper being used in the United States today must be imported from Canada.

Illustrations in American books of the seventeenth and eighteenth centuries were produced either from wood-cuts or from copper-plate engravings. Excellent work was produced in a few cases but for the most part American printers did not equal the Europeans in the quality of their book illustrations before 1800. On the other hand, illustrations were widely used by the American presses after that date, and they included not only portraits but maps, architectural drawings, cartoons, prints, and views of the larger cities.

Color prints were produced by 1800 or shortly after, and the works of outstanding artists were employed in book illustrations. The American edition of Rees' Encyclopedia, published in Philadelphia in 1797, was a particularly fine example of the copperplate engraver's art. Steelplate engravings were introduced after 1819, and although the resulting prints were not of the quality of copperplate engravings, the steel could be used almost indefinitely, producing many more copies than copper. A new method of reproducing illustrations was introduced early in the nineteenth century, but it did not become popular for many years. This was lithography, a process of reproducing pictures from a flat surface, originally smooth stone, but sometimes zinc or other metal. Color lithography was also possible by using a separate plate for each color desired or by the three-color process of over-printing with the three primary colors to produce almost all colors. The striking color prints of Currier and Ives, so illustrative of American life in the mid-nineteenth century, were produced by lithography.

The next great step in book illustration came with the development of photo-mechanical processes, particularly photo-engraving. This process employed chemical means to transfer pictures from the photographic film to the engraver's plate, permitting any photograph to be readily reproduced in print. Photography had been invented or developed before 1840, and was fairly common by 1860, but it was not until 1873 that the first photograph was printed lithographically in the New York Daily Graphic. The half-tone process, which enabled a photograph to be reproduced by regular printing, was developed in the 1870's, and from about 1880 on the photograph was an accepted feature in most newspapers and magazines. Color printing, rotogravure, and off-set printing were all coming into use by 1900, or were well beyond the experimental stages. Rotogravure was the photo-engraving adapted to the high-speed rotary presses for newspapers, while off-set was a process of lithography also adapted to a cylinder rather than a plate. In off-set, the picture is transferred from the original plate to a rubber covered cylinder and from this to paper revolving around a third cylinder. The off-set process has the advantages of reproducing both picture and text at the same time and also of printing on cheaper paper than that required for regular lithography.   In the twentieth century chemistry, photography and electronics have combined to produce methods of transmitting pictures or texts by wire or by television over long distances and printing them almost simultaneously with reception. Even more recently the introduction of communications satellites makes it possible to transmit television across the Atlantic.   Pictorial communication has come a long way from the cave man's drawing!

In the book-making process the final step is the binding.   In this field the changes have not been so radical but there have been many developments in the last century.   Before 1800, the printed sheets of four, eight or twelve leaves were folded, stitched in signatures, then sewn together in volumes, and finally bound in boards covered with leather or vellum.   The early printed books simply followed the binding methods of the later medieval manuscript volumes and although the book-binder became an artist in the fifteenth to eighteenth centuries his artistry lay more in his technique of decorating the leather covers of the book rather than in departures from earlier binding methods.   The nineteenth century saw the replacement of leather by cloth as the outside book covering and the wooden or stiff leather boards by heavy cardboard.   Machine stitching took the place of hand-sewing, and stronger glues were used to strengthen the spine.   As the printing presses became more mechanized and their output more prolific, the process of binding also began to be done by machinery and by the 1860's the hand-bound edition was a rarity.   The late nineteenth century saw the introduction of wire-stapling for pamphlets and smaller books, and the twentieth introduced the paperbacked, non-sewn, book that relied entirely upon glues or plastics for its binding.   Finally, plastic-impregnated fabrics are being used to form an attractive and durable type of book cover that can be printed as easily as paper yet has the lasting qualities of the finest leather.

One of the results of the change from leather-bound books to cloth bindings was the necessity for a protective cover over the cloth to prevent it becoming soiled before the book was sold.   This

problem found a solution in the paper book jacket, which was first
introduced in the 1840's but which did not come into common use
until the last decades of the nineteenth century. The paper jacket
or wrapper provided a place for advertising, and for information
concerning the book and its author, as well as for attractive illustrations. The design of book jackets has become an art but, for
the most part, jackets have tended toward becoming merely advertising matter. With the coming of the paper-bound books, the jacket merged with the binding boards and resulted in a stiff paper cover, often luridly illustrated in several colors. An interesting point
concerning the book jacket is that libraries are now protecting it
with a clear plastic cover, since it is often attractive and enhances
the attractiveness of the book.

The nineteenth century printing firm was usually a corporation employing anywhere from a half-dozen to several hundred workers, and often combining under one roof both printing and binding
processes. Publishing became a business distinct from printing,
with the latter often being performed on contract by other firms.
Printing workers were among the first to organize into labor unions
and by the late nineteenth century they were a powerful force in the
printing industry. Also, the printing industry tended to specialize,
with some publishers producing only newspapers, others magazines
or books and some firms doing only job printing. Newspapers increased in numbers until there was at least one for every county in
the United States and some of the larger metropolitan dailies were
issued in hundreds of thousands of copies daily. Magazines also increased in numbers, from a bare half-dozen around 1800 to several
score by 1850, several hundred by 1900, and more than ten thousand by 1960. The illustrated weekly appeared in the 1860's and
proved very popular, while monthly magazines appeared for all interests, including popular, juvenile, professional, technical and
trade; with circulations ranging from a few hundred to several million. Book printings went from a few hundred in the early nineteenth century to several thousand for a popular work before 1900
and even into the millions for a best-seller in the mid-twentieth
century. The broadside disappeared in the nineteenth century, but

the almanac held its own and the pamphlet became more versatile
and more plentiful than ever.

Whereas much of the early literature printed in the United
States was borrowed from European or classical authors, the tendency in the nineteenth century was toward the production of works
by American authors.   Particularly after 1850, the writers of American birth, whether in literature, history or science, far outnumbered those of European origin in the output of the American press.
New types of publications, including encyclopedias in many volumes,
collected works, and the illustrated gift book or annual, entered the
field and the book-seller, long associated with the printer, emerged
as a separate profession.   Not content with waiting for the customer,
both publisher and bookseller sent salesmen throughout the country
to advertise their products and increase their sales.   Many books
were published on a subscription basis, with orders being taken in
advance of publication.   After about 1840, the publication of text-
books for schools and colleges became a major business, as those
institutions of learning increased in number and size.   Books written and designed especially for children appeared in larger numbers
after 1850, and by 1900 the illustrated children's book was an accepted stock in trade for both publisher and bookseller.   For popular reading, the paper-backed "dime novel" appeared after the Civil
War; in the form of western, adventure and mystery thrillers they
were sold by the hundreds of thousands.   In the output of the nineteenth century presses, quality may have been lacking to a large extent, but quantity was there and the literate American could scarcely complain of a lack of reading matter.

Among the larger and better known publishers of the early
nineteenth century were a few that survive in present-day firms.
Matthew Carey and Sons, for example, was a firm founded and directed by a Philadelphia economist and politician.   When the father
withdrew from the company in 1822, it became the firm of Carey
and Lea, which lasted down through the nineteenth century and survives today as Lea and Febiger, Inc.   D. Appleton and Company,
founded as a publishing house in New York in 1831, survives in
Appleton-Century-Crofts.   J. and J. Harper, beginning in 1817, later

became Harper and Brothers, and survives after almost a century
and a half as Harper and Row. By the 1830's, Harper's was intro-
ducing the assembly line into the printing and binding of books and
employed over 300 workers in one building, a very large undertak-
ing for that time. In the same decade, Harper's began publishing
its Family Library, a series of popular books on many subjects,
low in price and wide in appeal. It was one of the first of many
such series, represented today by the Modern Library and the
Home University series.

      Some of the larger publishers in the later nineteenth century
experimented with the publication of both books and magazines. Harper's for example, published not only Harper's Monthly but at different times, Harper's Weekly, Harper's Young People, and Harper's Bazaar. D. Appleton and Company not only published a periodical, but added the New American Encyclopedia to its list, and
for a long time issued an annual supplement volume. Charles Scribner and Sons, another pre-Civil War publishing firm, began issuing
Scribner's Monthly in 1870 and made of it one of the most important
periodicals of its day. The twentieth century saw a proliferation of
publishing companies, with a tendency toward specialization. Publishers tended to publish either periodicals or books, and if books,
to specialize in particular types of books, such as technical, popular, religious or juveniles. The strictly commercial publishers
were joined by a new type of publisher - the university press.
These partly subsidized presses were able to publish scholarly works
that were not commercially feasible and hence added considerably to
publication of serious books. Two types of reprint publishers have
also added to the totals of books published. One of these is the
publisher of inexpensive reprints of popular fiction and non-fiction,
while the other is the reprinter, usually by photo-offset, of out-of-
print but still needed scholarly works. All told, American publishers, as of the mid-twentieth century, were producing from ten
to fifteen thousand titles per year, in printings of from a few hundred to several hundred thousand copies. Bibliographic control over
these publications has been made possible by H.W. Wilson Company's Cumulative Book Index, and R.R. Bowker Company's Books

in Print series.

The vital link between the publisher and the buyer of books is, of course, the bookseller. This occupation is little appreciated in the American economic and cultural scene. It is important and despite book clubs, direct mail order sales by publishers, and cut-rate competitors, it still remains a valuable part of the book industry. The book clubs of which there were some 112 in 1962, by-pass the local bookseller, and deal directly with the book buying public, offering low prices or premium books in return for continued buying. This has resulted in more books reaching the average reader, but it cuts down on the sales of the average book store. Many retail units must rely on the sale of greeting cards, toys or other merchandise in order to remain in the book business while others have found the rapid turnover of sales in the paper-back field enough to allow them to continue selling the slower moving trade volumes. The larger towns can usually support one or more good book stores, but many smaller towns, and many rural areas of the United States are without the benefits of a good book store. Although the best-seller, in original, reprint and paper-back editions, may sell over a million copies, many good and well-reviewed works of non-fiction will sell only a few thousand. Fortunately, better sales methods, more advertising, and a larger book-buying public are combining to improve the lot of the book seller as of the 1960's.

Thus we see that from a few scattered printers in the thirteen colonies of 1775, the American publishing industry has become by the 1960's a gigantic business, employing thousands of workers and producing nearly a billion copies of books per year. Magazines of five to ten million circulation are not uncommon, while the larger daily newspapers number their subscribers in the hundreds of thousands. The typewriter was a mechanical miracle of the nineteenth century, and the teletype added electronics to the graphic processes in the twentieth century, making the transmission of information in written form as instantaneous as the radio or television. But these innovations are already being surpassed by newer developments in the field - developments such as electrostatic printing, which does away with both press and type and prints directly from film; tape-

controlled type-setting; and wireless transmission of both pictures
and text so that copy can be set up in New York and printed in Chicago.   Add to these advances in the field of graphic communication
all those in the area of instantaneous communication, such as telephone, telegraph, radio and television, and the result is truly amazing.   Signals have been received from artificial satellites millions
of miles out in space, and regular communication has been maintained with astronauts circling the earth, 180 miles out, at 17,000
miles per hour.   Television programs have been broadcast from
Europe to America via the communications satellite Telstar and
this same method may soon make undersea cables obsolete in the
transmission of telephone and telegraph messages.   It is perfectly
conceivable that the voice of one man could today be heard simultaneously by radio by every human being on earth and in a few years
he could probably be seen on television as well.   The videophone,
long a science fiction specialty, is rapidly becoming a fact, and it
is possible to develop a radio-newspaper that for the price of a
television set would produce newspapers in the home directly from
a central news room in New York if there were a demand for it.
Moreover, any and all of this instantaneous communication can be
preserved in print, on film, disk, tape or wire for use tomorrow
or a hundred years from now.   The development of television programs on electronic tape rather than on photographic film has brought
about the instant replay of televised events.   Truly, the progress in
all methods of communication has been remarkable in the twentieth
century, but as of the 1960's, the book and its related graphic materials are still the basic means of continuing communication and
their presence seems assured throughout the foreseeable future.
Books and printing may be supplemented, but as yet man has no
tool to replace them completely.

Bibliography

Books

Bennett, Paul A.: Books and printing. New York, 1951.   258 p.

Fabey, Herbert: Early printing in California.   San Francisco,
          1956.   141 p.

Green, Ralph: The iron hand press in America. Rowayton, Conn.,
      1948.   40 p.

Greenhood, David: Chronology of books and printing. New York,
      1936.   186 p.

Halsey, R. V. : Forgotten books of the American nursery: a his-
      tory of the development of the American story book.   Boston,
      1911.   245 p.

Hunter, Dard: Papermaking; the history and technique of an an-
      cient craft. New York, 1947.   680 p.

Jackson, Holbrook: The printing of books. London, 1938. 285 p.

Lehmann-Haupt, Helmut: The book in America: a history of the
      making and selling of books in the United States. New York,
      1964.   2nd ed.   512 p.

McMurtrie, Douglas C. : The book. New York, 1943.   676 p.

Marianaccio, Anthony: Exploring the graphic arts.   Scranton, Pa.,
      1946.   275 p.

Miller, William: The book industry. New York, 1949. 156 p.

Morison, Stanley: Four centuries of fine printing. London, 1924.
      243 p.

Mumby, Frank A. : Publishing and bookselling; a history from the
      earliest times to the present day. New York, 1956. 4th ed.
      500 p.

Pitz, Henry C. : A treasury of American book illustration. New
      York, 1945.   255 p.

Pottinger, David: Printers and printing. Cambridge, Mass., 1941.
      143 p.

Reiner, Imre: Modern and historical typography. New York, 1946.
      125 p.

Rosner, C. : Printers progress, 1851-1951. Cambridge, Mass.,
      1951.   119 p.

Schick, Frank L. : The paperbound book in America and its Euro-
      pean antecedents. New York, 1958.   262 p.

Sheehan, Donald: This was publishing. Bloomington, Ind., 1952.
      288 p.

Shove, R. H. : Cheap bookproduction in the United States, 1870-
      1891. Urbana, Ill., 1937.   155 p.

Simon, Oliver: Introduction to typography. Cambridge, Mass.,
    1937. 155 p.

Steinberg, S.H.: Five hundred years of printing. New York, 1959.
    286 p.

Stern, Madeleine B.: Imprints on history; book publishing and
    American frontiers. Bloomington, Ind., 1956. 492 p.

Thompson, Ralph: American literary annuals and gift books, 1825-
    1865. New York, 1936. 183 p.

Weeks, Lyman H.: A history of paper manufacturing in the United
    States, 1690-1916. New York, 1916. 352 p.

Weitenkampf, Frank: The illustrated book. Cambridge, Mass.,
    1938. 314 p.

Wentz, Roby: Eleven western presses; an account of how the first
    printing press came to each of the eleven Western states.
    Los Angeles, 1956. 57 p.

Wroth, Lawrence: A history of the printed book. New York, 1938.
    507 p.

Periodical Articles

Green, Ralph: "Early American power printing presses," Studies
    in Bibliography, IV, (1951-52), 143-154.

Hagedorn, Leo H.M.: "The first century of photo-engraving," Pen-
    rose's Annual, XIX, (1917), 189-197.

Morison, Stanley: "Towards an ideal type," The Fleuron, II, (1924),
    57-75.

"Printing--ancient craft is stirring with technological innovations,"
    Fortune, XL, (Oct., 1949), 100-109.

Ransom, Will: "Five hundred years of printing," Publishers'
    Weekly, CXXXVI, (Aug. 5, 1939), 381-384.

Rollins, Carl P.: "A survey of the making of books in recent
    years," The Dolphin, I, (1933), 288-301.

Tanselle, G.T.: "The historiography of American literary publish-
    ing," Studies in Bibliography, XVIII, (1965), 3-40.

XIII

Modern Foreign Libraries

Library service in other countries varies considerably from that which we consider normal in the United States. In many countries individual libraries and library service in general approach and even surpass ours, but in others and in most of the world, great steps must be taken to reach even minimum standards of acceptable library service. Generally speaking, library services are best in northern Europe and in the British Commonwealth nations and poorest in the tropical and former colonial areas. All around the globe library progress is being made and any general statement today may be far from true even a year later.

Canada

As one might expect, library service in Canada, our nearest neighbor, has developed in much the same way that it has in the United States. There was a library at the Jesuit College in Quebec as early as 1635 and the legislature of Ontario (Upper Canada) had a library as early as 1791 but there was little movement toward public or school libraries until the later nineteenth century. There were subscription libraries and libraries in private academies earlier, but the first public library service dates from the Ontario Free Libraries Act of 1882. A School Libraries Act was passed in 1848 but it was generally ineffective until after 1900. By the 1950's most secondary schools had centralized libraries, while the elementary schools were served by classroom collections. School library supervisors, both on the provincial and municipal level, are to be found in several areas. Since the National Library Act of 1953, Canada has a central national library as well as a Library of Parliament and government departmental collections. The National Library of Canada in 1963 had some 250,000 volumes, slightly larger than the Library of Parliament but it is designed to hold some

750,000 volumes when in full operation and will service other libraries with micro-materials and bibliographic aids.   The Canadian Department of Agriculture with its nearly 250,000 volumes is the
largest of the department libraries but there are several other departmental research collections of notable size.   Each of the provinces has a provincial library, with the largest being that of Quebec.   Prince Edward Island has the distinction of providing library
service for 100 per cent of its inhabitants through its provincial library system, and other provinces are making use of regional libraries in order to reach more readers.   There are several large
public libraries, including those of Toronto (nearly 1,000,000 volumes), Montreal, Ottawa, Winnipeg, and Vancouver (480,000 volumes).   In all Canada there were over 800 public libraries in 1963.
Most of these are in Quebec and Ontario, but the western provinces
are rapidly improving with traveling collections, regional libraries,
and inter-library cooperation.   Package libraries are available from
several of the provincial libraries for the benefit of citizens who
live far from the centers of population.

The largest Canadian university library is that of the University of Toronto, with well over a million volumes but several others
including McGill University, Carleton University, Queen's University,
and the Universities of Manitoba, Saskatchewan, and British Columbia have collections in the hundreds of thousands.   Two universities,
Laval University and the University of Montreal, and several colleges serve the French-speaking Canadians and Laval in particular
is known for its outstanding collection of French language and literature.   The best known Canadian library schools are those at Mc-
Gill University and at the University of Toronto but a number of
other Canadian colleges offer some training in the field, and many
Canadians receive their library training in the United States.   Special library service is rapidly expanding in Canada and there are
some 200 scientific, hospital, business and industrial collections of
a thousand or more volumes.   Besides their own library associations,
Canadian librarians also take part in the activities of the American
Library Association and their standards of library service and librarianship are as high as those of the United States.

Latin America

The library picture in our southern neighbor, Mexico, is not as favorable as that in Canada. The National Library in Mexico City was first opened in 1861, and although its history has been one of slow growth, with many periods of disinterest on the part of the government, it now numbers some half-million volumes, many of which are quite valuable, along with more than 100,000 manuscripts relating to the history and development of the nation. Since 1929, the National Library has been under the direction of the University of Mexico and it is now housed on the new university campus. There it constitutes the core of the library materials available to the university, supplemented by the central university library and many departmental collections to form a research center of nearly a million volumes. Elsewhere in Mexico there are a number of college and university libraries but with a few exceptions their libraries are usually merely storehouses of valuable old volumes that are inadequate for current needs. Since 1921 a Department of Libraries has been included in the Ministry of Public Education and this agency has encouraged the development of public libraries throughout the country. Many small collections have been formed but outside of the Federal District, which includes Mexico City, very few of them approach anything like adequate service. Mexico City has four children's libraries as of 1963 with more planned in the future. Other types of libraries in Mexico include church libraries, few in number and small in size but often including great rarities; special libraries, almost all in Mexico City; and a few remaining private libraries of importance. Among the special libraries, that of the National Museum of Anthropology contains some 200,000 books and pamphlets, while the Mexican Society of Geography and Statistics has a library of 80,000 volumes. The United States has operated the Benjamin Franklin Library in Mexico City since 1943, and it has been quite effective in demonstrating American ideas in librarianship. In 1963 it contained some 30,000 volumes in English and Spanish, while the British Council Library contained about half as many. Library service in the public schools is almost non-existent

in Mexico, but a few attempts are being made to at least demonstrate what can be done where books and funds are available.

Elsewhere in Latin America, the library picture is more or
less the same as that in Mexico. Each country has a national library of some size but few public or institutional libraries of note.
Library service is hampered by the generally poor educational facilities, the low economic status of the majority of the population,
and the lack of trained personnel. The general philosophy of library
service in most cases tends toward protection and preservation of
the books rather than towards the encouragement of their use. To
help meet the need for trained librarians the Inter-American Library
School was established at Medellin, Colombia, in 1956 and in 1960,
sixteen graduates completed their course work there. Other graduate library schools are needed but in the meantime most Latin
American librarians receive their training through experience, short
courses and institutes conducted in the major libraries and in schools
in other countries.

In recent years, Brazil, Argentina, and Chile have taken the
lead among the Latin American countries in the field of library service. Brazil in particular has several outstanding libraries, including federal, provincial, municipal, school, institutional, and special.
The National Library at Rio de Janeiro contains over a million and
a half volumes, including over 600,000 bound volumes of journals,
and over 600,000 manuscripts. This library also contains the Bra-
zilian copyright office and operates a school of librarianship. At
Brasilia, the new capital of Brazil, there are separate libraries for
the Senate and the Chamber of Deputies. The latter is slightly the
larger of the two with about 80,000 volumes. In some of the larger
cities, such as Rio de Janeiro and Sao Paulo, there are municipal
public libraries, but in other areas public library service is the responsibility of the state. In Sao Paulo, the municipal library,
which contains over a quarter million volumes, is housed in a building, towering twenty-four stories, which was completed in 1942 at
a cost of over a million dollars. It and a few other libraries in
Brazil are thoroughly modern in organization and management. Brazil has also taken the lead in library extension, and has developed

bookmobile service in some of its rural areas. Sao Paulo has a
bookmobile service for its suburban areas and a large free library
especially for children.   The city of Recife has a modern collection
of phonograph records and musical scores and serves the public
through four branches and a bookmobile.   The libraries of the universities in Brazil vary considerably in size and usefulness, and
there is, as in other Latin American countries and in much of Europe, a strong dependence upon departmental and "institute" collections instead of in a central library.   However, there is a movement toward the building of new campuses, in the form of "university cities," to modernize the universities and centralized library
service will play a larger role in most of these.   One proposed university, at Brasilia, is planned to have a graduate school of Librarianship and Documentation, the first in the country.   There is,
in Rio de Janeiro, a National Catalog Exchange Service which provides centralized cataloging with printed catalog cards for subscrib-
ing libraries all over the nation.   There is also a National Federation of Library Associations to bring together the many smaller associations of librarians in the various states and cities.

In Argentina, the largest and most important library is the
National Library at Buenos Aires, with its more than a half million
volumes and over 50,000 manuscripts. It was founded in 1810, and
preserves some of the rarest historical materials in any of the Latin American countries.   In 1946 the Argentine government created a
national Commission for the Promotion of Popular Libraries and
this group made a survey of popular library facilities in the nation.
Some 1508 public and institutional libraries, most of them small,
were listed at that time, and their total book collection came to
some five million volumes.   Since that date the number of libraries
has increased and through the National School Library Service, an
attempt has been made to supply books, mostly reference works, to
the schools.   The libraries of the University of Buenos Aires, including the main library and those of the various faculties, contain
over a million volumes while the National University of Cordova,
the oldest university in Argentina, has a bookstock of some 200,000.
The National University of the Littoral in Santa Fe has over a mil-

lion volumes and there are seven other public universities and five
private ones with libraries of smaller size.   There is a school of
library science in Buenos Aires, a national library association, and
several regional library associations.   In the cities and towns popular subscription libraries, many associated with bookstores, provide
a welcome supplement to public library service, much of which is
non-circulating.   There are a number of growing special and technical libraries, particularly in Buenos Aires.   Among these are the
libraries of the National Academy of Medicine with 25,000 volumes,
and the National Aeronautical Institute with 35,000.   Argentina has a
number of excellent libraries but it lags in popular and school library service.

The National Library of Chile has nearly a million volumes,
and there are over 500 other public and institutional libraries in that
country.   With the exception of 21 of the larger municipal libraries,
all public library services in the nation are under the direction of
the National Library Service.   The University of Chile at Santiago
has a central library and 22 faculty libraries, containing in all nearly 450,000 volumes.   Courses in library science are offered here
and at some of the national teachers colleges.   The new Southern
University of Chile, established in 1954 at Valdivia, has for its library a "Documentation Center" of some 25,000 volumes.   Santiago
has nine libraries for children associated with its school system and
a number of special libraries of growing importance.   Generally
speaking, Chilean libraries, both public and educational, are among
the best in Latin America and for this the national library association deserves a great deal of credit.

In Peru, the National Library was burned in 1943 but it reopened in 1947 and rapidly grew back to 400,000 volumes by 1963.
In the library of the San Marco National University Peru has what
is probably the oldest library in the western hemisphere since it is
known to have been founded before 1600, possibly as early as 1575.
The central library of San Marcos has fewer than 100,000 volumes
but there are a number of faculty libraries almost as large.   Public libraries are to be found in the larger cities but most of them
are small and school library service is particularly poor.   Courses

for librarians are taught in an institute connected with the National
Library.   In Medellin, Colombia there is a public library sponsored
by Unesco as a pilot project in public library service for all Latin
America.   This library in the city of Medellin, operated as a joint
project by the Colombian government and Unesco from its opening
in 1954 until 1959, but it is now a completely local public library.
It has provided an example of modern free library service, with
strong service for children and young people, a collection of phonograph records, a public meeting room, and a branch library in a
working-class suburb.   Colombia has opened a similar modern public library in the industrial town of Bello and others are planned.

In the Caribbean area Cuba took the lead in librarianship in
the twentieth century with strong collections in the National Library,
founded in 1901, and in the Havana University Library.   Before
1959 Cuba's libraries were patterned on those of the United States,
but since the Castro regime has been in power, the libraries are
developing along the lines of those in the Communist countries.
More attention is being paid to workers' libraries, and the Economic Society Library in Havana, one of the largest in the nation, is
now known as the Library of the Economic Society of the Friends of
Peace.

Panama is taking the lead among the Central American countries in planning a regional library system to cover the entire country.   When completed the regional plan will comprise ten systems,
each with its own central library, with branches, traveling libraries,
and book stations, all directed from the national Library under the
direction of the Ministry of Education.

Elsewhere in Latin America, each country usually has a national library, a national university with several faculty libraries
and public libraries, usually non-circulating, in the larger cities.
Many of the more important libraries are simply repositories of valuable but poorly organized and seldom used volumes, while popular
circulating libraries are few, under-staffed, and lacking in funds.
Since World War II a number of outside forces have been felt in the
development of Latin American libraries, including those stemming
from Unesco, from the Organization of American States and from

the Alliance for Progress sponsored by the United States.   The
United Nations Educational, Scientific and Cultural Organization
(Unesco) has been particularly active; sponsoring inter-American library conferences, seminars on library training, inter-library cooperation, and other topics, as well as cooperating in founding the
Pilot Library in Medellin, Colombia.   Even with this outside aid
and advice, library service in Latin America still has a long way to
go before it becomes reasonably adequate.   The true value of the
public library as an asset to education and cultural communication
is yet to be generally realized in most areas south of the Rio Grande.

The United Kingdom

The West European countries have, as one might expect from
history, some of the largest and most important libraries in the
world.   In England the most important single collection is that of
the British Museum.   It is one of the largest libraries in the world
with more than 6,000,000 printed volumes, including some 10,000
incunabula and more than 75,000 manuscripts.   Its holdings in many
fields, ranging from Anglo-Saxon manuscripts to Egyptian papyri,
are among the best in the world.   Other great English libraries include those at Oxford and Cambridge Universities, the former with
the Bodleian and various college libraries together totaling nearly
three and a half million volumes and the latter almost as large.
The universities at Edinburgh, Manchester, Liverpool, Aberdeen and
London all have notable libraries, ranging in size from 300,000 to
750,000 volumes.   Some of the newer and smaller municipal, technical and liberal arts colleges have libraries in the 100,000 volume
range.   The National Library of Scotland in Edinburgh has over two
million volumes, while the National Library of Wales at Aberystwyth
is nearly as large.   Scotland's national collection grew out of the
Faculty of Advocates' Library, founded before 1684 and turned over
to the government in 1923.   There are several hundred institutional,
special and government libraries in London alone, many of them
quite large and containing valuable collections.   One interesting special library, a subscription library surviving from the pre-public library days, is the London Library with over 700,000 volumes avail-

able to members only.   Many of its members live in distant parts
of the British Commonwealth and borrow books by mail.

The National Central Library in London is a bibliographical
center and a clearing house of inter-library loans throughout the nation.   It also houses a Union Catalog of the holdings of all major
London libraries.   The most recent development in London libraries
is the creation of the Greater London metropolitan area with 32
boroughs, each of which has a separate public library system directed by a Chief Librarian.

England's Public Libraries Act of 1850 resulted in the formation of public libraries in more than 200 of the larger urban areas
in 1915, but the great majority of rural residents were still without
library service at that time.   In 1919 a new Libraries Act allowed
the county councils to provide library service for rural areas and
since that date service has been gradually extended until today it is
nationwide.   In 1955, there were no less than 577 central libraries
in England, Scotland, Wales and Northern Ireland, containing over
60,000,000 books and serving a population of over 50,000,000,
through 31,000 service points including branches, village centers,
mobile libraries, hospitals, prisons and schools.   For reference
purposes the public libraries are supplemented by other millions of
volumes in college, university and government libraries, all tied
together by a national inter-library loan system.   One of the largest
public library systems outside of London is that in the Liverpool
metropolitan area.   Here in an area of 2,200,000 population is
served by 21 library authorities with 3,500,000 books and some 700
staff members with a budget around $3,000,000.   On a smaller
scale, the City Libraries of Newcastle-on-Tyne serve a population
of some 300,000 with a library of 475,000 volumes and eleven
branches.   Library use in England is very high, with a total circulation of books from public libraries roughly equalling that of the
United States although its population is only one-third as great.

The libraries of Great Britain suffered great losses during
World War II.   The British Museum lost a wing which housed some
150,000 books and 30,000 volumes of bound newspapers, many of
which were not duplicated elsewhere.   Some sixty British libraries

were completely destroyed and the public libraries at Coventry, Exeter, Liverpool, Manchester, Plymouth, Portsmouth and Southampton suffered severe damage. The total book loss of the war, including libraries, bookstores, and publishers' stocks, was estimated at over 20,000,000 volumes. Since the war, British libraries have concentrated on replacing war losses, on extending library service to working people, particularly through trade union reading clubs and factory library deposits. The Public Libraries Act of 1965 places all public libraries in the United Kingdom under the Ministry of Education and Science. This agency can now establish standards for public libraries, control library service in smaller towns and rural areas, and require local government units to provide efficient library service at all times. British librarians have their professional organization, the Library Association which was founded in 1877 and now has over 10,000 members. There is also an active Association of Special Libraries and Information Bureaux, founded in 1924. Professional library education courses are given at the School of Librarianship and Archives at University College, London and at several technical schools throughout the country. Generally speaking, library service in England ranks with the best anywhere in the world.

France

In France, the great national library, the Bibliothèque Nationale, is another of the world's outstanding cultural treasures. Having developed over a period of some 500 years, it has received books by virtually every possible means, including gift, purchase, copyright law, expropriation and military conquest. The Bibliothèque Nationale was modernized considerably during the late nineteenth century, and again in the 1920's. The Bibliothèque Mazarine was joined with the Bibliothèque Nationale and the two work closely with the three other great national libraries in Paris, those of the University of Paris, the Bibliothèque Ste. Geneviève, and the Bibliothèque de l'Arsenal. Together these libraries form a research center of over 10,000,000 bound volumes, plus additional hundreds of thousands of manuscripts, engravings, periodicals and newspapers.

Elsewhere in Paris there are at least 33 other libraries of over 100,000 volumes each, including the library of the Chamber of Deputies with over 1,000,000 volumes, the library of the National Museum of Natural History with 450,000 volumes and the library of the Ministry of Foreign Affairs with over 400,000 volumes. Counting all school, government, special, institutional and large private collections, there were at least 1200 libraries in Paris in 1965.

Outside of Paris there are many other important university and municipal libraries. The universities at Grenoble, Bordeaux, Lille, Lyon, and Toulouse, to name but a few, have collections numbering from 300,000 to 1,000,000, while that at Strasbourg has nearly 3,000,000 volumes in all of its campus libraries. In addition to books, these libraries have large collections of manuscripts, some dating back many centuries. The large cities, such as Marseilles, Bordeaux, and Lyon have magnificent libraries, some of them based on collections founded centuries ago. These are, however, mainly reference collections and many smaller towns and villages have no public library service at all. Since the early 1900's, when a national library survey was made and a library association was formed, considerable effort has been made by the national and departmental governments to extend library service to all citizens of France but this movement has had limited success. Even where there are public circulating libraries, hours are short, physical quarters are poor, and library staffs are inadequate. School libraries, in public elementary and secondary schools are also poor but they have improved considerably since 1945. In that year a library division was set up in the Ministry of Education to coordinate and improve library service, both school and public, with particular emphasis on service in rural areas.

Germany

In the mid-nineteenth century Germany was probably the most advanced nation in the world in library service. Not only in the size of its book collections and in the number of its libraries but in its library methods and general philosophy of librarianship it was far ahead of both England and the United States. The outstanding

municipal and university libraries of the world patterned themselves
after the German libraries in the late nineteenth century.   This was
true, however, only for the scholarly libraries since free circulating public libraries were not widely developed in Germany until the
twentieth century and even then they lagged considerably behind
those of England and the United States.   Prior to World War II, the
major German libraries were the National Library in Berlin, with
2,850,000 volumes, including one of the largest collections of incunabula in the world; the State Library of Bavaria at Munich, almost
as large; and the State Libraries at Dresden and Breslau with about
750,000 volumes each.   University libraries at Munich, Heidelberg
and Göttingen contained about 1,000,000 volumes each while several
others were around the half million mark.   Some of the German
municipal libraries, particularly in the larger cities, had better research collections than most American universities but many of
them were non-circulating and available only a few hours daily.
Public circulating libraries, sometimes charging small fees to borrowers, were developed in many cities after 1900, but they were
usually small, poorly housed and served only a small percentage of
the potential reading public.   Much popular reading came from commercial rental libraries.   The Deutsche Bücherei at Leipzig, founded
in 1912, was unique in the way of libraries since it was a non-circulating copyright collection which attempted to obtain a copy of
every book published in Germany or in the German language.   It
contained nearly 2,000,000 volumes before World War II, but about
a fifth of these were lost when the building was largely destroyed in
1943.

When the Nazis came to power in Germany the development
of libraries was seriously curtailed, except for a few favored institutions.   All public libraries, whether popular or research, were
placed under strict government control and censorship over their
contents was rigidly maintained.   Many books were ordered destroyed or restricted from circulation and acquisitions were hampered, particularly in the case of non-German publications.   The popular circulating libraries were used as propaganda outlets by the
Nazis.   During the military action of World War II, many German

libraries were wholly or partially destroyed. Of 14,000,000 books
in 31 major German libraries, nearly 8,000,000 were destroyed
during the war and damage to buildings ran to millions of dollars.
Since 1945, however, remarkable results have been achieved in rebuilding German libraries and in developing new ones, particularly
in the public library field. The American Memorial Library was
opened in West Berlin in 1954, as a model public library patterned
after American practice and built largely with American funds. In
1965 it had about 300,000 volumes and circulated nearly 700,000 volumes, more than any other public library in Germany. American
aid has also been extended to the new Free University of West Berlin and U.S. Information Service libraries in the major German
cities have demonstrated the American idea of public library service. With this stimulus, Germany has been developing more public
libraries with open stacks, free circulation, and service for children. As an example, the city of Hamburg now has, in addition to
its scholarly libraries, a public circulating library of some 750,000
volumes. It has 49 branches and 25 other circulating collections in
suburban areas. Public library service still lags in Germany, and
there is still a different approach to library service in the sense
that research libraries and public libraries are considered to be entirely separate institutions, even to the extent that there are separate library associations for the personnel of the two services. As
for special libraries, however, Germany has hundreds, ranging
from a few hundred volumes to a hundred thousand or more, on almost all conceivable subjects.

The division of Germany after World War II into the two separate countries of West Germany and Communist-controlled East
Germany, with Berlin itself divided, brought about a number of
changes in the German library world. The former National Library
was in East Berlin and much of it was destroyed but some of its
more valuable contents were sent into western Germany for safe-
keeping. After 1945, the books belonging to the former National Library but located in West Germany were used as a foundation for a
West German Library in Marburg, and by 1965 this collection numbered about 2,000,000 volumes. The former National Library has

been rebuilt as the East German State Library and this also had about 2,000,000 volumes in the early 1960's. Elsewhere in East Germany, books and libraries are under strict control of the Communist government. Under the pretense of removing pro-Nazi books from the public and institutional libraries after 1945, a general house-cleaning of books unacceptable to the Communist commanders was made, and thousands of volumes were confiscated or destroyed. Russian and pro-Communist works were substituted and their reading was made practically compulsory. Many private and institutional libraries were expropriated by the Russians on one pretext or another and either taken to Russia or turned over to the new workers' libraries. At Potsdam, outside Berlin, a new Communist university was opened and its library was selected to conform to the new political philosophy. Other universities in Eastern Germany, including Humboldt University in Berlin, Ernst-Moritz Arndt University of Greifswald, Martin Luther University of Hall-Wittenberg, and Karl Marx University of Leipzig, have libraries of more than a million volumes each. Throughout East Germany, as in other parts of the Communist dominated world, books and libraries are considered a definite part of the propaganda war. This means that although there is more reading matter available to the average citizen than ever before it is a strictly controlled reading matter and the average reader has little choice. There is little or no freedom of either speech or press and the librarian is at once a tool and a victim of the government propaganda machine. A Central Bureau for Scholarly literature controls purchases for technical and reference libraries, particularly for materials coming from outside East Germany. Similarly, the Central Institute for Librarianship advises the public libraries and coordinates their activities through a system of administrative district libraries. There is an advanced School of Librarianship in East Berlin, a professional library organization, and a professional journal, Der Bibliothekar, published by the Central Institute.

Italy

In Italy the library situation in the twentieth century has been somewhat similar to that in Germany. As of 1900, some of the finest libraries in the world were in Italy, but two World Wars and two decades of dictatorship have taken their toll, and although not as much physical damage was done to Italian libraries as to the German ones, deterioration due to lack of proper care has been almost as destructive. Although the larger reference and research libraries of Italy contain some of the most valuable books and manuscripts in the world, popular library service has not been widely developed and public libraries as we know them in the United States do not exist in most Italian towns and cities. Italian libraries suffered some damage during World War II but some of their most valuable possessions were sent to the Vatican Library for safekeeping.

Of all the libraries in Italy, the Vatican Library is the most outstanding. With more than 900,000 printed books, including 7,000 incunabula, and nearly a hundred thousand valuable manuscripts, it is a treasure house of knowledge concerning the history and culture of the western world. However, down to the 1920's, it was just that, a treasure house, largely unorganized and almost entirely unavailable to any but the most important scholar. During the decades after World War I, a major effort was made to modernize the Vatican Library. American and other experts in library services were invited in to advise, and in 1926 the Carnegie Corporation sent William Warner Bishop to survey the Library and to make recommendations for its future growth and development. Dr. Bishop's visit came while Pius XI was Pope and since the Pope was himself a former librarian his interest and influence favored the modernization of the Library. Modern book stacks were installed, new quarters were added, cataloging and classifying were intensified, and in general the purposes and aims of the Library were redefined to make it not only more useful, but more used. Since then, thousands of new books and manuscripts have been added and scholars from all over the world have made use of its facilities. Printed catalogs of books and manuscripts in several areas have been prepared and the Vatican Library is becoming noted as a bibliographic center as well as a research collection.

The major public libraries of Italy are all controlled by the

National Library Service, including the National Central Libraries
at Rome and Florence and some thirty other state libraries, many
of which were formerly important private or ecclesiastical collections.   In 1875, the majority of the monastery libraries in Italy
were taken over by the government and these formed the basis of
the present state library system.   The National Central Library of
Rome has some 2,000,000 volumes, while the one at Florence is
even larger, with 3,500,000.   Among university libraries, the Alex-
andrine Library at the University of Rome has over 900,000 volumes, while other large collections are owned by the universities
at Bologna, Naples, Padua, Pisa and some twenty others.   A few
of the large privately endowed libraries have survived into the
twentieth century.   The Biblioteca Casanatense at Rome and the
Mediceo-Laurenziane Library at Florence are now under government control.   The former is a strong reference library containing
some 300,000 volumes in literature, religion, law, economics, social sciences and history.   The latter was formed from the collections of the Medici princes in the sixteenth century and although it
currently contains only about 50,000 printed volumes almost all of
them are rare.   Its great treasures are in its 10,000 manuscripts,
more than 700 of which date from before 1000 A.D.   The Biblioteca Ambrosiana at Milan, still under private control, now has over
600,000 printed volumes and 25,000 manuscripts, including holo-
graphs of Petrarch and Leonardo da Vinci.   There are a number of
specialized government libraries in Rome including the library of
the Italian Senate, with some 350,000 volumes, and various departmental libraries.   Most of the libraries mentioned above are strictly reference collections or at least have restricted circulation.   Popular circulating libraries have developed only slowly.   Since World
War II both private and governmental agencies have prompted the
development of popular libraries and some progress has been made
in this direction.   Public reading rooms have been established in
most cities and towns and they are relatively popular among the
younger people.   They are usually small, however, and reach only
a few people.   School libraries and children's libraries, in the
American style, are also seldom found in Italy.   In northern Italy,

where the Communist party is strongest, reading rooms have been widely used in its propaganda programs aimed at the working classes.

Other Western European Countries

In other western European countries, the development of library service has in general followed one of two patterns. In Switzerland and the Scandinavian countries, and to a lesser degree in Belgium and the Netherlands, library service includes strong state libraries together with many small popular libraries.

Denmark has probably the best public library service of any country in Europe. The Royal Library in Copenhagen has over 1,250,000 volumes and it is only one of several large government libraries. The University Library at Aarhus, with some 650,000 volumes, also serves as a national public library, and is a part of a library system that serves every citizen of Denmark. The University Library at Copenhagen is divided into two major systems, one for classics and general reference, the other for the sciences and between them they contain over 1,000,000 volumes.

Sweden has a strong public library system, with major research libraries in the Royal Library in Stockholm (850,000 volumes) and in the universities of Lund, Goteborg and Uppsala.

Norway and Finland are not as advanced in public library service as their neighbors and both suffered considerable library damage during World War II but they have improved rapidly since 1945. In both Norway and Finland the national libraries are also the libraries of the major national universities, in Oslo and Helsinki respectively. Oslo has a rather unique library in the Deichman Library, an endowed institution with government support, which serves as the city's public library. It now has some 475,000 volumes.

Switzerland has a somewhat complicated system of local, cantonal and national libraries, further confused by the four national languages, but it nevertheless provides excellent library service for its whole population. The National Library at Berne contains over 1,000,000 volumes as does also the University Library at Geneva. The League of Nations library at Geneva is now the European branch of the United Nations Library, and contains some 650,000 volumes.

In southern Europe, including Spain, Portugal and the Balkans, a second pattern of library development can be seen. Here there are a few large research libraries, but there has been little or no attempt to supplement them with popular circulating libraries.

The Spanish National Library at Madrid, for example, has about 1,500,000 volumes and the combined libraries of the University of Madrid total about one half as many. The University libraries at Barcelona contain about 500,000 volumes. The historic library of San Lorenzo del Escorial, founded in the sixteenth century, has only about 40,000 books but has many thousand valuable manuscripts. Some progress is being made in school libraries and popular circulating collections, especially since 1945, but outside the larger cities most of these collections are small and poorly supported.

In Portugal, the National Library in Lisbon has about a million volumes. The University of Coimbra, with its central and faculty libraries, has about 1,450,000. Oporto has a large municipal library but it is mainly a reference collection and, as in Spain, Portugal has yet to make much progress in popular and school libraries.

In the Balkans, the Greek National Library at Athens contains some 1,000,000 books and pamphlets but there are few other libraries of any size outside of the capital city and Salonika and very few books are available for the average reader.

Yugoslavia has a "national" library for each of its six major states, and these are sometimes both "national" and "national university" libraries. The largest, as of 1960, was that at Ljubljana, serving the Slovene Republic, but others at Belgrade (Serbia) and Zagreb (Croatia) were almost as large. Yugoslavia, like other Communist nations, has emphasized books and libraries considerably since 1945 and popular reading rooms have sprung up by the hundreds. These are small in most cases, poorly staffed and supported and, of course, contain only government-approved reading matter.

Eastern Europe

In Eastern Europe, behind the Iron Curtain, library service
is strictly controlled by the governments and is a prominent part of
the political system.   Emphasizing the power of the printed word
and the importance placed on it by the Communists, Russia claims
to have the largest library in the world in the National Library in
Leningrad (the Saltykov-Shchedrin Library), the largest number of
libraries of any country in the world, and the largest number of library books in use.   The Saltykov-Shchedrin Library has been built
up since 1917 on the base of the Russian Imperial Library and it ab-
sorbed many private, government and church libraries in the 1920's.
It is now reported as containing over 14,000,000 volumes.   Another
very large Russian library is the Lenin State Library in Moscow,
with over 13,000,000 volumes.   The Gorky Library at the University of Moscow contains some 6,000,000 volumes and the library of
the Russian Academy of Science at Leningrad almost 5,000,000.
Elsewhere in the Soviet Union there are a number of other national,
republic and university libraries of over a million volumes each.

Generally speaking, the libraries of Russia can be divided into four types.   First there are the large state or national libraries
headed up by the one in Leningrad, but including others in the capitals of the constituent republics of the U.S.S.R., such as those in
Kiev, Minsk or Alma Ata.   Next there are the public or "mass" libraries ranging from large city libraries and tremendous regional
depositories down to small collections of books in factories and col-
lective farms.   All told there were more than 400,000 of these "library outlets" containing over 600,000,000 books in the early 1960's.
The third group consists of the special or research libraries, ranging from large central subject libraries in Moscow down to research
shelves in individual laboratories.   Finally, there are the libraries
of educational institutions, from nursery school to university.   From
the Caspian to the Arctic and from White Russia to Kamchatka,
Russia is dotted with libraries -- one for every 500 population according to the latest estimates.

There are library schools at the larger universities, particu-

larly at Moscow, Leningrad and Kharkov. In 1961 there were 3,300
students at the Leningrad school alone and new library schools were
being established at Ulan Ude and at Tashkent. In addition to the
professional librarians trained at the universities, there are also
courses for library clerical and sub-professional workers, and in-
service training for minor library positions. Several library and
bibliographic journals are published, and there are national, regional and local library associations. The successful Russian librarian
must be more than a bibliophile or an administrator; he must be a
propaganda expert, politically conscious and socially active. He
must take the library services to the people rather than waiting for
them to come to his library. Books are weapons and the Russian
librarian must be fully aware that he is on the idealogical firing
line.

In Poland, many libraries were destroyed during World War
II but by the 1950's library reconstruction was well under way. A
National Library Law, passed in 1946, laid the foundations for widespread public library service. Poland obtained two library centers,
Danzig and Breslau, from Germany after World War II. Both of
these cities contained numerous libraries, both ancient and modern.
Among the larger university libraries are those at Warsaw
(2,300,000 volumes); Cracow (Jagellonian University, 1,200,000),
and Torun (Copernicus University, 1,000,000 volumes). The public
library system is well organized, with central public libraries,
branch libraries, and book deposits in industrial plants. Overall
there are more than 30,000 public library service points in the nation and virtually every citizen is reached by one or more of the library units. Some 27,000 school libraries supplement the public library system and in addition there are a number of government and
special libraries in Warsaw. In 1962, the capital city of Warsaw
had a main library of over a million volumes and 112 branches -
approximately one branch for each 10,000 people. These public libraries were supplemented by 136 scientific or learned society libraries, 455 school libraries, and 148 trade union libraries. Poland has library schools in its main universities and there are also
training classes for library workers in the larger public libraries.

Libraries in Bulgaria and Rumania are almost entirely under control of the national government. In these countries there were a few important reference collections but little popular library service prior to World War II. Since then, under Communist domination, they have been introduced to library service in the best Russian traditions. The largest library in Rumania is the library of the Rumanian People's Academy in Bucharest, with over 3,000,000 volumes and many rare manuscripts. This serves as a national research library, while the Central State Library, also in Bucharest, heads up a national public library system and contains about 1,000,000 volumes. Important university libraries are to be found at Bucharest, Iasi, and Cluj, each with about 1,000,000 volumes. The two largest libraries in Bulgaria are both in Sofia: the Kolarov State Library with about 750,000 volumes, and the Sofia State University Library with about 500,000. There are a number of special and government libraries in Sofia, most of them small, and some 5,000 popular libraries and reading rooms scattered throughout the country. In both Rumania and Bulgaria there is a strong emphasis on providing library services, and both popular and technical libraries are growing rapidly.

In Czechoslovakia, much library progress had been made in the period between the country's independence in 1919 and World War II. A public library organized along American lines was developed in Prague. It contained some 400,000 volumes by 1938, by which time the combined National-University Library in the same city had about 1,000,000 volumes. After 1945, under Communist domination, Czech libraries went through a drastic upheaval. There was drastic censorship of bookstocks, some old libraries were closed and many new ones were opened. Historic reference libraries were thrown open for public use, including those at the universities of Olmütz, Brunn and Bratislava. In the early 1960's, the National Library in Prague possessed over 3,000,000 volumes, while the university libraries at Brunn and Bratislava had about 1,250,000 and 750,000 volumes respectively.

In Hungary the National Library in Budapest, and other major libraries, were also rebuilt along Communist lines after 1945.

By 1960, the National (Szechenyi) Library had nearly 1,500,000 volumes, while the university at Budapest had some 1,750,000 volumes in central and faculty libraries and the municipal library in the same city had some 600,000. In both Hungary and Czechoslovaki librarians are considered "educators of the masses" and their libraries, whether government, public, technical or school, are designed to fit into the national political program.

The Near East

Elsewhere in the world, with a few exceptions, library service is far behind that in Europe and America. Much progress is being made and often in unexpected places. In the Near East, the new nation of Israel has made great library progress since its founding in 1948. The National and University Library in Jerusalem had over 1,000,000 volumes by 1964, and this institution included the largest collection of Hebraica in the world. Other large research libraries are at the Universities of Tel-Aviv and Bar-Ilan and at the Technion Institute in Haifa. Public library service is provided from some 700 public and endowed libraries and reading rooms, while the Ministry of Education and Culture provides school libraries and libraries for some rural settlements.

Egypt has its National Library at Cairo with some 800,000 volumes and important university libraries at Alexandria, Cairo, and for Upper Egypt, at Assiut.

Turkey has at Ankara its National Library with some 425,000 volumes, and university libraries in Ankara and Istanbul. Turkey is increasing the number of its public libraries but most of them are small.

In both Iran and Iraq library service is very backward by western standards but, with some aid from American library advisors in the 1950's, a progressive trend has been established. Iran has a national library of some 100,000 volumes, and the Iranian Parliament (Majlis) Library is somewhat larger. Both countries have universities with individual college library systems and most of their collections are small.

In Syria and Lebanon modern libraries are being established

in the larger cities, and there are several college and university libraries patterned after western library systems.

British Commonwealth Countries

In the British Commonwealth Nations libraries on the whole are good. Australia and New Zealand have progressive library programs which include public, school and university libraries.

In Australia the public libraries are under state rather than national control and each of the Australian states has a large central library. It serves both as a reference collection and as a circulating library in some cases. This state library also provides extension services, in the form of interlibrary loans and package libraries to outlying villages and farms. The National Library in Canberra, founded in 1927, is a fast growing collection designed to serve both as a national library and a parliamentary reference collection. With about 700,000 volumes, it is smaller than some of the state libraries. There are also municipal circulating libraries in the larger cities, and public libraries in most of the smaller cities and towns. The state libraries of New South Wales at Sydney and of Victoria at Melbourne, each with about 750,000 volumes, are the largest in Australia and the libraries of the Universities of Sydney, Melbourne and Adelaide are almost as large. Much progress has been made in Australian library service since World War II, especially in the fields of public and special libraries. The University of New South Wales offers a degree in librarianship, and there are also training schools for librarians in some of the state libraries and in the National Library in Canberra. New Zealand also has a library school. Australia has a national library association which supervises the examination and certification of librarians.

In Australia and New Zealand both there are numerous subscription libraries in the cities and towns. New Zealand in particular has a wide variety of these semi-public collections, some of which receive small public appropriations but still charge for the use of their books. On the other hand, the strictly public libraries also have large rental collections of fiction and popular non-fiction. Between the two, however, urban New Zealand has fairly adequate

library service and since 1945 the National Library Service has
entered the scene, supplying bookmobile and package library service
to virtually all citizens of its two major islands.   The National Library Service is divided into four divisions: the National Library
Centre, the Country Library Service, the School Library Service,
and the National Library School.   Independent of this service, but
relying on it for inter-library loans and bibliographic services, are
the municipal libraries in the larger towns and cities.   The National Library Centre and its four branches have over 2,000,000 books
at their disposal.   The General Assembly Library in Wellington has
some 250,000 volumes, and there are four major universities and
two colleges in the University of New Zealand system.   Their combined libraries total about 1,000,000 volumes.   The National Library Service maintains a union catalogue of non-fiction in the major New Zealand libraries, and also a union list of serials available
in the same institution.   It publishes an Index to New Zealand Serials, and a current national bibliography of New Zealand books and
pamphlets as well as many subject bibliographies and reading lists.
The New Zealand Library Association is quite active and has been
prominent in recent years in a national movement to improve rural
school and public libraries.

Africa

                In the Republic of South Africa there are excellent public li-
braries in Johannesburg and Cape Town, and several large university
libraries as well.   The Johannesburg Public Library has about
800,000 volumes, with 29 branches in 1963 and provides services to
hospitals, as well as bookmobile service to outlying suburbs.   This
library operated on a fee system until 1938 but since that date it
has been a free circulating library.   Other public libraries in South
Africa are following this lead but subscription libraries are still
popular in most towns and cities.   The National Library in Pretoria
has some 600,000 volumes, but the South African Library at Cape
Town is also considered a national library and with its 300,000 volumes it is the most important historical library in the Republic.
There are strong university libraries at Cape Town, Pretoria, Stel-

lenbosch, Johannesburg and Durban.   There are regional library
systems in the Transvaal and in Natal, providing library service to
small towns and rural areas.   Service to Africans (Negroes) is limited, although Johannesburg does have a branch library for non-
whites, and other public libraries are open to them on certain days.
There is a South African Library Association, a library journal,
and a library school at Cape Town.

On the frontiers of the modern library world are the newly
independent countries of Central Africa and their older free neighbors, Liberia and Ethiopia.   Here the major problems stem from
low incomes, scarcity of trained educators and librarians and high
illiteracy.   Some of the larger coastal towns have European-type
public libraries, and there is usually at least one college or university in each geographic unit.   Nigeria has a modern public library
at Lagos, a university library of some 150,000 volumes at Ibadan,
and a Regional Central Library of 30,000 volumes at Enugu.   Ghana
has a national Library Board with a central collection of some
300,000 volumes at Accra and a regional branch at Kumasi with
some 40,000 volumes.   Through these libraries and some 30
branches, plus box libraries and mail service, books are available
to serious readers throughout the nation.   The Balme Library at
the University of Ghana, Accra, has about 150,000 volumes, and
there are several government departmental libraries of a few thousand volumes each.   Liberia has a new university library, and also
a public library, at Monrovia, but both are small.   The former
French colonies in West Africa are provided with some library service by the IFAN (Institute Français d'Afrique Noir), but these are
mostly small reference libraries except for the headquarters library
in Dakar.   In East Africa, there are small public and college libraries in Kenya and Tanzania, and the East African Literature Bureau has libraries of about 40,000 volumes each in Nairobi and Dar-
Es-Salaam.   Ethiopia has a small national library and a university
library in Addis Ababa, with about 35,000 volumes.   In Moslem
North Africa there are national and university libraries in Algiers,
each with about 500,000 volumes, while Morocco has an ancient and
valuable library in the Kairoween University Library in Fez, founded

in the thirteenth century.   There is also a national library (Bibliothèque Générale) in Rabat, with 170,000 volumes.   Tunisia has a
national library in Tunis, and there are public libraries on the
French style in the larger towns of Tunis, Algiers and Morocco.

Otherwise, much of Africa between South Africa and Egypt is
without libraries of notable size.   The new nations are attempting
to develop schools and libraries, and are securing aid from Unesco
and other international sources.   In many of the African nations the
United States and Great Britain provide information service libraries
and the Soviet Union is also entering this field in some cities.   In
1953 Unesco sponsored a seminar on public libraries in Africa at
Ibadan in Nigeria.   This was a working conference which attempted
to ascertain just what library services were needed, and how they
could be obtained.   The results of this seminar were published in
the Unesco manual, The Development of Public Libraries in Africa.

China

Turning to the library scene in Asia, it can be seen that library history in China is nearly as ancient as that nation itself, for
the Chinese have always respected learning.   There was an imperial library before the beginning of the Christian era and a catalog in
book form has survived from a library of 11,000 volumes in the
first century, A.D.   But modern China, partly because of wars and
economic troubles, has not had a chance to develop a widespread library system.   In the 1920's some progress was made, with the development of several large university libraries and over 500 public
libraries in the larger towns and cities.   The years between 1930
and 1950 saw China torn in wars between Nationalists and Communists, and between both and the Japanese, so that library service
went backwards instead of forwards.   Many libraries were destroyed
or suffered from moving and neglect.   Since 1949 the new Communist government has placed considerable importance on books and
has set up a Bureau of Libraries in its Department of Cultural Affairs.   There are at least fifteen major universities and more than
a hundred technical colleges in Communist China as of 1965, and
each of them has as strong a library as can be obtained.   Public

library service has lagged comparatively but with a system of provincial libraries heading up public, communal and factory collections an attempt has been made to make China as library-minded as Soviet Russia. The largest libraries are the Peking State Library with 2,500,000 volumes (based on the former Chinese Imperial Library), the Mukden Central Public Library with 1,200,000 volumes, and the Shanghai Municipal Library with 900,000 volumes.

On Taiwan, where the Free Republic of China has existed since 1949, there has been considerable library progress. There is a National Library at Taipei with some 175,000 volumes, provincial libraries at Taipei and Taichung, and 17 other municipal public libraries. The National University in Taipei has a library of about 700,000 volumes and there are several other universities and colleges with respectable libraries. There are several special and government libraries of note and also a Central Educational Materials Center which supplies books and other teaching materials to educators throughout the island.

Japan

Japanese libraries, before 1945, consisted mainly of government and university collections, and the Imperial Library in Tokyo with some 500,000 volumes was the largest and most important. Tokyo had a municipal reference library established in 1908 but it was burned with its some 400,000 books during World War II. It was not reopened until 1957, but by 1963 it was again approaching its pre-war size. Although public library service in the western style is still somewhat foreign to Japan, much progress has been made, especially since the passage of a national Library Law in 1950. Under this act public libraries are under general government control but with considerable local autonomy and libraries are to be established at the prefectural, city and town levels. As of 1963 there were some sixty city and prefectural libraries with bookstocks in the neighborhood of 100,000 volumes and many smaller town and community libraries. Bookmobile service has been started in some rural areas but circulating libraries are still the exception rather than the rule and much public library service is in the form of ref-

erence service for high school and college students.   There are
some fifty major university libraries with libraries ranging from
2,000,000 volumes and there are several hundred minor universities, colleges and institutes.   The National Diet Library, which now
includes the former Imperial Library, contains some 3,000,000 volumes and there also are growing libraries for each of the major
government agencies.   For example, the Ministries of Agriculture
and Education each have libraries of about 100,000 volumes.   A library school has been established in Tokyo, and courses for librarians are also available in several other colleges.

The Philippines

In the Philippines, libraries suffered considerably during
World War II when an estimated 95 per cent of all library books in
the city of Manila were destroyed.   Since 1945, aid from the United
States has helped in the rebuilding of Philippine libraries, and considerable progress is being made.   The former National Library,
considerably damaged in World War II, has been reorganized as the
Bureau of Public Libraries, and under its direction an attempt has
been made to establish public libraries throughout the islands.
Some success has been achieved but most of the libraries are small.
The Manila City Library has about 15 branches but had only about
60,000 volumes in its central collection in 1963.   Among the major
university libraries are those of the University of the Philippines
with about 300,000 volumes in all collections, the University of
Santo Tomas, and the Far Eastern University.   There is an Institute of Library Science at the University of the Philippines, a Philippine Library Association, and an Association of Special Libraries.

India

In India, where the British were in power for more than two
centuries, the larger cities have municipal libraries and there are
some fifty large universities, many with dozens of constituent colleges and thousands of students, as well as several hundred smaller
colleges and technical institutes.   Since 1950 a model public library
has been in operation in Delhi, with lending services, a children's
department, books for the blind and other western library customs.

It has some 200,000 volumes and serves some 300,000 library users
per month and it is slowly being adopted as a prototype by Indian
public libraries.   Most Indian public libraries still resemble European municipal reference libraries.   The National Library of India
is in Calcutta and has some 1,100,000 volumes.   India's special libraries range from the ancient and exotic to the extremely modern.
Among the former is the Madras Oriental Manuscripts Library with
some 80,000 bound volumes and many thousands of manuscripts in
Sanskrit and south Indian languages.   Representing the modern is
the Indian Council of World Affairs Library in New Delhi, founded
in 1950 and already containing over 75,000 volumes, 1,100 current
periodicals, and 100,000 government documents.   Development of
school and public library services in India faces almost insurmount-
able obstacles.   There are many different languages spoken in various parts of the heavily populated country, economic standards are
extremely low and illiteracy is extremely high - almost 85 per cent
of all adults in 1950.   Despite this pessimistic outlook, Indian library leaders have planned for the eventual establishment of a nationwide system of school and public libraries under the direction of
a national library service.   Dr. S.R. Ranganathan, a leading Indian
librarian, wrote widely on library subjects, including a volume on a
Library Development Plan: Thirty-five Year Programme for India.
There is also an active Indian Library Association which is encouraging library development, the formal training of librarians, and the
translation of library literature into the major Indian languages.

Pakistan

Elsewhere in southeast Asia, the library picture is even less
advanced than that in India.   In Pakistan there is the new Liaquat
National Library in Karachi, with about 40,000 volumes in 1962,
but one of the largest libraries is the Panjab Public Library in Lahore, founded in 1884 and containing about 125,000 volumes in 1960.
Among the larger university libraries are those at Dacca, Karachi,
and Lahore (Panjab University), each with over 100,000 volumes.
There are also a number of government colleges with small working
libraries and there are municipal libraries in the larger towns and

cities.   Pakistan has several small but efficient special libraries in
Karachi and Lahore, including a National Scientific and Technical
Documentation Centre but adequate public and school library serv-
ices are slow in developing.

Other Countries of Southeast Asia

The young Republic of Indonesia has been very active in attempting to develop public and school libraries.   There are eight
major universities, most of them established since Indonesian independence, and the usual pattern in these new institutions has been
to form faculty libraries before setting up a central collection. Special libraries have progressed more rapidly than public and school
services but this is typical of a young nation interested in technical
and scientific advancement.   The city of Djakarta has a good public
reference library and much progress has been made in the establishment of public reading rooms throughout the Republic.   This is
more a matter of adult education than the establishment of permanent public libraries but it is a step in the right direction.   A national library which will be both a bibliographic and an archival center is in the process of establishment and major government departments are developing specialized libraries for their own use.   There
is a national library association, and a library school in Djakarta.

Thailand and Burma each have national libraries that are
both archives and libraries, and neither is very large.   There are
universities in Burma at Rangoon and Mandalay, and in Thailand at
Bangkok (two), each of which have libraries of around 40,000 volumes.   Public and school libraries in both countries are slowly being established, with aid from the United Nations and from other
countries.

Singapore has a public and national library, formerly the
Raffles Library founded in 1844, which had about 175,000 volumes
in 1960.   Branch libraries for suburbs and outlying areas are
planned, and there is the University of Singapore Library with about
300,000 volumes.   In Malaysia there are sizeable public libraries at
Penang and Kuala Lumpur, with a university and government libraries also at the latter city.   Finally, off the coast of Africa, in the

new island Republic of Malagasy, there is an excellent example of
a new nation learning to fly before it learns to walk. A new national library in Tananarive is entitled The Office of Documentation.

The United States and Great Britain have placed information
libraries in major cities all over the world since World War II.
These institutions have served dual purposes as cultural ambassa-
dors and as model libraries and have done much to promote the idea
of free public library service. Equally important has been the work
of Unesco. This cultural agency of the United Nations was established with the thesis that since war begins in the minds of man, it
is in the minds of men that war must be prevented. Educated citizens and free libraries are twin weapons in fighting the prejudices,
falsehoods and fears that lead to wars, and for this reason, Unesco
is doing everything it can to promote education and library development all over the world. In order to promote library service it
conducts seminars and conferences on library development and library problems and aids in the establishment of model public libraries such as those at Delhi, India, and Medellin, Colombia. It publishes the Unesco Bulletin for Libraries which serves international
exchange of library information. It also publishes two series of library aids: the Unesco Public Library Manuals and the Unesco
Bibliographic Handbooks. To aid intercultural understanding it en-
courages the translation of major literary works into other languages,
and publishes the Index Translationum, a current bibliography of
translated works. In its "Public Library Manifesto," Unesco has
stated the aims of library service for all countries and in years to
come it should be a major factor in the development of library service throughout the world.

Bibliography

Books

Bostwick, Arthur E., ed.: Popular libraries of the world. Chi-
        cago, 1933. 316 p.

Burkett, J., ed.: Special library and information services in the
        United Kingdom. London, 1961. 200 p.

Burton, Margaret: Famous libraries of the world; their history, col-
        lections and administrations. London, 1937. 458 p.

Canada.   Commission on Inquiry: Libraries in Canada; a study of
    library conditions and needs.   Chicago, 1933.   153 p.

Carnovsky, Leon, ed. :   International aspects of librarianship.   Chi-
    cago, 1954.   132 p.

Danilewicz, Maria: The libraries of Poland.   St. Andrews, Scot-
    land, 1943.   63 p.

Danton, J. P. :   Book selection and collections; a comparison of
    German and American university libraries.   New York, 1963.
    204 p.

Danton, J. P. :   U. S. influence on Norwegian librarianship, 1890-
    1940.   Berkeley, Calif. , 1957.   91 p.

Esdaile, Arundell, ed. :   National libraries of the world, their his-
    tory, administration and public services.   London, 1957.
    430 p.

Evans, Evelyn J. A. :   A tropical library service; the story of
    Ghana's libraries.   London, 1964.   174 p.

Friis, T. :   The public library in South Africa, an evaluative study.
    Capetown, 1962.   357 p.

Harrison, K. C. :   Libraries in Scandinavia.   London, 1961.   248 p.

Horecky, Paul L. :   Libraries and bibliographic centers in the
    Soviet Union.   Bloomington, Ind. , 1959.   307 p.

Irwin, Raymond, and Staveley, Ronald: The libraries of London.
    London, 1961.   2nd ed.   332 p.

Jackson, William V. :   Aspects of librarianship in Latin America.
    Champaign, Ill. , 1962.   119 p.

Kesavan, B. S. :   India's national library.   Calcutta, 1961.   300 p.

Library Association of China: Libraries in China.   Peiping, 1929.
    43 p.

McColvin, L. R. :   The chance to read; public libraries in the world
    today.   London, 1956.   284 p.

McColvin, L. R. :   Public libraries in Australia.   Melbourne, 1947.
    120 p.

McColvin, L. R. :   The public library system of Great Britain.
    London, 1941.   218 p.

Munn, Ralph: Australian libraries, a survey.   Melbourne, 1935.
    139 p.

Munn, Ralph: New Zealand libraries, a survey of conditions and
    suggestions for their improvement. Christchurch, 1934.
    68 p.

Newcombe, Luxmoore: The university and college libraries of
    Great Britain and Ireland. London, 1927. 220 p.

Orcutt, William: The magic of the book. Boston, 1930. 315 p.
    (See pp. 63-104: "The resurrection of the Vatican Li-
    brary.")

Osborn, Andrew: New Zealand library resources, report of a sur-
    vey... Wellington, 1960. 70 p.

Ottervik, Gösta: Libraries and archives in Sweden. Stockholm,
    1954. 217 p.

Pan American Union: Books and libraries in the Americas. Wash-
    ington, 1963. 287 p.

Ranganathan, S.R. : Library development plan for India. Delhi,
    1950. 462 p.

Richardson, E.C. : Some aspects of international library coopera-
    tion. Yardley, Pa., 1928. 168 p.

Rivera, Rodolfo: Preliminary list of libraries in the other Ameri-
    can republics. Washington, 1942. 181 p.

Ruggles, Melville J., and Swank, Raynard C. : Soviet libraries and
    librarianship. Chicago, 1962. 147 p.

Schurer, H. : Public libraries in Germany. London, 1946. 23 p.

UNESCO: Developments of public libraries in Africa: the Ibadan
    seminar. Paris, 1954. 154 p.

UNESCO: Development of public libraries in Latin America; the
    Sao Paulo conference. Paris, 1952. 192 p.

UNESCO: Public libraries for Asia: the Delhi seminar. Paris,
    1956. 166 p.

UNESCO: Directory of archives, libraries and schools of librarian-
    ship in Africa. Paris, 1964. 112 p.

UNESCO: National libraries, their problems and prospects. Paris,
    1960. 125 p.

Periodical Articles

In addition to the volumes above, there is a wealth of articles on
    modern foreign libraries in current library periodicals, such
    as Library Quarterly, Library Trends, College and Research

Libraries, and particularly in the UNESCO Bulletin for Libraries. The following are a few examples:

Alksnis, Gertrude: "Soviet Russian children's libraries: a survey of recent Russian sources," Library Quarterly, XXXII, (1962), 287-301.

Campbell, H.C., ed.: "Metropolitan public library problems around the world," Library Trends, XIV, (July, 1965), 1-116.

Daniels, Marietta: "The promotion of libraries in the Americas," Library Quarterly, XXX, (1960), 201-208.

Galloway, R.D.: "Library experiment in Iran," Library Quarterly, XXX, (1960), 188-200.

Hoppes, Muriel: "The library of the League of Nations at Geneva," Library Quarterly, XXXI, (1961), 257-268.

Jordan, Alma: "Public libraries in the British Caribbean," Library Quarterly, XXXIV, (1964), 143-162, 258-263.

Kase, Francis J.: "Public libraries in Czechoslovakia under the unified library system," Library Quarterly, XXXI, (1961), 154-165.

"Libraries in Latin America," Library Journal, LXXXVI, (Nov. 15, 1961), 3887-3915.

Mearns, David C., ed.: "Current trends in national libraries," Library Trends, IV, (July, 1955), 3-116.

Plumbe, Wilfred J., ed.: "Current trends in newly developing countries," Library Trends, VIII, (Oct., 1959), 125-341.

Rao, K. Ramakrishna: "Library developments in India," Library Quarterly, XXXI, (1961), 135-153.

Reichmann, Felix: "The catalog in European libraries," Library Quarterly, XXXIV, (1964), 34-54.

Sawamoto, T.: "Recent Japanese library developments," College and Research Libraries, XXIV, (1963), 213-218.

Strauss, W.P.: "The Mitchell Library of Sydney, Australia," Library Quarterly, XXX, (1960), 124-129.

Tauber, Maurice F.: "Survey of resources of Australian libraries," Stechert-Hafner Book News, XVI, (1962), 53-55.

Thompson, S.O.: "American library in Paris: an international development in the American library movement," Library Quarterly, XXXIV, (1964), 179-190.

Vosper, Robert: "European university libraries: current status
    and developments," Library Trends, XII, (April, 1964),
    475-623.

XIV

Modern American Libraries

Library services have made tremendous progress in twentieth century United States. Free public library services have almost covered the nation; school libraries are an accepted part of the educational process; government and research libraries are fulfilling a vital role in the nation's progress; and new special libraries are joining in a multiplicity of ways in strengthening the neverending process of storing and retrieving knowledge. Graphic communication, in all its forms, is the province of today's libraries. The task is immense but libraries are making a valiant effort to keep the collection, organization and use of all graphic communication under control.

The public library in particular has grown from a nineteenth century experiment into an increasingly important segment of the modern cultural scene. In this respect, the largest public library in the country is typical, for the New York Public Library is almost entirely a twentieth century achievement. The Astor Library, a public reference collection donated by the Astor family, had been in the possession of the city since 1848, and had been open to scholars a few hours daily. Since 1870, the Lenox Library, a smaller but somewhat more popular reference collection donated by James Lenox, had also been available. Neither of these libraries loaned books for outside reading. In 1879 a Free Circulating Library was formed, with partial public support, and by 1895 this institution had eleven branches. In addition, there were literally dozens of other libraries in New York, semi-public in nature but receiving little or no public assistance and being supported almost entirely by charitable or professional organizations. In 1866, Samuel Tilden left the bulk of his estate, including his own library of some 20,000 volumes to the Tilden Trust, with the power to found a free public library in New York City. When the Tilden Fund became available

in the 1890's, the city fathers of New York decided to combine all
their libraries into one centrally controlled system.   This was done
in 1895 with the creation of the New York Public Library, with Dr.
John Shaw Billings as the first Chief Librarian.   At first there was
no central library and the Tilden collection was housed in the Astor
building, while the Lenox Library remained in its own quarters.   In
1901, Andrew Carnegie donated $5,200,000 to the city of New York
for the erection of 65 branch libraries and these were erected in
the next few years.   A movement for a centrally located main library building had been under way since 1897 but it was not until
1911 that this was completed and opened to the public.   This building, now known as the New York Public Library, is mainly a reference library, housing the Lenox, Astor, Tilden and other research
collections.   By 1913, the entire public library system contained
over 2,000,000 books and pamphlets, and circulated more than
8,000,000 items to 343,000 registered borrowers.   Its annual budget had already passed $1,000,000 and it was rapidly becoming one
of the most important libraries in the nation.   By 1965 the metropolitan area of New York City was served by the central reference
library and by three circulating library systems (including the
Brooklyn Public Library and the Queens Borough Public Library)
whose 187 branches and 9 bookmobiles placed nearly 8,000,000
books at the disposal of 2,226,000 registered borrowers.

Elsewhere in the nation the first decade of the new century
saw public libraries firmly established in the larger cities, including Boston, Chicago, Cincinnati and San Francisco, and well under
way in many others.   The subscription libraries continued to decline as the public libraries increased in size and services and
many of them merged into the newer institutions.   This was not always easily accomplished, as for example in Philadelphia.   There
was a move in that city to merge the strong Mercantile Library into the Philadelphia Free Library as early as 1900, but it was not
until 1944 that it was finally accomplished.   Old established libraries were offering new services -- open stacks, children's libraries, public catalogs -- while new public libraries were being created.   For example, Louisville, Kentucky, opened its Free Public

Library in 1902, and Galveston, Texas, did likewise in 1904. A
few brave librarians were experimenting with branches and even
with rural library service. The U.S. Office of Education, taking
stock of the nation's libraries in 1913, proudly reported 3062 free
public circulating libraries of over 1000 volumes each. It is interesting to note though, that the great majority of these were in the
Northeast and Middle West while in the South and West public libraries were few and far between.

        The coming of the First World War slowed down the develop-
ment of public library service somewhat, but it did bring about another event in library history that was to have a lasting effect.
This was the development of libraries for the use of service men in
camps, on ships, and overseas. Over $1,600,000 was raised by
public subscription to finance this venture and its direction was
placed into the capable hands of the American Library Association
and the American Red Cross. With the A. L. A. -A. R. C. books thus
purchased or donated by libraries and individuals, 47 major camp
libraries, staffed by trained librarians, were set up at training
bases and overseas headquarters. In addition to these, 261 smaller
libraries and over 2,500 supply points, deposits of 50 to 100 books
each, were placed at smaller posts, on board ships, and at Red
Cross canteens. These books were well used, and there can be little doubt that many soldiers and sailors, who were thus introduced
to library service during their military careers, came home with an
increased interest in reading and libraries. At any rate, the return
of peace and relative prosperity in the 1920's saw many smaller
towns opening their first public libraries, while others extended their
services to rural areas, acquired new buildings, or explored new
fields of service to the public. Library extension, in particular,
came into its own during the post-war decade and county libraries
in many parts of the nation moved out of the experimental stage.
State library commissions were active but public funds for library
service remained small and trained and experienced help was still
scarce.

        In 1926, the American Library Association published a seri-
ous study of the libraries of the nation in its Survey of Libraries in

the United States. It was mainly a factual summary but it emphasized the fact that library service was still far from what it should
be. Over 3000 libraries of 5000 volumes or larger were queried
as to administration, staff, services and facilities and a wide variety of replies were received. This report made few recommendations as to how services could be improved but it did serve as a
solid basis on which to plan for the future, and had it not been for
the depression years that followed, it would have quite probably
been followed by a period of noticeable library progress.

The depression years that began in 1929 at first brought severe difficulties for public libraries. Budgets were reduced and
services were curtailed. Branches were closed in many cases, and
bookmobiles discontinued. But the depression also brought with it
new demands for library services from unemployed who desired to
improve their chances for jobs or who simply wanted reading matter for their enforced leisure. After 1933 the Federal government
entered the library scene with the Work Progress Administration
which aided local libraries in many ways. Library workers both
skilled and unskilled became plentiful under the W. P. A. and National Youth Administration programs and funds were available in some
cases for new buildings. Eventually statewide W. P. A. library programs were set up to demonstrate public library service where
there had previously been none and many of these "demonstration libraries" became permanent. New books were purchased, old ones
mended, and bookmobiles made available to many new areas. Library extension services throughout the nation were given new
strength, and more people became library conscious than ever before. Another Federal agency, the Tennessee Valley Authority, began a regional library experiment in the seven states touched by the
Tennessee River and brought public library service to many counties
that had hitherto had none. All in all, 1939 found 3,000,000 more
Americans with library services than in 1934, thanks largely to those
"emergency" efforts on the part of the Federal government. However, there was still nearly one-third of the nation without library
service, with only about 400 counties, one in eight, that offered
county-wide library service in 1940. One more important library

development of the depression years was the establishment in 1936
of the Library Services Division in the U. S. Office of Education.
This gave the nation a central clearing house for library planning,
and a source of information and guidance for all types of libraries.
A number of states began to provide direct aid for public library
service in the 1930's and this added considerably to the improved
library scene.

The effects of the depression years, both favorable and un-
favorable, can be seen in the U. S. Office of Education's public library statistics for 1938-1939. Bookstocks and circulation were up
but staffs were still small, and budgets considerably stretched to
meet the demands. Statistically, there were 6,880 public libraries
reporting in that year and their bookstocks totalled more than
104,000,000 volumes. Some 24,000,000 registered borrowers had
taken home over 400,000,000 volumes, and 7,000,000 new books had
been added to public library shelves in the last year reported. The
Northeastern and Middle Western states still had the largest number
of libraries but the remainder of the nation was increasing its library service at a rapid rate. The South lagged most noticeably in
this respect but its larger cities were developing stronger libraries
and rural library services were expanding.

Between the depression years and the mid-twentieth century
came the long years of the Second World War. Unlike the First
World War, however, this world conflict did not hamper the development of public library service in the United States and, indeed,
tended to encourage it. There were shortages of personnel in most
libraries and in some war industry areas the rapid growth in population resulted in restricted library service. But generally speaking,
public library service expanded and went far beyond the usual pas-
sive offering of educational and recreational reading. In maintain-
ing public morale, in serving business and industry, and in the
broad fields of adult education and public information, the wartime
services of libraries can hardly be underestimated. Without exaggeration it can be said that America's public libraries more than
proved their worth to the nation during the trying days of World
War II.

After the war public libraries saw a rapid return to normal conditions and then a progressive surge ahead with new buildings, new branches, and new services offered to the public. New problems arose with television and the millions of paper-backed reprints that flooded the book market. Post-war shifts in population added thousands of patrons to some libraries and subtracted them from others. Two groups in particular -- those under twenty-one and those over sixty-five -- increased out of proportion to the remainder of the population and they provided a ready and willing public for the library's services. But in the main, these problems have been met, and the public library is the stronger for them. Television has been welcomed as an ally and even as a tool for library service, with book reviews and book talks reaching additional thousands of people. The paper-backed thriller relieves the public library in part of its task in supplying purely entertainment reading and, in reinforced library bindings, it often supplements the library bookstock at economical prices. The population changes have been met with improved services to children, special departments for teen-agers and for those over sixty-five.

For library service in rural areas and in towns of 10,000 or less population the Library Services Act of 1956 has provided a remarkable advance. It provided for Federal government aid to library extension in those areas over a trial period of five years, and its aid has been extended by subsequent acts. The results of the Library Services Act will long be felt. As an example of one immediate effect, the book circulation in one rural Georgia county jumped from 35,000 in 1955 to over 300,000 in 1959. New books, new branches, new personnel and even new library systems have resulted all over the United States from the assistance provided by the Library Services Act. By 1963 only 10 per cent of the population of the United States was without library service (as compared to 36 per cent in 1940), but over half of those with libraries had inadequate ones. Still there were 5,770 public libraries with incomes of over $2000 each and they contained some 190,000,000 volumes for the use of 44,000,000 registered borrowers. The unhappy corollary to these statistics is that there were 2500 other book col-

lections called public libraries, with less than $2,000 each per
year for all expenses.

One progressive step in the recent development of public library service has been the improved services available to the Negro
population in the South.   In 1913, only fourteen public libraries in
the South offered library service to the Negroes of their areas.
Later the larger cities opened separate branches for Negroes but as
late as 1947 only 188 out of a total of 597 Southern libraries offered them any type of library service at all.   After the Supreme
Court decision in the school segregation cases in 1954, a few Southern libraries gradually opened their doors to Negroes and this number has increased over the next decade.   Various restrictions were
still placed on the use of public library facilities by Negroes until
the passage of the Civil Rights Act of 1965.   Since that time most
Southern libraries have complied with the Federal laws concerning
segregation and are now finally open to all citizens.

College and university libraries have also progressed rapidly
since 1900.   The average college library of that date was small and
consisted almost entirely of the classics and contemporary textbooks.
It was staffed with only one or two librarians, was little used by
the students and was usually housed in a room or wing of the college administration or classroom building.   With the exception of a
half-dozen major universities, the concept of the college library as
a research center was almost entirely absent.   The idea of the college library as a storehouse of knowledge, where books were preserved rather than used, was still common and the concept of the
librarian as a curator of a repository of ancient tomes was still
prevalent.   But changes were rapidly taking place in college library
concepts, with more liberal lending policies, hours of opening and
types of services rendered.   Students and faculty alike were demand-
ing and receiving more books and more service, and the twentieth
century college library was gradually taking shape.

Harvard University Library had, by 1900, been surpassed in
size by the Library of Congress, but it was still by far the largest
university library in the nation.   Its bookstock then numbered
560,000, including the main library and all department or special

libraries on the campus, and it was far ahead of Yale with 285,000 volumes and the University of Chicago with 329,000. Other major university libraries at the turn of the century included those at Princeton, Cornell, Johns Hopkins, Dartmouth, and the Universities of Michigan, California and Pennsylvania. In 1915, Harvard moved into the new Widener Library building, designed to fill its library needs for an indefinite period. But within fifteen years it was filled to overflowing, and it has been supplemented by the Houghton Library for rare books and manuscripts, the Lamont Library for undergraduates and no less than seventy other departmental and associated libraries elsewhere on the campus.

On other university campuses, the library scene in the first half of the twentieth century was similar to that at Harvard, although in most cases it was on a much smaller scale. There was a constant striving, with varying success, to keep bookstocks, buildings, and staffs in line with the growing numbers of faculty and students. Gradually the college library ceased being a museum and became an active part of the academic program. Newer teaching methods called for more student use of the library and more faculty participation in book selection. For the undergraduates, the college library had to provide reserved books for required course readings and a wide variety of source materials for term papers. For the graduate students there was no end to the demand for research materials, rare and expensive books and periodicals and the publications of learned societies. Above all, the books had to be readily available and to this end libraries had to be better organized and, in many cases, completely recataloged and reclassified. Open stacks, seminar rooms, faculty studies and student carrels became more common as new buildings were constructed. Fortunately, the changes came at a time when library philanthropy was still alive, and most of the major university libraries and many of the minor ones received substantial gifts in books, buildings and money. The Carnegie Corporation, in particular, gave money for buildings, for books, library surveys, recataloging projects and publications.

The 1920's saw a number of university libraries in the South and West beginning to compete in size and importance with the older

ones in the Northeast. Similarly, the libraries of teachers' colleges, and technical and agricultural institutions took on more importance, and although not equal in size to those of the universities,
they increased their significance in their own fields. Library and
laboratory were growing together and their interdependence was being widely recognized. On many campuses there was a conflict between those who wanted departmental libraries, and those who
wanted everything in a central collection. Each type of organization
had its good points and its weak points, but down to 1940 the departmental libraries were the more common in the larger institutions. As the donations of books and funds from the library philan-
thropists became smaller and fewer, many libraries turned to the
formation of Friends of the Library groups, where many could make
small gifts to take the place of the few large ones formerly received. The coming of the depression decade of the 1930's hurt the
college and university libraries as much as it had the public libraries. Staffs and budgets were curtailed, and plans for expansion
and improvements were often put off indefinitely. Here too the
W. P. A. and the N. Y. A. programs brought temporary relief and
some colleges were able to go ahead with binding, cataloging, indexing and other long delayed projects. The W. P. A. public records
projects provided outstanding research materials in their indexes
and abstracts of public records on the local, state and Federal levels. In some cases, particularly in the case of public institutions,
Federal funds were available for the construction of library buildings.

In order to extend the services which their strained budgets
could not provide, university libraries experimented with cooperative
buying programs, in which neighboring collections shared expensive
materials or coordinated their buying of rarer works. Union catalogs and inter-library loans furthered this cooperation, and photo-
mechanical means of reproducing printed materials were introduced
in the larger libraries. By the time the effects of the depression
were wearing off, World War II came with all its problems. Colleges and universities were called upon to supply the special training needed for soldiers and specialists in a nation at war and their

libraries felt the strain. Funds were usually plentiful but staff problems increased and the demands for books and services for the new programs, the newly organized academic departments, and the war information centers severely taxed the abilities of all but the largest libraries. Under the pressure of need, however, new methods were employed, new tools were developed, thousands of new workers were introduced to the library field, and the end of the war saw the nation's college and university libraries stronger than ever. Everywhere academic libraries were taking stock of their assets, accomplishments and aims, and were planning for sound and useful service in the postwar years.

After 1945 thousands of war veterans flooded the college campuses and both undergraduate and graduate enrollments rose to new highs. Moreover, these older students were usually more serious than their non-veteran contemporaries and they made full use of all library facilities. Hard put at first to meet this demand, the libraries soon adjusted, and once again went into a program of new buildings, annexes and departmental collections. Scores of new buildings graced campuses from Maine to California, with most of them designed in the newer forms of modular construction, open shelf arrangement and subject divisional organization. Book stocks, library staffs, and library budgets far surpassed the expectations of even a decade earlier. The nation's largest university library at Harvard had by 1963 passed the 7,000,000 mark in its volume count, while Yale's collection approached 4,700,000. Some 33 other university libraries had passed the million mark, and the collection of half million volumes was becoming almost a norm. Two university libraries -- Harvard and California at Berkeley -- had annual budgets of over $4,000,000, while 29 others had passed $1,000,000 in their annual expenditures. Some 40 American university libraries had staffs of over 100 employees, and at least seven had staffs of over 300. On the other end of the scale, dozens of junior and "community" colleges were getting along with only one staff member and hundreds of others were woefully under-staffed. Each year new colleges were being established and each of these required staff, books and quarters to add to the sum total of library facilities avail-

able for higher education. In the academic year of 1962-1963,
some 2100 college and university libraries served 4,200,000 students
with a total of 214,000,000 books. It was a far cry from 1900, but
it was still a rapidly growing and rapidly changing library scene in
American higher education.

As bookstocks reached unmanageable proportions, many of
the nation's university libraries turned to various types of storage
plans for little used materials. Some found storage on their own
campuses or in nearby buildings, while others made more use of
microfilming and discarding. In two areas, however, the storage
problem was met by the formation of cooperative inter-library centers, jointly owned and controlled by several libraries. The New
England Deposit Library in Boston is maintained by the major libraries of the Boston area, including Harvard, Massachusetts Institute of Technology, the Boston Public Library, and the Massachusetts State Library. In it are deposited newspapers, state and foreign documents, as well as runs of periodicals, sets of little used
works, and other marginal materials. Much of this material is not
duplicated in any of the member libraries, but is available to any
of them. The Midwest Inter-Library Center in Chicago (now the
Center for Research Libraries) is the result of cooperation between
a dozen or so middle western university libraries. It was formed
in 1951 and has a capacity of over 2,000,000 volumes. This center functions much the same as that in New England, but it also
has the task of collecting certain types of little used materials itself, thus relieving its constituent libraries of that operation. The
volume of printed material available in micro-form has increased
annually, so that even medium-sized research libraries can provide
rare or bulky research sources in a manner that is both economical and space-saving. Still another development on university campuses after the 1950's has been the construction of separate undergraduate libraries of around 100,000 volumes, thus providing most
of the needs of the average student away from the bewildering enor-
mity and complexity of the million-volume research collections.

A number of the larger universities are fortunate in having
special privately endowed libraries on their campuses. These are

often housed and staffed completely separate from the main libraries, but are available for research use to faculty and students.
Examples of these are the William Andrews Clark Memorial Library
at the University of California at Los Angeles, the Hoover Library
of War, Revolution, and Peace at Stanford University, and the Furness Memorial Library at the University of Pennsylvania.   The
Clark Memorial Library consists mainly of rare and important works
in English literature, and today contains some 60,000 volumes.   The
Hoover Library, endowed by former President Herbert Hoover, centers its holdings around primary source materials relating to the
theme of war, revolution and peace, especially since 1900.   It holds
thousands of volumes of periodicals and government documents from
other countries, including files of over 6000 newspapers, in addition to over 600,000 books, pamphlets and other printed items.
The Furness Library on the other hand is built around a Shakespearean collection and English literature of the sixteenth century.
At Baylor University in Waco, Texas, there is a Robert Browning
Library that is justly renowned.   The University of Cincinnati has
the Burnam Classical Library of some 80,000 volumes, and on
many other university campuses there are special libraries, privately endowed but available to students and faculty, that add considerably to the research materials available.   In almost every case
these collections owe their existence to the efforts of one man, a
book collector and scholar who made his own hobby and interest a
cultural asset for the benefit of thousands of future students.

        The school library as we know it today in the United States
is almost entirely a twentieth century development.   The nineteenth
century had seen academy libraries, school district libraries and
Sunday school collections, but at the turn of the century there were
few public schools with anything like workable libraries.   There was
still a debate as to whether the public library should serve the children with year round library service, or whether there should be
libraries in the school as well.   By 1910, however, changes in the
philosophy and methodology of public education had decided the question in favor of libraries in the schools, or at least in favor of
books in the school.   The introduction of such new educational pro-

grams as the platoon school, the Winnetka plan and the Dalton plan, all involving the development of initiative on the part of the pupil, called for books at hand at all times.   The concept of developing and educating the child through freedom rather than compulsion made the use of books, both for instruction and for pleasure a ne- cessity in the new methods of classroom teaching.   By 1910, the standard goal of schools was a centralized library of at least one thousand volumes, supervised by a librarian or teacher-librarian and under the general direction of the school principal or superin- tendent.   Unfortunately, this goal was not reached to any great ex- tent until well after World War I.

In 1913, the nation's schools reported only 3,265 libraries of over 1,000 volumes, and only 607 of those were staffed by full-time librarians.   The total bookstock of some 6,000,000 volumes sounds impressive, but a description of the average secondary school li- brary, which was included in the report, gives another picture:

> Secondary school libraries are weighed down with books
> long since out of date, or with antiquated books...
> Most of them are small collections of reference and text
> books, poorly quartered, unclassified, and neither cata-
> loged or readily accessible for constant use.

The better libraries were in the larger cities, where they were of- ten organized into city-wide systems with trained library supervis- ors.   On the other hand, the small town and rural areas, particu- larly in the South, had schools where library service was either weak or entirely lacking.

School libraries progressed gradually in the 1920's and most of the new school buildings of that decade provided quarters for li- brary service.   But still services were not up to the demand, and in 1935 when the U.S. Office of Education compiled what was prob- ably the most complete set of statistics ever gathered on the nation's schools, there was a noticeable deficit in libraries.   A total of 27,724 schools reported libraries containing more than 28,000,000 volumes in all, for an average of slightly more than 1,000 each. But of these only 3,808 reported full-time librarians, and 8,770 were in charge of part-time librarians, leaving some 15,000 "libra- ries" that were little more than unsupervised book collections.

There was still a long way to go in school library service and in most cases the individual schools were financially unable to find the answers to their library problems.

Fortunately, aid and advice on school library service has been available from a number of outside sources. On the national level both the American Library Association and the National Education Association have been most active in encouraging the development of school libraries, the training of librarians and the establishment of school library standards. Particularly in the publishing of helpful handbooks and texts these organizations have supplied a long felt need. The National Council of Teachers of English in 1914 appointed a standing committee on school libraries, and the A. L. A. in the same year established its School Library Section. N. E. A. in 1920 published a pamphlet on Standard Library Organization and Equipment for Secondary Schools, giving librarians and school administrators a goal toward which they could aim their library development. This report received the endorsement of the A. L. A. and provided standards of size and contents for libraries of junior and senior high schools of various enrollments. This was followed by another N. E. A. pamphlet in 1925 which was on Elementary School Library Standards, also approved and re-published by the A. L. A. In addition to these, state departments of education, state education and library associations, and library schools made surveys, studies and reports that added to the information available on school library services and standards.

Aside from standards and statistics, however, there were other significant developments in school libraries, often on a more practical level. Charitable foundations, such as the General Education Board and the Rosenwald Fund, gave financial aid to school library demonstration projects in various parts of the nation, particularly in those areas where school library service had lagged behind. For example, in 1929 the Rosenwald Fund provided aid for eleven county libraries in the South to demonstrate public library service to rural schools. The Carnegie Corporation's aid to library schools also furthered the training of school librarians and the improvement of school libraries. Most of the states gave aid and encouragement

to the development and improvement of school libraries in one form
or another.   In some cases this took the form of a state school library supervisor, in others the supplying of books for school libraries, either in permanent deposits or in rotating collections.   Almost all states published school library standards, handbooks, and
booklists and gave some form of certification or recognition to those
schools whose libraries met certain requirements.   The Federal
Government aided the schools and their libraries through the Office
of Education, which published literature, collected statistics and
after the 1930's, provided a school library specialist in the national
office.

In many cases, particularly in rural areas, cooperation between school and public libraries has provided answers to many of
the problems of both.   This has taken several forms.   In some
cases there is a single library system, including a public library in
the county seat, which supplies all county schools with books.
There are many advantages to this including lower administration
costs, lower processing and operating costs and the advantage of
having to supply only one set of children's books for both school and
public library use.   In other cases, public libraries or branches are
located close to the schools, and the children are allowed free use
of public library facilities.   In some cases the reverse is true --
the libraries are in the schools and are open to the public after
school hours.   Either way, the benefits are obvious, particularly
when the cooperative system includes centralized purchasing and
cataloging.   Professional libraries for teachers are often incorporated into the larger library systems.   By the 1950's, many public
libraries, particularly in the larger cities, were being deluged with
high school students whose school libraries were inadequate in bookstock or open hours or both.   In these cases compromises have had
to be made between school and library officials and often better libraries for both have resulted.

Recent years have found the public school library expanding
beyond the medium of books and into the field of audio-visual and
other teaching aids.   In fact, the instructional materials center,
supplying all needs of the classroom teacher including books, peri-

odicals, pamphlets, pictures, slides, films, filmstrips, maps, pictures, disk recordings, tape recordings, television tapes, programed teaching materials, and even three dimensional models is, to a large extent, replacing the conventional type of school library. A large high school library today may well consist of a suite of rooms (or even a separate building on the new campus-type high school grounds) including reading rooms, reference room, browsing room, conference rooms and work rooms. It may have an audiovisual room adjacent to it where projection equipment and television reception is available. In individual study carrels it may provide teaching machines, television (either educational or closed circuit), earphones from tape and record players and other learning devices. Among its 20 to 30,000 books and other items it may make use of microfilm, microprint, and miniprint. Its field of service will include all the graphic and auditory arts, its staff will include librarians and materials specialists as well as clerical and mechanical aides and its budget will run well over $50,000 annually. This of course is not the average but it is the desirable level of good school library service, and many school libraries are approaching it.

As of 1963, only 59% of the nation's schools had central libraries and only about 40% had school librarians. Of the elementary schools, only 45% had school libraries, and only about 21% had school librarians. Over 10,000,000 elementary children had no school libraries and of all the school children in the United States fully 25% attended schools with no central libraries at all. This meant that whereas some schools had excellent libraries, many had none at all, and in the 1960's the efforts of the nation's educational leaders have been directed toward equalizing and improving school opportunities all over the nation. One significant attempt to show what excellent school libraries can do has been demonstrated by the Knapp School Libraries Project. In 1964 the Knapp Foundation of New York City made a grant of over $1,000,000 to the American Library Association for a five-year project in demonstration school libraries. These pilot libraries will show how schools that meet the national standards for school library service can im-

prove their educational programs.   The first two demonstration
projects were at Central Park Road School in Plainview, New York,
and at Marcus Whitman School in Richland, Washington.   The Federal Government has also entered the library picture with federal
aid for the development of school libraries.   This aid has come in
several forms, including the National Defense Education Act (particularly the amendments of 1964), the Elementary and Secondary
Education Act of 1965, and various other federal laws.   In form,
this assistance varies from outright grants of funds for the purchase
of books and other materials, to aid in the training of school librarians through fellowships, loans and summer institutes.   Probably the greatest shortage of all lies in the number of trained librarians so, despite the funds available, progress in the expansion
of school library service must hinge on the effectiveness of the program for training more school librarians.

Paralleling the growth of public, college and school libraries
in the twentieth century has been the rapid development of special
libraries, particularly those of the Federal government.   The real-
ization that necessary books and source materials should be at hand
for all government agencies has led to the establishment of a number of libraries not only in Washington, but at regional headquarters
throughout the nation.

The Library of Congress is the nation's greatest library and
one of the two or three largest in the world.   In 1964 its holdings
numbered over 40,000,000 items, including over 13,000,000 books
and pamphlets, over 15,000,000 manuscripts, and millions more of
photographs, slides, maps, prints, music scores, motion picture
films, recordings, microfilms and microprints.   Its acquisitions increase at a rate of almost 2,000,000 items per year.   Its services
directly or indirectly are available to every citizen of the United
States through its inter-library loans, its services to the blind, its
bibliographic publications, and its printed catalog cards.   Two other
major libraries in Washington, the National Agricultural Library
and the National Library of Medicine, are among the greatest libraries in the world in their respective fields.   The former serves
the U.S. Department of Agriculture and the nation with its

1,200,000 volumes and over 20,000 files of periodicals and newspapers.   The latter, which moved into a new building in nearby
Bethesda, Maryland, in 1962, makes its 1,100,000 volumes available
to all medical and health agencies in the country and in the form of bibliographic services to all the nation.   Since 1963 it has operated
MEDLARS (Medical Literature Analysis and Retrieval System), a
computer based program of storage and retrieval of bibliographic
citations.

Other federal departments operate major libraries in Washington, ranging from about 100,000 to 1,000,000 volumes in size,
and also many minor specialized collections.   Each is designed to
serve a particular purpose and a relatively limited clientele but almost all are available to the general public in one way or another.
All told, the government libraries in Washington form together a
national bibliographic center that can hardly be surpassed anywhere
in the world.

Many departments of the Federal government have branches
or regional offices scattered throughout the United States, and these
often have libraries of their own.   The Department of Defense has
libraries all around the world, at its various Army, Navy and Air
Force posts.   The Air Force Library Service, for example, had in
1964 some 7,000,000 books available to its personnel through 8,000
distribution points.   There are large libraries at the service academies, and all permanent military and naval bases have both popular
and technical libraries, as do all the service hospitals.   The larger
naval vessels have libraries on board and the smaller ones have rotating collections made available through the Navy Department's Library Services Branch.   Other Federal agencies, such as the Tennessee Valley Authority, the Atomic Energy Commission, and the
National Aeronautics and Space Administration have developed notable
research libraries.   The TVA has since its founding in 1933 developed a technical library of some 56,000 volumes in Knoxville and
has, besides, maintained libraries at each of its construction points
and encouraged the development of public library service throughout
its area.   The Atomic Energy Commission has some 21 libraries
scattered throughout the United States, with the largest at Hanford,

Washington; Oak Ridge, Tennessee; and at its headquarters at Germantown, Maryland. NASA has seven major libraries at its research centers, each of which has several thousand books and journals, with additional thousands of classified and unclassified technical reports.

Not to be ignored in a discussion of government libraries
are those of the states. State libraries are usually devoted primarily to history or law or both, but they have in many instances
grown into important reference and research collections. Ordinarily they serve as reference libraries only but their books may be
available to citizens of the state through mail or inter-library loans.
In many cases the state library also serves as a library commission to promote and encourage the development of library service in
all parts of the state. Other libraries operated by states include
such special collections as Supreme Court libraries, legislative reference libraries and libraries of various state departments, such as
agriculture and education. In many cases the best collection of public documents can be found in the library of the secretary of state.
State archival agencies, which are in fact specialized manuscript libraries, are sometimes connected with the state library and sometimes are maintained as separate organizations. In the state of
Hawaii a Governor's Committee on State Library Resources in 1965
recommended that a statewide library system be developed, with all
public, school and governmental libraries developed into a coordinated and cooperative system headed up by the state library.

In a general sense, government libraries are all special libraries in that their collections are specialized, or their functions,
or their reading public, or all three. However, the libraries most
generally considered as special libraries are those of professional
associations, technical schools or departments of universities, public institutions such as hospitals and prisons, and those of industrial
or financial corporations. These libraries, many of which are quite
large, serve only a limited clientele but are considered so important
to that small number that they often have large staffs. Outstanding
among the special libraries are the endowed libraries, often semi-
public in nature, such as the Newberry and Crerar libraries in Chi-

cago, the Folger Shakespeare Library in Washington, and the Huntington Library in California.   The John Crerar Library is a technical and scientific reference library of over 1,000,000 volumes.
The Newberry Library is a reference collection devoted to literature, history, philosophy and music.   It is particularly strong in
American history, and contains some 800,000 volumes.   In San Marino, California, the Huntington Library and Art Gallery is largely
a rare book collection but as such it is one of the finest in the nation, and many of its 400,000 volumes are not duplicated elsewhere.
The Folger Shakespeare Library, opened in Washington, D.C., in
1932, is devoted to material by and about William Shakespeare, the
theater and the era in which Shakespeare lived.   It has included
among its 250,000 volumes the largest single collection in the western hemisphere of books printed in England or in English before
1641.   The Pierpont Morgan Library in New York City is another
endowed reference library, strong in incunabula, history and early
Americana, while the Lloyd Library and Museum in Cincinnati has
some 165,000 volumes, largely devoted to botany, chemistry and
pharmacy.   One of the most recently established of these endowed
research libraries is the Linda Hall Library of Kansas City, Missouri, which is devoted largely to science and technology.   These
libraries and a few other similar ones throughout the nation are usually open to serious students, although almost all are strictly reference libraries and some have other restrictions as to use.

Almost as valuable as the endowed libraries are those of the
historical and other professional societies throughout the nation.
Many of these had their beginnings in the nineteenth century or earlier, and their holdings are extensive and important.   The Wisconsin State Historical Society in Madison is one of the largest, with
over 350,000 volumes, an equal number of pamphlets, and some
2,000,000 manuscripts.   The New York Historical Society Library
has over 400,000 volumes and 1,000,000 manuscripts, and other important historical society collections include those of Missouri,
Minnesota, Illinois and Massachusetts.   The Boston Athenaeum, essentially an historical library, contains over 420,000 volumes, and
several other historical collections in the nation number over

100,000 volumes each. In addition to the historical societies, many scientific organizations have libraries noteworthy for their size and contents. The New York Academy of Medicine library has some 350,000 volumes, plus an additional 150,000 pamphlets; while the Engineering Societies Library in the same city has nearly 200,000 volumes. In Philadelphia, the Academy of Natural Sciences Library and the American Philosophical Society Library are noted for their research collections, and throughout the country there are hundreds of other technical, scientific, legal and religious libraries ranging in size from a few hundred to several hundred thousand volumes. A recent addition to this type of library is the Presidential library, containing the books and papers of ex-Presidents of the United States. The Franklin D. Roosevelt Library at Hyde Park, New York, is the oldest of these and contains some 30,000 bound volumes and nearly 20,000,000 manuscripts and other miscellaneous items. Other Presidential libraries are those of Harry S. Truman at Independence, Missouri; Dwight D. Eisenhower at Abilene, Kansas; and Herbert Hoover at West Branch, Iowa. These are all under the general supervision of the National Archives and Records service. A very special international library is that of the United Nations in New York. This library, named in honor of the late Dag Hammarskjold, U.N. Secretary General, had some 225,000 volumes in 1964.

In the past few decades another type of special library has appeared on the American scene. This is the business or technical library maintained by the large corporation. Consisting of highly specialized books and materials, this type of library is ordinarily used by the personnel of a particular company but it may be available to other serious students. Banks, insurance companies and newspapers were among the first businesses to realize the importance of having their own reference libraries but industrial firms were soon to follow. The New York Times has a large library of books and pamphlets, backed up by information files containing more than a million items. The DuPont Company has libraries at each of its major plants in addition to a large one at its headquarters in Wilmington, Delaware. The General Electric Company Library in

Schenectady, New York, is outstanding in the field of electronics, while the American Telephone and Telegraph Company library in New York City is equally strong in the field of communications. Most of the large oil companies have technical libraries to serve their staffs of researchers, as do also the steel, rubber, chemical, automotive and mining corporations. These technical libraries range from a few hundred volumes to many thousands and from part-time librarians to large staffs of specialists. Besides books, periodicals and pamphlets, they must deal with micro materials, thousands of processed reports, and various other forms of mechanically and electronically recorded information. To control this multitude of materials and to "file and find" it readily and easily, technical librarians are turning to punched cards, machine literature searching, and other advanced mechanical and electronic methods. The special libraries are taking the lead in experimenting in new methods of information storage and retrieval and are pointing the way that all librarians and "information specialists" may eventually follow.

Library service has made tremendous strides in the United States since 1900. Whether in public, school, college, government or special libraries, progress has been made in both numbers and size that could hardly have been imagined a half century ago. Yet in spite of this growth, and partially because of it, the library profession is faced with even greater problems today than ever before. The combination of a superabundance of recorded information and a shortage of personnel to control it is only one of the many problems confronting the librarian of 1965. While the problems are great, the facilities for meeting them are also increasingly available and the future of librarianship in the world of communication is bright.

Bibliography

Adams, Frederick B., Jr.: An introduction to the Pierpont Morgan Library... New York, 1964. 64 p.

Adams, Joseph Q.: The Folger Shakespeare Memorial Library. Washington, 1942. 61 p.

Aldrich, Frederic D.: The school library in Ohio. New York, 1959. 236 p.

American Library Association: College and university libraries and
    librarianship. Chicago, 1946. 152 p.

American Library Association: A national plan for public library
    service. Chicago, 1948. 168 p.

American Library Association: School libraries for today and to-
    morrow, functions and standards: Chicago, 1945. 43 p.

American Library Association: A survey of libraries in the United
    States. Chicago, 1926. 4 v.

Antrim, Saida B.: The county library. Van Wert, Ohio, 1914.
    306 p. (Largely on the history of this pioneer county li-
    brary.)

Asheim, Lester, ed.: Forum on the public library inquiry. New
    York, 1951. 281 p.

Bostwock, Arthur E.: The American public library. New York,
    1929. 471 p.

Bronson, Barbara: Bibliographical guides to the history of Ameri-
    can libraries. Urbana, Ill., 1953. 32 p.

Brough, Kenneth: Scholars' workshop; evolving concepts of library
    service. Urbana, Ill., 1953. 197 p.

Cecil, H. L.: School library service in the United States, an inter-
    pretative survey. New York, 1940. 334 p.

Daniel, Hawthorne: Public libraries for everyone: the growth and
    development of library services in the United States... New
    York, 1961. 192 p.

Ellsworth, Ralph E.: The school library. New York, 1965. 116 p.

Erickson, E. W.: College and university library surveys, 1938-
    1952. Chicago, 1961. 115 p.

Evans, Luther H., ed.: Federal departmental libraries, a summary
    report... Washington, 1963. 150 p.

Barker, Tommie Dora: Libraries of the South, a report on devel-
    opments, 1930-1935. Chicago, 1936. 215 p.

Gleason, Eliza A.: The Southern Negro and the public library.
    Chicago, 1941. 218 p.

Henne, Frances: Youth, communication and libraries. Chicago,
    1949. 233 p.

Humble, Marion: Rural America reads; a study of rural library service. New York, 1938. 101 p.

Jackson, Lucille, ed. : Technical libraries, their organization and
    management. New York, 1951. 202 p.

Jamieson, John: Books for the army; the army library service in
    the Second World War. New York, 1950. 335 p.

Joeckel, Carleton C. : The government of the American public li-
    brary. Chicago, 1935. 393 p.

Johnson, Alvin: The public library, a people's university. New
    York, 1938. 85 p.

Johnson, Elmer D. : A history of libraries in the western world.
    New York, 1965. 418 p.

Landheer, Bartholomeus: Social functions of libraries. New York,
    1957. 287 p.

Kroll, Morton, ed. : College, university and special libraries of
    the Pacific Northwest. Seattle, 1961. 310 p.

Kroll, Morton, ed. : Elementary and secondary school libraries of
    the Pacific Northwest. Seattle, 1960. 330 p.

Kroll, Morton, ed. : Libraries and librarians of the Pacific North-
    west. Seattle, 1960. 271 p.

Leigh, Robert D. : The public library in the United States. New
    York, 1950. 273 p.

Leigh, Robert D. : Governor's study of public and school libraries
    in the state of Hawaii. Honolulu, 1960. 83 p.

Lydenberg, Harry M. : History of the New York Public Library.
    New York, 1932. 643 p.

Marshall, John David, Jr. , ed. : The American library history
    reader; contributions to library literature. Hamden, Conn. ,
    1961. 464 p.

Marshall, John David, Jr. , ed. : In pursuit of library history.
    Tallahassee, Fla. , 1961. 86 p.

Rossell, Beatrice S. : Public libraries in the life of the nation.
    Chicago, 1943. 116 p.

Salamanca, Lucy: Fortress of Freedom. Philadelphia, 1942.
    445 p. (A popular history of the Library of Congress.)

Schenck, Gretchen K. : County and regional library development.
    Chicago, 1954. 272 p.

Stanford, Edward B. :   Library extension under the W. P. A.   Chicago, 1944.   284 p.

Temple, Phillips: Federal services to libraries.   Chicago, 1954. 227 p.

United Nations: The Dag Hammarskjold Library.   New York, 1962. 167 p.

Wilson, Louis R. :   The geography of reading.   Chicago, 1938. 481 p.

XV
The Growth of the Profession of Librarianship

A profession is usually characterized by having a body of specialized knowledge, advanced facilities for specialized education and a professional association to improve services and to increase the quality and quantity of services and of professional personnel. In each of these respects, the field of librarianship qualifies eminently as a profession.

The development of a body of specialized knowledge, in the form of professional tools and technical aids for librarians, has closely paralleled the growth of libraries themselves, particularly in the modern era. Classification manuals, subject heading guides, bibliographies, indexes and textbooks in library methods all aid the librarian in serving the reading public. These are a basic part of the literature of librarianship, and a vital part of the history of libraries.

It has already been noted that 1876, the year so important in American library history, saw the beginning of the Library Journal and the first edition of Melvil Dewey's Decimal Classification System. These useful library aids were followed in a few years by the first volume of the American Catalog, a current record of books in print. The American Catalog continued to appear at intervals until 1910, but before that date it had been superseded by the H.W. Wilson Company's United States Catalog. In its last one volume edition, which appeared in 1928, the United States Catalog listed more than 190,000 titles. Its supplement, the Cumulative Book Index, keeps this national bibliography up to date, and provides a current author, subject and title index to books and pamphlets published in the United States or elsewhere in the English language. Another exhaustive bibliographic tool is the R.R. Bowker Company's Publishers' Trade List Annual, which is a compilation of all available publishers' catalogs for a given year, bound together. In recent

years this has been made more useful by means of an author and
title index, Books in Print, and by a Subject Guide to Books in
Print.

The Dewey Decimal Classification System went through several editions before 1900 and by that date it had been widely adopted
by public, school and college libraries throughout the nation.   As
the new editions grew longer and more complex, an abridged edition was issued for the use of smaller libraries.   The development
of the Library of Congress Classification System provided a more
easily expanded arrangement for larger collections.   Many of the
university and technical libraries turned to this system and the Library of Congress aided them by publishing the L. C. Classification
in frequently revised and expanded editions.   To supplement the
classification guides came the A. L. A. Catalog Rules of 1908, and
Subject Headings for Use in Dictionary Catalogs.   Just as important
to the average library was the service provided by the Library of
Congress in preparing and selling printed catalog cards.   These
cards, available after 1901, provided full author information, title,
collation, L. C. classification number, and suggested subject headings.   In later years the Dewey classification number has been
added.   L. C. cards are available for most American publications
and many foreign ones, and have gradually been expanded to include
all cataloged books in the Library of Congress.   The average library
can now purchase cards for almost all books added to its collection.
The Library of Congress also publishes its own Guide to Subject
Headings, and other indexes and bibliographic aids for the use of its
own staff and other librarians who care to purchase them.   Since
the 1940's a printed catalog of all Library of Congress holdings has
been available, and this has been kept up to date by both author and
subject supplements.   After 1956 this was expanded into the National Union Catalog, which includes not only books cataloged in the Library of Congress but many more received by other major libraries
in the nation.

Other sources of bibliographic aids for librarians appeared
early in the twentieth century.   Possibly the most used book selection tool was the A. L. A. Catalog.   First published in 1893, it was

revised in 1904 to include some 8,000 titles, all suitable for use
in the public library.   It remained the standard guide for small libraries, and was continued by new editions and supplements down to
1949.   Another useful aid in book evaluation and selection is the
Book Review Digest, which first appeared in 1905.   It provides a
brief summary of several reviews for each of hundreds of the more
popular and important books published each year.   Serving as an index to book review literature, as well as a selected subject guide
to the new books, the Book Review Digest has proved to be a most
valuable library aid.   Even more selective in approach is the H.W.
Wilson Company's Standard Catalog series.   This series began with
the Children's Catalog in 1909, when for the first time an extensive
but selective bibliography of current children's literature was made
available.   The Children's Catalog was followed by the Standard Catalog for Public Libraries in 1918, and the High School Catalog in
1926.   Each of these provides a classified selection of the latest
books in each field, with a dictionary catalog of authors, titles and
subjects and is kept up to date by supplements and new editions.
There are brief annotations, and some collections are analyzed to
provide further information for librarians.   Classification numbers
and subject headings are included to make them even more indis-
pensable, with the result that they are basic purchases for libraries
in their respective fields.   Along with other Wilson publications,
they appear in cumulative form, with a basic volume about every
five years, kept up to date by semi-annual and annual supplements.

        The H.W. Wilson Company aids already mentioned are only
a small part of the library service program provided by that organization.   In the field of periodical indexing, Poole's Index to Periodical Literature, begun in the mid-nineteenth century, was the only
thing in its field before 1900.   This was not too satisfactory, since
it was very selective, difficult to use, inaccurate in places and
rather erratic in its publication.   After many tribulations, it
ceased publication in the early 1890's.   Several attempts at a successor failed, and finally in 1901, H.W. Wilson took over the task
and began the publication of the Reader's Guide to Periodical Literature.   This succeeded after some difficulties, largely because the

Wilson Company adopted the custom of charging for its publications according to the value of each to a particular library. This service basis of prices enabled smaller libraries to obtain the Wilson publications at lower prices; hence their use was widespread. Another useful feature of the Wilson publications is the system of cumulative issues, and cumulative indexes that reduce the number of places to look for a particular bit of information.

The next Wilson index after the Reader's Guide was the International Index to Periodicals, begun in 1907. This index, started as a supplement to the Reader's Guide, indexed a selected list of periodicals largely of a scholarly or technical nature in the humanities and pure sciences. These were periodicals not usually received in the smaller libraries and did not need to be included in the Reader's Guide, but which were needed in the larger public and college libraries. The need for special indexing in another field was met in 1908 with the Index to Legal Periodicals, and other subject fields have been covered by the Industrial Arts Index, begun in 1913; the Agricultural Index (1916); the Art Index (1929); the Education Index (1929); Library Literature (1936); and the Bibliographic Index (1938). In recent years, the Industrial Arts Index has been divided into the Applied Science and Technology Index and the Business Periodicals Index, while the International Index came to concentrate more on two specific fields and took the name Social Sciences and Humanities Index in 1965. Meanwhile the Agricultural Index has broadened its field somewhat and become the Biological and Agricultural Index.

Current Biography, a collection of sketches of currently important people, was begun in 1940, and this was supplemented in 1946 by the Biography Index, which lists biographical material appearing in some 1500 periodicals, plus numerous collected biographies and pamphlets. Other important Wilson library aids include the Essay and General Literature Index, started in 1931, which indexes books of essays and collected articles in all fields; the Fiction Catalog (1908); the Abridged Reader's Guide (1935); the Educational Film Guide (1936); the Catalog of Reprints in Series (1940); and the Filmstrip Guide (1938). The Union List of Serials, begun

in 1927, contains about 120,000 serial titles and indicates the holdings in these titles for some 650 large libraries. This was compiled with the aid of an American Library Association committee,
and was revised in a 1943 edition with later supplements. The
Vertical File Service, begun in 1932, is an annotated subject index
and buying guide to pamphlets.

Aside from its indexes, the H.W. Wilson Company provides
other reference aids, including the Reference Shelf, and the University Debaters Annual. The former is a series of volumes of collected essays and articles on topics of current interest, while the
latter is a similar work but one devoted to current national debate
topics. In 1938, Wilson added to its already impressive list of library services the production of printed library catalog cards.
These cards, available currently for several thousand of the more
popular adult and children's books, are simpler in form than the Library of Congress cards and less expensive. They are available
either with or without printed call numbers and subject headings.
The Wilson cards meet the need of the small public and school libraries for catalog cards, and provide what amounts to a centralized, subscription cataloging service. In addition, Wilson has published over the years several hundred books and pamphlets on various phases of library service, along with many study guides and
bibliographies. By no means the least important of their publications is the Wilson Library Bulletin, a monthly periodical devoted
to the interest and needs of school and public librarians.

Another important firm in the library publishing field is the
R.R. Bowker Company of New York, which since 1870 has issued
the Publishers' Weekly, a current index to books and pamphlets appearing in the United States. This is a most complete record of
current and forthcoming books, and as such is a standard tool both
for booksellers and librarians. The Bowker Company also has published the Library Journal since early in that periodical's history,
and has made of it one of the most generally useful of all library
periodicals. Regular features of the Library Journal include selected and annotated lists of new books, news about libraries and
librarians, and articles of practical interest to the library profes-

sion. Since 1954 Bowker has also published the School Library Journal, appearing monthly from September to June. Other Bowker publications include the American Library Directory, which is a guide
to the location, personnel and resources of libraries, large and
small, all over the United States and Canada; and Ulrich's Periodicals Directory, which lists periodicals of all types and all countries.
Many important books for the library and book-trade professions
have appeared under the Bowker imprint.

The American Library Association is also a major publisher
of library tools. These include the Booklist and Subscription Books
Bulletin, long separate publications but now joined together; and the
A. L. A. Bulletin, which is the professional journal of the association. The Booklist is a selected and annotated list of current books
suitable for purchase by the average library, while the Subscription
Books Bulletin is a critical guide to new reference works, particularly those sold on a subscription basis. The Bulletin provides
news of the association's activities, publishes articles of general library interest, and serves as a sounding board for discussion of
current library problems. Since 1904, A. L. A. has published a
Guide to Reference Books, first edited by Alice B. Kroeger, later
by Isadore G. Mudge, and now by Constance M. Winchell. Through
several editions this has been a standard textbook for students in
reference classes, and a handy guide for all librarians. A list of
Subject Headings for the Use in Dictionary Catalogs was issued in
1893, with later editions to 1911. When the Library of Congress began publishing its own greatly expanded list of subject headings, the
A. L. A. allowed its list to go out of print. Fortunately, the Wilson
Company filled in the gap in 1923 with the publication of Minnie E.
Sears' List of Subject Headings for Small Libraries. In addition to
the publications of A. L. A., which include many books on all phases
of librarianship, the various divisions of the national library organization also have publications of their own. For example, the Association of College and Reference Librarians publishes a quarterly,
College and Research Libraries. Other divisional publications include the Association of Hospital and Institution Libraries Quarterly,
the Journal of Education for Librarianship, Library Resources and

Technical Services, R. Q. (Reference Services Division); School
Libraries, and Top of the News. In addition, most of the state
and regional library associations have their own publications, as
do also the national special library groups.

Several other important periodical and bibliographical aids
for the librarian have been, and are, published by other companies.
The Library Bureau from 1896 to 1921 published a general library
periodical entitled Public Libraries (later simply Libraries), which
was ably edited by Mary Eileen Ahern. The University of Chicago
Press has published a number of important books in the library
field, especially the symposiums of its various annual library institutes, and has issued the Library Quarterly since 1930. The F. W.
Faxon Company of Boston publishes the Bulletin of Bibliography,
and has also published such indexes as the Dramatic Index and the
Annual Magazine Subject Index. In 1952 another most useful library
periodical was started by the University of Illinois Press, with the
title Library Trends. The Scarecrow Press of New York, the Shoe-
string Press of Hamden, Connecticut, and Gale Research Company
of Detroit, all publish indexes, bibliographies and general works of
particular interest to libraries and librarians. In addition to the
American library publications, there are a number of excellent
works published in England by the Library Association and others,
so that the library profession in the English-speaking world is fairly well supplied with professional literature. Most of the European
countries are also well supplied with indexes, bibliographies and library literature in general, but elsewhere around the world such is
not usually the case. To meet the need for library tools in Asia,
Africa and Latin America particularly, UNESCO is aiding in the developing and translating of such works in all the major languages.

As far as specialized education is concerned, the field of library service also qualifies as a profession. Before the twentieth
century the librarian was for the most part a scholar, more concerned with learning than with the techniques of librarianship. His
interest was in the contents of books, their subject matter, and he
worked with books because he loved and needed them. His interest
in the use of books by others was secondary to his own use of

books or to his desire to preserve them for future use.   Hence,
even in the nineteenth century the librarian was often considered to
be a book keeper, a protector of the storehouse of knowledge, rather than an educator, eager to have books used and read.   Good librarians of that century became such because they trained themselves or were fortunate enough to have worked under other great
librarians.   Library processes and methods varied from institution
to institution and, usually, each one developed its own method of arranging books and of circulating them.   Librarianship was an occupation but it was hardly a profession in the nineteenth century.

Library education in England in the nineteenth century took
the form of apprenticeships and the prospective librarian simply
learned his trade by working in a library.   This method of library
training was also preferred by many American libraries during the
same period and it was widely held that apprenticeship was preferable to classroom training even as late as 1900.   In Germany, on
the other hand, the education of the librarian was the same as that
of the scholar, and considerable emphasis was placed upon a wide
range of training in the liberal arts, with knowledge of languages,
bibliography of all subjects, rare books and even paleography.   In
the United States, library education, when it did develop, generally
took the form of a combination of these two plans, with training
both in the liberal arts and in the practical techniques of library
operation.

Some American colleges had offered courses in bibliography,
particularly historical bibliography, in the years immediately after
the Civil War.   The U. S. Bureau of Education's monumental report
on Public Libraries in the United States in 1876 had some interesting notes on the subject of library training:

> It is clear that the librarian must soon be called upon
> to assume a distinct position as something more than a
> mere custodian of books, and the scientific scope and
> value of his office be recognized and estimated in a be-
> coming manner...   To meet the demands that will be
> made on him he should be granted opportunities for in-
> struction in all the departments of library science.

This instruction in library science was slow in coming,
however.   A few universities did begin to offer courses in "refer-

ence and bibliography" or "books and reading," but it was not until 1887 that the first school of librarianship was opened. This was Melvil Dewey's library school at Columbia University which survived at the institution for two years in the face of strong opposition. In 1889 Dewey moved to Albany where he became Librarian of the New York State Library, and he carried his library school with him. He gradually built up a staff of teachers and a student body of thirty to fifty each year. His curriculum was a practical one, in line with the general educational tendency toward technical training that was then in vogue. He taught the actual processes of selecting, acquiring, processing, arranging and circulating library books. His courses included phases of library work now considered clerical rather than professional, such as typewriting, library handwriting, book lettering and book repairing.

In the 1890's, three "institutes" began offering courses in library science. These were Pratt in Brooklyn, Drexel in Philadelphia, and Armour in Chicago. They were joined in the next decade by Carnegie at Pittsburgh, Syracuse University, Western Reserve at Cleveland, University of Wisconsin, and University of Illinois (transferred from Armour). About the same time several public libraries began formal training classes for librarians, including those at New York, Atlanta, St. Louis and Los Angeles. Still another type of library training could be obtained at summer schools or "institutes" held at several colleges and universities before 1920. Wherever it was taught, library training in the early years of the twentieth century emphasized the practical aspects of librarianship, and the highest prerequisite for library courses was usually the junior year of college.

In 1913, the U. S. Bureau of Education reported rather fully on the status of library training in the nation and noted the small number of colleges offering library science courses. Of some 900 colleges and universities queried, only about a dozen offered full courses in the field, with a few more offering summer library institutes or courses designed especially for teacher-librarians. About one college in ten offered some type of training in the use of books and libraries. There was considerable variance in the length and

content of the courses given and in the credit or degrees granted
for library training.   Courses ranged anywhere from a few months
to two years in length and most classwork continued to emphasize
the practical side of library work.

Prior to 1920, library training continued to present a most
confused picture.   There was no general agreement on what should
be taught in library science courses or at what stage in one's formal education they should be given.   Library training was being offered variously in public libraries, technical institutes, liberal arts
colleges, teachers colleges, and universities, and no one was sure
as to who was doing the best job.   Some thought that any educated
person could learn the necessary routines to run a library in short
order, while others considered sound training in the techniques of
operating a library more important than knowledge of the contents
of books.   This confusion tended to work against the professional
standing of the graduates of the various schools, so there soon
arose a demand for standardization of library schools and their curricula.   In 1915, ten library schools joined together to form the
Association of American Library Schools, with the purpose of standardizing entrance requirements and reforming curricula.   This still
did not solve the problems, however, and in 1919, Carnegie Corporation aid was obtained for a thorough study of the library training
field.   Charles C. Williamson, then on the New York Public Library
staff, had been an outspoken critic of current library training methods, and was selected to do the necessary research for the Carnegie study.

Williamson's report was completed and published in 1923, and
in many respects it marks a turning point in the modern era of library training.   Williamson surveyed the library school curricula,
entrance requirements, teaching staffs, methods of instruction, and
textbooks.   He found confusion between professional and clerical
training and recommended that library schools teach professional
courses only, while training classes conducted by libraries could be
used for teaching library techniques to clerical workers.   He recommended more standardization in the library school curricula, particularly in the first year.   He found only two library schools that

required a college degree for admission, and he recommended that
all should have this requirement. Concerning the teaching staffs in
the library schools, Williamson noted that only 52 per cent were
college graduates themselves, only seven per cent of them had ever
had any training in teaching and nearly a third had had little or no
practical experience in library work. He particularly noted the lack
of adequate textbooks and the reliance on the lecture method of teaching. He recommended better qualified teachers, more class discussion, more and better supervised field work, and improved text-
books. The need for more library schools and more students was
pointed out, as well as the need for certification of professionally
trained librarians. Finally, the need for postgraduate library
courses in specialized and advanced fields was recognized and considerable emphasis on cultural rather than technical courses was encouraged. On the whole, Williamson's findings concerning library
training were not flattering to the profession but his recommendations were sound and they were adopted gradually over the next decade in considerable degree.

Along with the funds for Williamson's study, the Carnegie
Corporation provided support, over a ten year period, for the promotion and extension of library training. A Board of Education for
Librarianship was established by the American Library Association
in 1924 and this group proceeded to plan for the accreditation of library schools. It also aided and encouraged the development of new
library schools. In 1926, the New York State Library School at Albany was returned to Columbia University where it became the
School of Library Service. Dr. Williamson became its head and was
able to carry out some of his own recommendations. The Carnegie
Corporation made available funds for the establishment of two Southern library schools, one at Hampton Institute, Virginia, for Negroes,
and one at the University of North Carolina. It also aided in the
establishment of the graduate school of library science at the University of Chicago. By 1930, graduate library courses, that is
courses beyond the first year, were offered at Michigan, Illinois,
California, Columbia and Chicago, and Carnegie fellowships were
available for the best qualified students applying for admissions at

any of those schools. With the beginning of advanced library study leading to M. A. and Ph. D. degrees in library science, the training of librarians entered a new phase.

In 1926, there were only 14 library schools accredited by the Board of Education for Librarianship, but this figure had reached 30 by 1942. These accredited schools were divided into three classes. Type I schools required college graduation for admission and/or gave advanced library courses beyond the first year. Type II schools had the same entrance requirements, but gave only one year of library training. Type III schools admitted college undergraduates, usually at the senior year and gave only one year of library courses. In addition to these, however, there were a number of other colleges, particularly teacher training institutions, that offered courses in library science, usually for the training of school librarians.

Along with the idea of accreditation for library schools came the plea for certification of librarians, although this was somewhat slower in gaining general approval. By 1938, 21 states and the District of Columbia were legally requiring certification for school librarians, while a few states were beginning to certify public and county librarians or librarians in state owned colleges and universities. By 1952, school librarians in 31 states were required to hold certificates, while 14 states called for legal certification of public librarians. Standards for libraries, relating holdings, staff, buildings and hours to population or clientele served, were also slow in being adopted, but progress was made. In 1933 the American Library Association adopted standards for public libraries and in 1937 the Carnegie Corporation Advisory Group drew up recommended standards for junior college libraries. State departments of education and regional associations of colleges and secondary schools have set up standards for high school libraries and the regional associations have also drawn up standards for college libraries. Various national accrediting groups also have requirements for library holdings and service in their respective fields. The American Library Association and its various divisions have continued to provide standards for all types of libraries, as for example the Standards for

School Library Programs, published in 1960. Much of the progress
made by American libraries in the last few decades can be attributed to this development in certification and accreditation.

The Second World War brought on an increased demand for
trained librarians, and to meet this demand more non-accredited library schools were begun, and various innovations were introduced
into the curricula of the established schools. This led to a period
of confusion in the years after 1945, and to several attempts to
straighten out this confusion. As early as 1926, most of the library schools had agreed to offer only an A. B. or B. S. degree in
library science for the first year of graduate work and to require
two years for the M. A. or M. S. in L. S. After the war, some
schools began to offer the masters degree for the first year of
graduate library courses in order to make the library degree equal
to the fifth year M. A. available in most other fields. This trend
gradually met general acceptance and by 1952 the majority of the
accredited schools were also giving the fifth year M. A.

In 1946, Joseph L. Wheeler, retired librarian of the Enoch
Pratt Free Library in Baltimore, surveyed the field of library education again at the expense of the Carnegie Corporation, and reported on his findings. In his volume, Progress and Problems in
Education for Librarianship, Wheeler noted that there was still much
criticism of library schools for teaching too much detail, for being
too elementary, too theoretical, and too slow in meeting the changing demands of the profession. He found also that not all these
criticisms were justified and that the library schools were making
headway in meeting those that were. However, he still felt that the
library education picture was confused and librarians themselves
were undecided as to what type of training they wanted for their new
assistants. Wheeler's recommendations included more strength and
life for the Board of Education for Librarianship and more standardization in methods, requirements and curricula for the schools. If
necessary, fewer and better library schools would be preferable to
more with lower standards. Yet he still called for a strong program for recruiting potential librarians and better salaries and working conditions to make the library field more attractive to young

people. And strong throughout all his recommendations was the
basic thought that, above all, librarians should know and love books.

Since the old standards of accreditation for library schools
were outmoded by 1950, the Board of Education for Librarianship
set up new standards in 1951 and began a program of school visita-
tion designed to set up a new accredited list. Thirty-three library
schools had been accredited under the new standards by 1964, along
with three schools in Canada. The new accreditation standards took
into consideration the organization and administration of the schools,
their faculty and staffs, their physical facilities and particularly
their curricula. In 1956, the Board of Education for Librarianship
was replaced by the A. L. A. Committee of Accreditation, and a poli-
cy of continuous re-appraisal of the library education field was
adopted. In at least 74 other colleges and universities, undergraduate majors in library science were available by 1964 and some of
these schools also offered graduate courses.

Other developments in library training in recent years have
been brought on by the changing demands in the library field. To
meet the demands for librarians who are specialists in subject
fields two approaches have been tried. Specialists have been re-
cruited to take library degrees and librarians have been encouraged
to return to graduate schools for further work in subject fields. In
the library schools themselves courses in subject bibliography have
been strengthened. The need for other special talents in library
services, such as public relations, adult education, and even library
architecture are being reflected in the course work offered in library schools. To reach librarians already in service, summer
workshops, special institutes and conferences are being held at
many institutions. Aid in the form of scholarships and expenses for
such institutes has been available in many cases from the Federal
government. The 1965 Higher Education Act, in particular, provides funds for aiding students to obtain library training. Many university libraries are offering "work while you learn" programs for
part-time students in library schools. The concept of the librarian
as both a scholar and a practical business man is being widely accepted, and the trend toward librarians who are "educated" as well

"trained" is strongly in evidence.

The third attribute of the profession, that of an active and
representative professional association, is very much in evidence in
the field of librarianship. In fact, the development of librarians'
professional association has been closely associated with the growth
of librarianship since the mid-nineteenth century. In the United
States, the major library organization has been, since 1876, the
American Library Association. From its hundred or so members
at the beginning, it has grown steadily, reaching about 2,000 members by 1920, and over 30,000 by 1965. Very early in its history
the organization saw the need of specialized sub-divisions, with a
College and Reference Library Section, and a Trustees' Section before 1890. Later on, sections for Catalogers and Classifiers, Public Librarians, Junior College Librarians, Children's Librarians
and other special groups were added. Committees and round-tables
were formed for special purposes, and for smaller segments of the
library profession. Outside of A. L. A., but cooperating with it in
many ways are such groups as the Music Library Association, the
Theatre Library Association, the Special Libraries Association, the
Catholic Library Association, the Medical Library Association, and
other special groups. In addition, the A. L. A. and its members often cooperate with such related groups as the National Education Association, the Adult Education Association, the American Documentation Institute, and the Bibliographical Society of America. American librarians are also active in international library organizations,
such as the International Federation for Documentation, the International Association of Music Libraries, and the International Federation of Library Associations.

Besides its component divisions, the American Library Association also ties together a nationwide system of state, regional and
local associations. Each of the states has a library association,
which usually meets annually or biennially and many of them have
their own publications. Moreover, several parts of the United
States have active regional library organizations, such as the South-
western Library Association and the Pacific Northwest Library Association. In many of the larger cities and metropolitan areas there

are local library organizations, sometimes largely social, but usually professionally active.

The organization of the American Library Association has been changed several times in its history, but its basic objectives have remained the same. The first goal of promoting library service for all Americans has still not been completely achieved, but great progress has been made so that today nearly 90 per cent of the people of the United States are in reach of library service. Other objectives of raising library standards, improving library methods, increasing the number of trained librarians, assuring the professional status of librarianship, and providing helpful professional literature and library tools for working librarians, have all been largely achieved, although most need continued attention. In recent years the A. L. A. , through its Washington office, has taken a prominent role in promoting federal legislation of benefit to libraries and education in general. The Library Services Act of 1956 and more recent legislation of value to libraries are at least partially the result of this activity. The promotion of international cooperation in library services and of international good will and understanding through books and libraries is another outstanding objective of the Association.

Professionally, the American librarian has come far since 1876. He has achieved professional recognition and a respected place in the cultural and educational structure of the country. There are still many problems concerning the recruitment and education of librarians and concerning their duties, salaries and welfare after they are professionally trained, but these problems are gradually being solved. Today, the leaders of the profession recognize that both quantity and quality are needed among potential librarians, and that better librarians as well as more librarians are needed to serve a nation of intelligent readers.

Bibliography

Books

American Library Association: College and university library accreditation standards. Chicago, 1957. 48 p.

American Library Association: In retrospect, a history of the Division of Cataloging and Classification. Chicago, 1950. 28 p.

American Library Association: The preparation of teacher-librarians. Chicago, 1937. 48 p.

Anders, Mary Edna: The Southeastern Library Association, 1920-1950. Atlanta, 1956. 58 p.

Anderson, F. : The Carnegie Corporation library program, 1911-1961. New York, 1963. 115 p.

Asheim, Lester: The core of education for librarianship. Chicago, 1954. 68 p.

Berelson, Bernard, ed. : Education for librarianship. Chicago, 1949. 307 p.

Beust, Nora E. : Professional library education. Washington, 1937. 95 p.

Bryan, Alice I. : The public librarian. New York, 1952. 474 p.

Butler, Pierce: Introduction to library science. Chicago, 1933. 118 p.

Danton, J. Periam: Education for librarianship. New York, 1949. 97 p.

David, Lily M. : Economic status of library personnel. Chicago, 1950. 117 p.

Dewey, Melvil: Simplified library school rules. New York, 1904. 96 p.

Evans, Henry R. : Library instruction in universities, colleges and normal schools. Washington, 1914. 38 p.

Fleming, Edward M. : R.R. Bowker, militant liberal. Norman, Okla. , 1952. 395 p.

Friedel, J. H. : Training for librarianship. Philadelphia, 1921. 224 p.

Joint Committee of the American Association of Teachers Colleges and the American Library Association: How shall we educate teachers and librarians for library service in the school? New York, 1936. 74 p.

LaMontagne, Leo F. : American library classification. Hamden, Conn. , 1961. 433 p.

Lawler, John: The H.W. Wilson Company; half a century of bib-
    liographical publishing. Minneapolis, 1950. 207 p.

Leigh, Robert D. : Major problems in the education of librarians.
    New York, 1954. 116 p.

Manley, Marian C. : The special library profession and what it of-
    fers. New York, 1938. 132 p.

Metcalf, Keyes D. : The program of instruction in library schools.
    Urbana, Ill. , 1943. 49 p.

Munn, Ralph: Conditions and trends in education for librarianship.
    New York, 1936. 49 p.

Munthe, Wilhelm: American librarianship from a European angle.
    Chicago, 1939. 191 p.

Pettee, Julia: Subject headings; the history and theory of the alpha-
    betical subject approach to books. New York, 1947. 191 p.

Plummer, Mary W. : Training for librarianship. Chicago, 1923.
    32 p.

Rantz, James: The printed book catalogue in American libraries,
    1723-1907. Chicago, 1963. 144 p.

Reece, Ernest J. : Programs for library schools. New York,
    1943. 64 p.

Reece, Ernest J. : The task and training of librarians. New York,
    1949. 91 p.

Rider, Fremont: Melvil Dewey. Chicago, 1944. 151 p.

Sawyer, Harriet P. , ed. : The library as a vocation. New York,
    1933. 484 p.

Swanson, Don R. , ed. : The intellectual foundations of library edu-
    cation. Chicago, 1965. 98 p.

Trautman, Ray: A history of the School of Library Service, Colum-
    bia University. New York, 1954. 85 p.

Utley, George B. : 50 years of the American Library Association.
    Chicago, 1926. 29 p.

Vann, Sarah K. : Training for librarianship before 1923. Chicago,
    1961. 242 p.

Wheeler, Joseph L. : Progress and problems in education for li-
    brarianship. New York, 1946. 97 p.

White, Carl M. : The origins of the American library school.
New York, 1961. 211 p.

Wilson, H.W. : The bookman's reading and tools. New York,
1932. 53 p.

Williamson, Charles C. : Training for library service, a report
prepared for the Carnegie Corporation. New York, 1923.
165 p.

Periodical Articles

Gitler, Robert L. : "Accrediting and education for librarianship,
developments of 1951-57," A. L. A. Bulletin, LII (1958),
273-274.

Graham, C. R. : "1876-1931, seventy-five years later," Library
Journal, LXXVI, (1951), 459.

Howe, Harriet E. : "Two decades in education for librarianship,"
Library Quarterly, XII, (1942), 557-570.

Keppel, F. P. : "The Carnegie Corporation and the graduate library
school," Library Quarterly, I, (1931), 22-25.

Lancour, Harold, and Harrison, J. C. : "Education for librarianship
abroad in selected countries," Library Trends, XII, (Oct.,
1963), 121-355.

Lancour, Harold: "The librarian's search for status," Library
Quarterly, XXXI, (1961), 369-381.

Mitchell, Sydney B. : "The pioneer library school in middle age,"
Library Quarterly, XX, (1950), 272-288.

"Philadelphia, 1876-1951," Library Journal, LXXVI, (1951), 1984-
1986.

Putnam, Herbert: "Education for library work," Independent, LII,
(Nov. 22, 1900), 2773-2776.

Scott, Edith: "IFLA and FID - history and programs," Library
Quarterly, XXXII, (1962), 1-18.

Walbridge, E. F. : "Milestones of library history," Library Journal,
LXXVI, (Mar. 15, 1951), 460-463.

Wilson, L. R. : "The American library school today," Library Quarterly, VII, (1937), 211-245.

Winger, Howard W. : "Aspects of librarianship: a trace work of
history," Library Quarterly, XXXI, (1961), 321-335.

XVI

Current Trends in Books and Libraries

The world of books and libraries currently finds itself in an odd position. With millions of people still not receiving the minimum in library service, the profession as a whole must prepare for new developments that seem far removed from that same minimum. Without enough books or libraries or librarians of the best mid-twentieth century type, we must concern ourselves with computers and automation, with electronic means of storing and retrieving information and with new developments in science and education that both challenge and dismay us. The library world is caught between two seemingly irresistible forces - the population explosion and the information explosion. On the one hand there are more people than we can serve with standard types of library service and on the other there is more information in recorded form than we can make available to the ones who must have it. There are more books, pamphlets, periodicals and papers than ever before - and more people to read them, and it would appear that the librarian would have to be more than human to bring the two together. Wherein lies the solution? Do we have to become information scientists instead of librarians? Do we have to put the books on tape and the tape into push-button machines? Or is there a place for both the book and the electronic brain, the librarian and the information scientist? Perhaps an analysis of the problems facing the library world today might be in order, even if the solutions are not necessarily forthcoming.

To begin with, not only are the numbers of people increasing, but the percentage of people using libraries is rapidly increasing. No longer can the library consider an educated ten per cent as its major clientele; it must serve all ages and all types of readers. From the kindergarten to the post-Ph.D., and from the casual Sunday reader to the astronaut, the library of today must serve the

total population. School children are increasing in numbers, and
more of them are reaching higher levels of formal education than
ever before. New methods and approaches to teaching require new
library services from the primary grades upward. Fifth graders
are doing "research" in a manner that once would have pleased high
school teachers and better high school students are writing papers
that once would have been accepted in college. Micro-materials
have joined the audio-visual aids in the high school library and the
library itself has undergone a transformation and emerged as the
"instructional materials center." The centralized library, once considered the utmost in school library service, now finds itself breaking down into divisional materials centers, with one each for the
sciences, the social sciences, the arts and the humanities. The
school library today finds itself in a position where ideals and standards, proven methods and plans, are available for the best of educational library service, but where public support, financial backing,
and qualified staff are still in short supply. There is, indeed, a
great and increasing need for educated, trained and dedicated school
library personnel.

　　　The public library is in much the same position. More
people are using public library resources, and their demands are
expanding in both volume and range. No longer will the latest nov-
els, a few children's books, and a "handyman's shelf" suffice to
meet the public's needs. Instead, the public library today must consider the ages, educational level, occupations and professions of its
readers, as well as meeting the cultural, business and technical demands of the community and its economy. The needs of the teen-
ager and the golden-ager, the drop-out and the genius must all be
met. The unemployed, the unskilled and the poorly educated require
attention as much as the successful and highly trained. Such a wide
range of needs strains public library staffs, budgets and buildings
with the volume and variety of the materials required and the services to be rendered. Young people's rooms and business branches,
bookmobiles and film collections are but a few of the many means
by which some of these demands are met. Public libraries of
greater than average size are finding that they not only need librari-

ans and clerical workers, but personnel managers, public relations
experts and business managers, as well as specialists in audio-visual aids, business services, work with the underprivileged, and
group relations.   Public libraries are finding more and more that
they are subdividing into multiple special service units, even though
many of them may be in the same building.   On the one hand they
are merging into the educational field through their increased work
with school and college students and in adult education, while on the
other hand they are moving into the special library field in many of
their activities.   At the same time, however, the public library is
gaining in professional stature and is taking its rightful place as the
educational and cultural institution it should be.   No longer can it be
considered the poor relation of the college and research libraries;
it is their equal if not their superior in general social significance.

The public library is, of course, faced with many of the
same problems as school libraries.   There are still the problems
of space, staff and funds, but many more as well.   How far should
the public library go in meeting the needs of school and college students?   Where does the responsibility of the academic library end
and that of the public library begin?   If public libraries offer special services for students and workers, for women's clubs and business men, why not for other professional, occupational or social
groups?   If professional collections are provided for some groups,
why not for others?   With the proliferation of professional and technical literature, not even the largest libraries can now provide all
the services required for all occupational groups.   Then, there is
the question of purely recreational reading.   How far should the public library go in meeting the public demand for multiple copies of
the latest "best-seller?"   Can it rely on the paper-back and the rental collection to fill this need or does it still owe a duty to the public in the field of reading for entertainment?   Different libraries
and different librarians have opposing viewpoints on this question
and practice varies considerably among libraries.   Then there is
the question of censorship.   Both public and school libraries are
meeting with the problem of self-appointed censors, who attempt to
say what should and what should not be on library shelves.   Public

libraries are particularly vulnerable to such attacks since their
services are open to all and since they have a duty to serve the very
people who attempt to censor their holdings.   Moreover, the librarian himself comes under the charge of censorship at times, since he
must, willingly or unwillingly, select some books and reject others
in the process of acquiring his library's bookstock.   The question of
censorship, entering as it does into the fields of morals and social
morés, is a difficult one at best and is one in which all forms of
communication are concerned.   Not only are court decisions and
permissive legislation necessary but more and broader education is
needed before a social climate in which censorship will not be a
problem can be achieved.

For the libraries in institutions of higher education, the population explosion means more students, more colleges and universities and more libraries; but it is the explosion of information that
brings on the greatest problems.   From the world's authors and
scientists the amount of literature and recorded research that appears each year is amazing, even to the largest libraries.   It is
virtually impossible for any library to keep up with all the literature appearing in even a few chosen fields.   Not only is it difficult
to procure the recorded information in the first place, because of
its volume, varied sources and forms, but the organization of this
material, the classifying and cataloging, the coding and indexing, is
a task that staggers the imagination.   Research libraries are looking in many directions for solutions.   One answer lies in cooperation in the field of acquisition, along the lines of the Farmington
Plan.   According to this arrangement, major research libraries di-
vide their acquisitions in certain fields so that all material appearing anywhere in the world is acquired by one or more of the institutions cooperating.   Along with this cooperative acquisition will go
services in photocopying and interlibrary loans, teletype and television, to make these materials available to researchers in any of the
cooperating units.   The greater use of micro-photography, and even
micro-micro-photography, will aid not only in acquisition and storage problems but also in information retrieval, through rapid scan-
ning, reading and copying devices.   The greater use of mechanical

and electronic aids will assist in all phases of library operations
from acquisition through arrangement and storage of information to
its ultimate retrieval in readable form.   Experiments have already
been made in a number of ways in which automation and electronics
can be used in library processes.

Even if there are possible solutions, by use of electronics, to
the problems of excessive amounts of information, what can be done
to serve the increased numbers of students who are not yet scientists or researchers?   Shall we install vending machines for required reading materials?   Program our computers to answer the
standard reference questions?   Or to print out recommended reading lists on any subject on demand?   Again the answer lies in value
versus costs.   Any of these and many other similar services could
be provided if it were felt that they were worth the cost.   But for
the ordinary needs of the multiplicity of students, we come back to
our same old problems - not enough trained librarians, not enough
library seating space, not enough of the right books at the right
time.   The magic of electronics can provide many answers, but not
all.   There is still a need for the librarian to bring the student and
the book together.

More than any others, the special library is feeling the force
of change, but fortunately it is in a somewhat better position to re-
spond.   In many respects, the special library has advantages over
the public or educational institution.   It has a restricted "public" to
serve; it usually has a limited type or subject field of information
to acquire and service; and it often has the necessary funds to promote rapid development and change.   Indeed, it has been the special libraries who have generally led the way in experimenting with
new library methods and devices.   From punched cards to punched
tape, these libraries have usually been the first to make use of   innovations, often while they were still in the experimental stage.
Two of the nation's greatest special libraries, the National Agricultural Library and the National Library of Medicine, have particularly taken a lead in the development of new methods of controlling
scientific bibliography and indexing.   Government libraries with specialized functions, which includes almost all of them, are finding

that their services are more in demand as the activities of their agencies become more complex. They serve a limited clientele, but much of their service must be of a highly technical nature. More coordination and planning of government library services is needed in order to insure the most efficient use of their many materials and services. Specialized libraries belonging to business and industrial firms have proven their value in purely economic terms and their numbers and importance have grown significantly, particularly since World War II. Their future seems assured, although their forms may undergo more change than those in any other type of library.

Somewhat different is the scene in the many special libraries associated with professional societies and institutions of higher learning. Here, in most cases, budgets are not keeping up with demands for service and with materials available for purchase. Many society and departmental libraries, once considered fairly adequate, are lagging behind as the flood of research materials in their fields outgrows their capacity to acquire and digest. Many of them are finding solutions in amalgamation, in joining larger collections, or in restricting their services.

In all fields of special library service, personnel is a major problem. Shall a special librarian be a subject specialist, with incidental library training? Or a trained librarian with incidental subject knowledge? Even with all available personnel of both types, there is still a shortage of special librarians. Moreover, the more complicated the processes of storing and retrieving specialized information becomes, the more difficult it is to secure the necessary staff members. Whether "special librarian" or "information scientist," there is plenty of room for the person who wants to be able to bring the specialist and his information together.

Since 1960, the American public has been introduced to the "library of the future" in two World's Fairs, at Seattle and New York. "Library 21" at Seattle provided the visitors with a pictorial history of communication from cave painting to computer, and then provided the latter with a staff to show how it could be used in dispensing information. There was also a conventional "ready refer-

ence center," an adult browsing area, and the Children's World, with
the latter being by far the most popular with the general public. At
New York, "Library/USA," the library exhibit, was a combination
of books, librarians and machines, demonstrating particularly the
potential role of the computer and other data processing equipment
in the modern library. Here, as in Seattle, one of the most successful parts of the library display was an exhibit of children's literature in a library atmosphere. Possibly the great success of the
two exhibitions was not so much the demonstration of the "library of
the future," as the impression made on the millions of visitors concerning the significance of libraries today.

Solutions to the many problems facing the library world in
the latter half of the twentieth century are not as simple as one might
hope them to be. It is easy to say that more librarians, larger
budgets, bigger buildings, and electronic wizardry will solve all our
problems. But although all these will help, they do not present all
the answers. Cooperation, planned coordination of library facilities,
constant search for new concepts of service as well as new machinery,
all must enter into the ultimate solution. The library of the twenty-
first century will undoubtedly be far different from that of today -
but so is the library of today far removed from that of the nineteenth century. Changes will come, particularly technological
changes, but the chances are that many of our present media of communication will still be around in only slightly changed forms. It
was predicted in the early nineteenth century that just as printing
had replaced the manuscript, so periodicals and newspapers would
make the book obsolete. Yet the book is still with us, in only
slightly changed format, and in greater numbers than ever before.

But what of other technological advances? The year 1965 has
found us familiar with the concept, if not the actual practice, of
computer controlled acquisition and circulation systems, with computer compiled and printed book catalogs, serials lists, and acquisition lists, and with machine location of information from reels of
tape or microfilm. The rapid advances in photocopying in all its
forms brings almost instant reproduction in normal reading size of
all types of graphically recorded information. Machine translation

of foreign languages and reproduction of reading materials in micro-
micro form seem to be just around the corner.   Hence, it does not
take much imagination to assume such relatively imminent developments as a "dial-a-book" service, where one could sit at home, dial
a coded number, and have his book flashed on a television screen,
rather than having to go to a library for it.   Perhaps the "book"
might be "published" in film or electronic form, rather than in paper
and print, but the chances are that it will still be in the same old
alphabet, or a reasonable facsimile thereof.   Mechanical, photographic, electronic - the future of these contributions to the field
of communications and information control may be easily envisioned
from their present status, but what of even more fantastic developments of the future?

A few far-seeing scientists are already anticipating such developments as the transferral of sensory perception directly to the
human brain, bypassing both eyes and ears.   The therapeutic value
of this for the physically handicapped or mentally disturbed, might
be remarkable, but for the normal human being, its possibilities
are frightening, to say the least.   Extending this line of reasoning,
one could foresee direct thought transferral from one person to another, thought control by one person of another, direct implanting of
knowledge in the human brain by electrical or chemical means, and
memory erasure by similar means - all equally frightening possibilities.   Mass indoctrination and complete control of society in a
manner never achieved by politics or force, could be easily expected if such a process were devised.   Suffice it to say that extra-
sensory means of communication are still in the realms of the im-
probable.   In other respects, however, man's potentialities in the
field of human communication are almost unlimited.   What he
chooses to do in the way of developing those potentialities is the
only question.

Whatever forms the recorded knowledge of the future may
take, there will always be the problem of preserving it, storing it,
organizing it, and making it available for future use.   Whether they
call themselves librarians, information scientists, or by some future term, the "keepers of the books" will still be needed, and

needed in greater numbers than ever before. The future of libraries and librarianship may not be crystal clear, but it will be exciting, and the role of the librarian in the future of human communication will be more vital than ever before.

Bibliography

American Library Association: National inventory of library needs. Chicago, 1965. 72 p.

Asheim, Lester, ed.: The future of the book. Chicago, 1955. 105 p.

Asheim, Lester, ed.: Persistent issues in American librarianship. Chicago, 1961. 114 p.

Becker, J., and Hayes, R. M.: Information storage and retrieval: tools, elements, theories. New York, 1963. 448 p.

Bolt, Cerenek and Newman, Inc.: Toward the library of the twenty-first century. Cambridge, Mass., 1964. 41 p.

Clapp, Verner: The future of the research library. Urbana, Ill., 1964. 124 p.

Coplan, Kate, and Castagna, Edwin, eds.: The library reaches out. Dobbs Ferry, N.Y., 1964. 430 p.

Gaver, Mary V.: Patterns of development in elementary school libraries today. Chicago, 1963. 27 p.

Humphrey, John A., ed.: Library cooperation: the Brown University study of university-school-community library coordination in the state of Rhode Island. Providence, 1963. 213 p.

International Federation of Library Associations: Libraries in the world: a long-term programme for the I. F. L. A. The Hague, 1963. 62 p.

Kenney, Brigitte L.: Cooperative centralized processing. Chicago, 1959. 98 p.

Lacy, Dan: Freedom and communications. Urbana, Ill., 1961. 93 p.

Licklider, J. C. R.: Libraries of the future. Cambridge, Mass., 1965. 219 p.

Lohrer, Alice, ed.: The school library materials center. Urbana, Ill., 1965. 109 p.

McLuhan, Marshall: Understanding media: the extensions of man.

New York, 1964. 359 p.

Mahar, M.H. , ed. : The school library as a materials center. Washington, 1964. 84 p.

Markuson, Barbara E. , ed. : Libraries and automation; proceedings of the conference on libraries and automation. . . Washington, 1964. 268 p.

National Educational Association: Mass communication and education. Washington, 1958. 137 p.

Perry, J.W. , and Kent, Allen: Documentation and information retrieval: an introduction to basic principles and cost analysis. Cleveland, 1957. 156 p.

Schick, Frank L. , ed. : The future of library service: demographic aspects and implications. Urbana, Ill. , 1961. 286 p. (Originally in Library Trends, July and October, 1961.)

Schultheiss, Louis A. : Advanced data processing in the university library. New York, 1962. 388 p.

Sharp, H. S. , ed. : Readings in information retrieval. New York, 1964. 759 p.

Shaw, Ralph R. , ed. : The state of the library art. New Brunswick, N. J. , 1960 -

Shera, Jesse H. : Libraries and the organization of knowledge. Hamden, Conn. , 1965. 216 p.

Taube, Mortimer, and Wooster, Harold: Information storage and retrieval: theory, systems, and devices. New York, 1958, 228 p.

Trinkner, Charles L. , ed. : Better libraries make better schools. Hamden, Conn. , 1962. 335 p.

White, Carl M. , ed. : Bases of modern librarianship: a study of library theory and practice in Britain, Canada, Denmark, Germany and the United States. New York, 1964. 126 p.

Index

Aberdeen, Scotland, University Library, 102, 208
Academy of Natural Science Library, Philadelphia, 179, 256
Acton, Lord, 102
Adams, James, 121, 129
Adams, John, 142, 162-3
Adams, John Quincy, 163
Advocates' Library, Edinburgh, Scotland, 105-6, 208
Ahern, Mary Eileen, 267
Alabama, University of, 150
Albany, New York, Institute of Science Library, 152
Albrecht V, Duke of Bavaria, 88
Alcuin, 51-2
Alexandrian Library, 33-7
Almanacs, 119, 121-2, 195
Alphabet, 16, 20-2, 287
Alsted, Johann Heinrich, 96
American Academy of Arts and Sciences, Boston, 152
American Library Association, 169, 176, 179-80, 182, 202, 238, 249, 251, 265-7, 271-2, 274-6
American Memorial Library, Berlin, 213
American Philosophical Society Library, Philadelphia, 140, 151-2, 256
American Red Cross, 238
Amherst College Library, 149
Amsterdam University Library, 93
Antiochus the Great, 34
Antwerp, Belgium, Municipal Library, 93
Appleton-Century-Crofts Company, 195-6
Archives, 30, 254. See also Manuscripts
Argentina, National Library, Buenos Aires, 205
Aristophanes of Byzantium, 35

Aristotle, 33, 49, 73, 76
Armaria, 48-9, 56
Armour Institute Library School, Chicago, 269
Ascham, Roger, 103
Association of American Library Schools, 270
Assurbanipal's Library, 32
Astor, John Jacob, 172
Astor Library, New York, 172-3, 180, 183, 236-7
Atlanta, Georgia, Carnegie Library, 269
Audio-visual aids, 250-1, 281
August, Duke of Wolfenbüttel, 89
Augustus Caesar, 37
Australia, National Library, Canberra, 223
Austria, National Library, Vienna, 89, 92
Azilian pebbles, 14

Balcarres, Earl of, 106
Barnard, John, Jr., 135
Baskerville, John, 111-3
Bates, Joshua, 172
Bavaria, State Library, Munich, 88-9, 212
Bay, Jacob, 27
Bayle, Pierre, 96
Behistun, Rock of, 19
Belgium, Royal Library, Brussels, 93
Benedict, Saint, 46
Benjamin Franklin Library, Mexico City, 203
Bentley, Richard, 103
Berkeley, George, 133
Bessarion, Cardinal, 84
Bible, 35, 49, 52, 68, 69-70, 74-5, 81, 111-2, 124
Bibliography and bibliographies, 35, 41, 92, 182, 196, 209, 224, 252-3, 261-2, 267, 284
Biblioteca Ambrosiana, Milan,

84, 216
Biblioteca Casanatense, Rome, 85, 216
Biblioteca Laurentiana, Florence, 57, 84, 216
Biblioteca Lindesiana, 106
Biblioteca Marciana, Venice, 84
Biblioteca Spenceriana, 106
Biblioteca Ulpiana, Rome, 37
Bibliothèque Mazarine, Paris, 87, 210
Bibliothèque Nationale, Paris, 70, 86, 210-11
Bibliothèque Ste. Geneviève, Paris, 88, 210
Bigelow, John P. , 172
Billings, John Shaw, 178, 237
Bingham, Caleb, 157
Bishop, William Warner, 215
Blair, James, 133
Block printing, 65-8, 70
Board of Education for Librarianship, 271-4
Bodleian Library. See Oxford University Library
Bodley, Sir Thomas, 100-1, 110
Bologna, Italy, University Library, 84-5
Book bindings, 45, 48, 53, 60, 83-4, 113-4, 193
Book clubs, 197
Book collectors, 53, 57-8, 61, 83, 89, 106, 182-3, 247. See Also Libraries, Private
Book forms, 24-6, 37, 45, 76-7, 83, 195-6, 283, 287
Book jackets, 193-4
Book of Kells, 48
Book of the Dead, 31
Book selection, 153, 263, 265-6, 283
Book trade, 32, 38-9, 55, 59-60, 82, 89, 111-2, 128, 142-4, 148, 195-6
Bookmobiles, 205, 224, 227, 239
Borromeo, Federigo, 84
Boston Athenaeum Library, 152, 170, 181, 255
Boston Public Library, 134-5, 139, 163, 169, 172, 177, 246
Boston Society of Natural History Library, 152
Bowditch, Nathaniel, 172

Bowdoin, James, 149
Bowdoin College Library, 149
Bowker, R. R. , Company, 196-7, 261, 265-6
Bracciolini, Poggio, 57
Bradford, Andrew, 126
Bradford, John, 129
Bradford, William (printer), 120-1, 127, 129
Bradford, Governor William, 138
Braud, Denis, 129
Bray, Reverend Thomas, 107-8, 135-6
Brazil, National Library, Rio de Janeiro, 204
Bristol, England, Public Library, 107
Bristowe, Reverend, 134
British Council Libraries, 203, 231
British Museum Library, London, 31-2, 48, 102-6, 111, 208-9
Broadsides, 75, 95, 105, 119, 121, 123-4, 194
Brown, John Carter, 148, 163
Brown, Nicholas, 148
Brown, Samuel, 109
Brown University Library, Providence, Rhode Island, 134, 148, 170, 175, 183
Browning Library, Waco, Texas, 247
Budé, Guillaume, 86
Buell, Abel, 127
Buenos Aires, University of, 205
Buffalo, New York, Public Library, 175
Bullock, William A. , 189
Burnam Classical Library, Cincinnati, 247
Bushell, John, 121
Byrd, William, 140-1

Caesar, Julius, 36-7
Caldwell, David, 164
California, University of, Berkeley, 175, 243, 245, 271
Callimachus, 35
Cambridge, England, University Library, 56-7, 100-1, 102, 111, 208
Camden, William, 106
Campbell, John, 124-5

Canada, National Library, Ottawa, 201
Carey, Matthew, 195
Caritat's Circulating Library, New York, 157
Carnegie, Andrew, 183, 237
Carnegie Corporation, 215, 243, 249, 270-3
Carnegie Institute Library School, Pittsburgh, 269
Carter, Robert, 141
Caslon, William, 111, 113
Cassiodorus, Magnus Aurelius, 46-7
Catalogs and cataloging, 10-1, 31-3, 35-6, 41, 49-50, 56, 86, 91, 103, 105, 134-5, 150, 153, 170, 177, 181-2, 205, 215, 226, 243, 248, 250, 252, 262, 265-6, 283
Catherine the Great, Queen of Russia, 94-5
Cave drawings, 13-4, 193
Caxton, William, 74-5, 80, 112
Cennini, Bernardo di, 80
Censorship, 111, 122, 128, 221, 282-3
See Also Freedom of the Press.
Center for Research Libraries, Chicago, 246
Certification of librarians, 250, 272
Chained books, 48, 50, 56
Chalkley, Thomas, 140
Chambers, Ephraim, 96, 113
Champollion, Jean François, 17-8, 20
Chap-books, 82
Chapman, Thomas, 149
Charlemagne, Emperor, 50-52, 86
Charles V, King of France, 58, 86
Charleston, South Carolina, Library Society, 137-8, 141, 155, 173
Chicago Public Library, 173
Chicago, University of, 175, 243, 271
Children's literature, 112-3, 195, 286
Chile, National Library, Santiago, 206
Chile, University of, Santiago, 206
China, National Library, Peking, 226-7
Christina, Queen of Sweden, 85, 90
Church, William, 189-90
Cicero, Marcus Tullius, 36, 38, 49, 57, 76
Cincinnati Public Library, 247
Civil Rights Act of 1965, 242
Clark Memorial Library, Los Angeles, 247
Classification, 56, 87, 154, 181-2, 261-3
See also: Library arrangement
Clay tablets, 18-9, 21-2, 31-3, 64, 105
Clog calendar, 15
Clymer, George, 188
Cobham, Thomas, 57
Codex, 24-5, 37, 45, 85
Cogswell, Joseph G., 172
Coimbra University, Portugal, 218
College of Rhode Island See Brown University
Collophon, 76
Columbia University, New York, 134, 139, 147, 148, 175
Columbia University School of Library Service, 180, 269, 271
Columbian press, 188
Colwell, Stephen, 163
Communication, Auditory, 5, 7-8, 12-13
See also: Speech
Communication, extra-sensory, 287
Communication, Graphic, 5-6, 13-4, 61, 77, 193, 198, 236
See also: Printing, Writing
Communication satellites, 193, 198
Computers, 253, 284-6
Constantine, Emperor, 40
Copenhagen, University of, 93, 217
Copperplate engraving, 76, 83-4, 113, 191-2
Copyright, 110, 164
Cordova, Argentina, National University, 205

Cornell University, 175, 243
Cos, Island of, 36
Cotton, Robert Bruce, 104
Coventry, England, Public Library, 107
Cracow, Poland, University (Jagellonian), 95, 220
Crantz, Martin, 80
Cremer, Heinrich, 70
Crerar, John, 183
Cromberger, Juan, 118
Cuba, National Library, Havana, 207
Cuneiform writing, 18-19, 21, 32-3
Currier and Ives, 192
Cutter, Charles A., 181-2
Czechoslovakia, National Library, Prague, 221

Dartmouth College, 134, 243
David Ibn Nachmias, 81
Davie, William R., 149
Davis, James, 120-1, 129
Day, Matthew, 119, 129
Day, Stephen, 119
Dead sea scrolls, See Qumran Library
DeBury, Richard, 56-7
Delhi, India, Public Library, 228-9
Demetrius of Phalerum, 35
Demotic script, 17
Denmark, Royal Library, Copenhagen, 93, 217
Deutsche Bücherei, Leipzig, 212
Dewey, Melvil, 179-82, 261-2, 269
Diamond Sutra, 65
Dickinson College, Carlisle, Pennsylvania, 149
Diderot, Denis, 96
Diptych, 25
Documentation, 206, 231
Draper, Lyman C., 178
Drexel Institute Library School, Philadelphia, 180, 269
Dummer, Jeremiah, 133
Dundee, Scotland, Public Library, 107
DuPont Company libraries, 256
Dürer, Albrecht, 83
Durham, England, University, 102

Dury, John, 103

East African Literature Bureau, 225
East German State Library, Berlin, 214
Ebert, Friederich A. (Fritz), 91-92
Economic Society Library, Havana, 207
Edfu, Temple of, 31
Edinburgh, Scotland, University of, 102, 106, 208
Egypt, National Library, Cairo, 222
Electrotype, 189
Elieser, Rabbi, 81
Elizabeth I, Queen of England, 100, 103
Elzevir Press, Leiden, 73-4, 83-4
Encyclopedias, 95-6, 113, 192, 195-6
Enoch Pratt Free Library, Baltimore, 183
Epaphroditus, 38
Erpenius, Thomas, 101
Essenes, 39, 46
Essex Institute Library, Salem, Mass., 179
Estienne, Henri, 73, 81
Eumenes II, King of Pergamum, 34
Euphorion of Chalcis, 34
Everett, Edward, 172
Exchanges, 165

Farmington Plan, 283
Federal aid to libraries, 239, 241, 244, 250, 252, 274, 276
Federigo, Duke of Urbino, 57, 85
Federov, Ivan, 81
Fitzhugh, William, 140
Flags, 8
Florence, Italy, National Library, 84, 216
Folger Shakespeare Library, Washington, D C., 255
Folsom, Charles, 170
Force, Peter, 163, 177
Foster, John, 119, 129
Fourdrinier brothers, 190

294

Fowle, Daniel, 129
Fox, Justus, 127
France, National Library, See:
  Bibliothèque Nationale
Francis I, King of France, 86
Franklin, Ann, 128
Franklin, Benjamin, 120-2, 126-
  7, 129, 136, 138, 140, 163
Franklin, James, 129
Franklin Institute Library, Phila-
  delphia, 151-2
Franklin D. Roosevelt Library,
  Hyde Park, N.Y., 256
Frederick William, The Great
  Elector, 88
Freedom of the press, 124, 129,
  214.
  See also: Censorship
Friburger, Michael, 80
Friends' Library, Philadelphia,
  140
Friends of the library groups,
  244
Froben, Johann, 74, 81
Fugger, Ulrich, 89
Furness Memorial Library, Phila-
  delphia, 247
Fust, Johann, 69-71, 76, 80

Galveston, Texas, Public Library,
  238
Garamond, Claude, 74
General Electric Company li-
  braries, Schenectady, N.Y.,
  257
George I-IV, Kings of England,
  102, 104
Georgetown, S.C., Library So-
  ciety, 156, 173
Georgia, University of, Athens,
  150, 175
Gering, Ulrich, 80
Germany, National Library, Ber-
  lin, 88, 212-3
Gestures, 7, 12
Ghana, University of, Accra,
  225
Gift books, 113, 195
Gilbert, Humphrey, 103
Gilpin brothers, 190
Glasgow, Scotland, University of,
  101-2
Glen, James, 141

Glover, Jose, 119
Goethe, Johann Wolfgang von, 92
Goldsmith, Oliver, 113
Göttingen, Germany, University,
  89-90, 212
Government publications, 122-4,
  162, 164, 170, 246-7, 254
Grace, Robert, 136
Granjon, Robert, 74
Grant, Seth Hastings, 170
Gray, William, 58
Gray's Inn Library, London, 107
Great Britain. Parliament. Com-
  mittee on Public Libraries,
  1847-1849, 109
Great Britain. Public Libraries
  Act, 1850, 209
Great Britain, Royal Library,
  See: British Museum Library
Greece, National Library,
  Athens, 218
Green, Bartholomew, 121
Green, Samuel, 119, 127-9
Gridley, Jeremiah, 126
Guild, Reuben Aldrich, 170, 181
Guildhall Library, London, 57
Gustavus Adolphus, King of
  Sweden, 89-90, 93
Gutenberg, Johann, 64, 69-71,
  74, 80, 188

Hamilton, Andrew, 123
Hamilton College Library, Clin-
  ton, N.Y., 149
Hamilton County, Ohio, Library,
  171
Hampton Institute, Virginia, Li-
  brary School, 271
Harley, Robert, 104
Harper & Row Company, 195-6
Harris, Benjamin, 124
Harris, Caleb Fiske, 183
Harris, John, 96
Harris, Thaddeus Mason, 153-4
Harvard, John, 132
Harvard University, 132-3, 147-
  52, 174, 242-3, 245-6
Hawaii, State Library, 254
Heidelberg, Germany, Palatine
  Library, 85, 89
Helsinki, Finland, University, 95
Hendreich, Christoph, 88
Henry VIII, King of England, 100

Hercalaeneum, 38-9
Hesse, Andreas, 80
Hewat, Alexander, 141
Hieratic script, 17
Hieroglyphic script, 16-7
Hochfelder, Caspar, 80
Hodgson, John, 141
Hoe, Richard M. , 189
Holbein, Hans, 74, 83
Hoover, Herbert, 247
Hoover Library, Stanford, Calif. , 247
Horn book, 113
Hume, David, 106
Humphrey, Duke of Gloucester, 58
Hungary, National Library, Budapest, 221-2
Huntington Library, San Marino, Calif. , 255

Ideographs, 15-6, 20
Illinois, University of, 175, 180, 267, 269, 271
Illumination, 45, 48, 59
Illustrations, 68, 76, 113, 188, 191-2, 194
See also: Copperplate engraving, Steel-plate engraving, wood-cuts.
Incunabula, 72-77, 85, 93, 215
Indexes and indexing, 77, 91, 261-7, 283-4
See also: Periodical indexes.
India, National Library, Calcutta, 229
Indian Council of World Affairs Library, New Delhi, 229
Indiana, University of, 150
Indians of North America, 7, 15, 132
Information storage and retrieval, 11, 253, 257, 280, 283-5
Ink, 23, 70, 127
Inner Temple Library, London, 107
Innes, Alexander, 139
Innes, James, 141
Innsbruck, Austria, University, 93
Institute Français d'Afrique Noir, 225
Instructional materials centers, 250-1
Inter-American Library School, Medellin, Colombia, 204
Inter-library loans, 92, 204, 209, 223-4, 244, 252, 254, 283
Iredell, James, 141
Ireland, National Library, 106
Israel, National Library, 222

Jackson, Andrew, 163
James, Thomas, 101, 110
Japan, National Diet Library, 227-8
Jefferson, Thomas, 77, 142, 150, 160
Jenson, Nicholas, 72-4, 80
Jewett, Charles Coffin, 169, 172, 176-7, 181
Johannesburg, South Africa, Public Library, 224
John Crerar Library, Chicago, 183, 254-5
John of Spires, 80
John of Westphalia, 80
John Rylands Library, Manchester, England, 106
Johnson, Samuel, 139
Johnston, Gabriel, 141
Johnston, James, 121, 129
Johnston, Samuel, 141
Johnston, William, 141
Julius, Duke of Brunswick, 88

Kairoween University, Fez, Morocco, 225
Keayne, Robert, 134
Ketalaer, Nicholaus, 80
King's Chapel Library, Boston, 135
King's College, See: Columbia University.
Knapp School Libraries Project, 251-2
Koberger family, 73
Koenig, Friedrich, 188
Kohlinger, Stephen, 80
Kolarov State Library, Sofia, Bulgaria, 221
Konig, Wilhelm, 80
Koster, Laurens, 70
Kroeger, Alice B. , 266

Language, See: Speech, Writing
Laud, Archbishop, 101
Laurens, Henry, 141
Laurentian Library, Venice,
See: Biblioteca Laurentiana.
Laval University, Quebec, 202
Lea and Febiger, Inc., 195
Leempt, Gerardus, 80
Legal deposit, 86, 92, 103, 105,
110, 164
Leibniz, Gottfried Wilhelm, 89,
91, 92
Leicester, England, Public Li-
brary, 107
Leiden, Netherlands, University,
93
Leipzig, Germany, University
Library, 90
Lenin State Library, Moscow,
219
Lenox, James, 172, 236
Lenox Library, New York, 172,
183, 236-7
Lessing, Gotthold Ephraim, 89
Lettou, John, 75, 80
Leypoldt, Frederick, 182
Librarians and librarianship, 6,
10, 11, 31, 36-8, 48-9, 52,
91, 103, 134, 138, 150, 169-
70, 174, 176, 179-80, 214,
220, 242, 245, 248, 249, 251-
2, 257, 261-88
Librarians' Conference of 1853,
Philadelphia, 169-70, 181
Libraries (arranged by location):
Africa, 224-6
Argentina, 205-6
Asia Minor, 32-4, 36, 40-41,
222
Assyria, 31-32
Australia, 223-4
Austria, 92-3
Babylonia, 30-2
Belgium, 58, 93
Brazil, 204-5
Bulgaria, 221
Burma, 230
Canada, 201-2
Chile, 206
China, 41-2, 226-7
Colombia, 207-8
Constantinople, 40-1, 51
Cuba, 207

Czechoslovakia, 56, 221
Denmark, 93, 217
Egypt, 30-31, 34-6, 222
England, 47, 51-2, 55-7,
100-117, 208-10
Ethiopia, 225
Finland, 95, 217
France, 47, 50-3, 55-6, 58,
86-8, 210-11
Germany, 52-3, 56, 88-92,
211-14
Ghana, 225
Greece, 33-36, 218
Hungary, 58, 221-2
India, 228-9
Indonesia, 230
Iran, 222
Iraq, 222
Ireland, 47, 102, 106, 109
Israel, 222
Italy, 47, 53, 56-7, 84-6,
214-7. See also: Rome.
Japan, 227-8
Kenya, 225
Latin America, 203-8
Liberia, 225
Malagasy Republic, 231
Malaysia, 230
Mexico, 203-4
Morocco, 225-6
Moslem countries (Medieval),
40-1, 46, 53
Netherlands, 93
New Zealand, 223-4
Nigeria, 225
Norway, 93, 217
Pakistan, 229-30
Palestine (Ancient), 39-40
Panama, 207
Peru, 206
Philippines, 228
Poland, 56, 95, 220-1
Portugal, 53, 94, 218
Rome, 36-8, 39, 45. See
also: Italy.
Rumania, 221
Russia, 94-5, 219-20
Scotland, 101-2, 104-5, 109,
208
Singapore, 230
South Africa, 224-5
Spain, 41, 53, 94, 218
Sweden, 89-90, 93, 217

297

Libraries (arranged by location) (cont.)

Switzerland, 47, 53, 217-8
Taiwan, 227
Tanzania, 225
Thailand, 230
Turkey, 222
United States, 132-87, 236-60
Yugoslavia, 218

Libraries (arranged by type):

Academy, 159-60, 201, 247
Apprentices', 152, 154
Armed services, 238, 253
Cathedral, 52-4, 100
Children's, 157, 176, 203, 206, 216, 237, 241. See also: Libraries, School.
Christian (Ancient), 36, 39-40, 46
Church, 6, 90, 135-6, 203
Circulating, 83, 92, 142-4, 148, 155-7, 212
Coffee house, 108-9
College and university, 46, 55-6, 87, 90-1, 94, 100-2, 132-4, 147-51, 173-5, 202-3, 205-6, 208, 210, 212, 214, 216-8, 220, 222-31, 242-7, 283-4
County, 171, 238-9, 249
Departmental, 151, 174, 244
Endowed, 247, 254
Government, 6, 30, 32-3, 42, 107, 160-2, 176-8, 216, 224, 228, 252-4, 284-5
Literary society, 151, 174
Mechanics', 108, 152, 171
Mercantile, 152, 154, 171
Monastery, 45-54, 87, 90, 100
Parish, 107, 135-6
Private, 6, 30, 33, 37, 45-6, 57-8, 84-5, 87-8, 94-5, 104, 106, 110, 138-42, 162-4, 165, 172-3, 182-3
Proprietary, 108-9, 170
Public, 33, 37, 87-8, 90-1, 107-10, 134, 158-9, 165, 170-75, 180, 183, 201-5, 207-10, 212-3, 215-6, 219-31, 236-42, 250, 280-3
Rental, 142. See also: Libraries, Circulating.
Rural, 109, 171, 202, 204, 209, 223, 225, 227, 238, 240-1, 249, 250
School, 159-60, 175-6, 201, 203-5, 211, 216, 218, 220, 227-8, 229, 247-52, 281
School district, 158-9, 175, 247
Social, 106-7, 152-5, 170-1, 202
Special, 151-2, 154, 173-4, 178-9, 203, 206, 208-9, 211, 213, 216, 219, 221, 228-30, 252-7, 283-5
State, 161-2, 178, 254-5
Subscription, 108-9, 136-8, 147-8, 155-6, 170, 201, 206, 208, 223, 237
Sunday school, 155, 159, 247
Temple, 6, 30
Undergraduate, 246
University, See: Libraries, College and university.

Libraries, Destruction of, 35-6, 39, 41, 45, 53, 58, 89-90, 100, 147-8, 173, 209-10, 212-5, 217, 220, 226-7
Libraries, Origin of, 6-7, 25, 30, 41
Library arrangement, 31-2, 37, 48-50, 56, 83, 150, 153, 243-5, 251, 268, 284. See also: Classification.
Library associations, 170, 180-1, 202, 205-6, 210-1, 213-4, 220, 223-4, 225, 228, 265-7, 275-6
Library bookstock, 49, 108, 133, 138-41, 148, 153, 155-6, 159, 246
Library buildings, 37, 55, 88, 91, 102, 105, 134, 137, 140, 149-52, 172, 174-6, 183, 243-5, 248
Library Bureau, 182, 267
Library commissions, 171, 238
Library education, 180-1, 202, 204-6, 210, 214, 220, 223-5, 228-9, 267-75
Library equipment and supplies, 182, 249
Library legislation, 109, 136, 158, 169, 171-2, 201, 209-10, 220, 227, 241, 252. See also: Federal aid to libraries;

298

State aid to libraries.
Library literature, 91-2, 103, 108-9, 153-4, 170, 181-2, 214, 220, 224-6, 229, 231, 249-50, 261-8, 273
Library philanthropy, 101-2, 104, 132-4, 141, 149, 172-4, 182-3, 243-4, 249
Library rules and regulations, 55-6, 150-1, 242
Library Services Act of 1956, 241, 276
Library standards, 248-51, 270, 272-4, 276
Library storage, 246
Library 21, Seattle World's Fair, 285-6
Library/USA, New York World's Fair, 286
Lincoln's Inn Library, London, 106-7
Linda Hall Library, Kansas City, 255
Lindisfarne Gospels, 48
Linear-B script, 19
Linotype machine, 114, 190
Lithography, 114, 192-3
Little, Clement, 102
Liverpool, England, Municipal libraries, 209
Liverpool, England, University, 102, 208
Lloyd Library and Museum, Cincinnati, 255
Logan, James, 139
London Library, 208-9
London, University of, 102, 208
Los Angeles Public Library, 269
Loudon, Samuel, 143
Louisiana State University, Baton Rouge, 175
Louisville, Kentucky, Public Library, 237-8
Lucas, Henry, 101
Lucullus, Lucius, 36
Luther, Martin, 77, 90

McCall, John, 129
McGill University, Montreal, 202
Machine translation, 286-7
Machlinia, William de, 75
M'Kenzie, John, 141
Madison, James, 150

Madras, India, Oriental Manuscripts Library, 229
Madrid, Spain, University, 94, 218
Magliabichi, Antonio, 84
Manchester, England, Public Library, 107, 210
Manchester, England, University, 208
Manila, Philippines, Municipal Library, 228
Manuscripts, 45-6, 49, 57, 85, 86, 88, 92, 94-5, 101, 104, 203, 205, 208, 210, 215-6, 218, 229, 252, 254, 286
Manutius, Aldus, 72-3, 81, 83
Marlborough, Duke of, 106
Marschalk, Andrew, 129
Martin, Esteban, 118
Mason, Robert, 102
Massachusetts Horticultural Society Library, Boston, 152
Massachusetts Public Library Act, 1851, 169
Mather, Cotton, 139, 141, 144
Mather, Increase, 139
Mather, Samuel, 135
Matthias Corvinus, King of Hungary, 58
Maximilian, Duke of Bavaria, 85
Maximilian I, Emperor of Austria, 92
Mazarin, Cardinal, 87
Maxwell, William, 129
Medici family, 57, 84, 216
MEDLARS, 253
Mein, John, 143-4
Mentelin, Johann, 80
Meredith, Hugh, 121
Mergenthaler, Ottmar, 190
Mexico, National Library, 203
Michigan, University of, 150, 175, 243, 271
Micro-materials, 202, 246, 252, 257, 281, 283, 287
Midwest Inter-library Center, See: Center for Research Libraries.
Minnesota, University of, 175
Mississippi, University of, 150
Missouri, University of, 150, 175
Mitchell, William H., 190
Mnemonic devices, 14-5

Monasteries, 45-7, 61
Monastic orders, 47, 54
Monroe, James, 163
Monte Cassino, 46
Moreri, Louis, 96
Morocco, National Library,
Rabat, 226
Morrill Act of 1862, 174
Moscow, Russia, Public Library, 95
Moscow, Russia, University of,
95, 219
Mosely, Edward, 141
Mudge, Isadore G. , 266
Museum materials, 6, 104
Musical instruments, 8
Mussey, W.H. , 163

Nairne, James, 106
Napoleon, Emperor, 17, 85-6
National Aeronautics and Space
Administration, 254
National Agricultural Library,
252-3, 284
National Central Library, London, 209
National Council of Teachers of
English, 249
National Education Association,
176, 249, 275
National Library of Medicine,
252-3, 284
National Youth Administration,
239, 244
Naudé, Gabriel, 87
Nebraska, University of, 175
Netherlands, Royal Library, 93
New England Deposit Library,
Boston, 246
New Hampshire State Library,
162
New Harmony, Indiana, Working
Men's Institute Library, 155-6
New Orleans, Louisiana, Library Society, 156
New South Wales State Library,
Sydney, 223
New York Academy of Medicine
Library, 256
New York Academy of Sciences
Library, 152
New York Apprentices' Library,
154, 173

New York City Hospital Library,
178
New York Engineering Societies
Library, 256
New York Historical Society,
173, 178, 255
New York Mercantile Library,
170-1, 173
New York Public Library, 173,
183, 236-7, 269
New York Society Library, 137-
8, 139, 147, 173
New York State Library, 162,
178, 180, 269, 271
New York Times Library, 256
New Zealand National Library
Service, 224
Newberry, Walter L. , 183
Newberry Reference Library,
Chicago, 183, 255
Newbery, John, 113
Newcastle-on-Tyne, England,
City Libraries, 209
Newspapers, 95-6, 112, 121-6,
128, 190, 192, 194, 197, 209,
210, 246-7, 286
Newton, Sir Isaac, 133
Nicholas V, Pope, 59
Niccoli, Nicolo, 57
Nigeria, Regional Central Library, Enugu, 225
North Carolina, University of,
149-50, 175, 271
Notary, Julian, 75
Nuremberg Chronicle, 73, 76
Nuremberg, Germany, Municipal
Library, 90
Nuthead, Dinah, 128
Nuthead, William, 120, 128-9

Octavian Library, Rome, 37, 39
Offset printing, 192-3
Omar, Caliph, 36
Oporto, Portugal, Municipal Library, 94, 218
Orsini, Fulvio, 85
Oslo, Norway, Free Public Library (Deichmann Library),
93, 217
Oslo, Norway, University of, 93
Oxford University Library, 56,
58, 100-2, 110, 134, 208

Pablos, Juan, 118
Paine, Thomas, 128
Pakistan, National Library, Karachi, (Liaquat Library), 229
Palatine Library, Heidelberg, 85, 89
Palatine Library, Rome, 39
Palimpsests, 49
Palmart, Lambert, 80
Pamphlets, 95, 112, 119, 123, 128, 195, 247, 256
Panizzi, Anthony, 104-5
Panjab Public Library, Lahore, Pakistan, 229
Pannartz, Arnold, 72, 80
Paper-bound books, 193-5, 197, 241. See also: Pamphlets.
Paper and paper-making, 41, 53, 65-7, 120, 127, 190-1, 193
Papyrus, 17, 22-3, 25, 30-1, 37, 45, 66, 93, 105, 208
Parchment, 23-4, 25, 45, 49, 55, 66, 193
Paris, University of, 55, 60, 210-11. See also: Sorbonne.
Parker, James, 129
Parker, Matthew, Archbishop, 101
Parks, William, 120, 129
Paulus Aemilius, 36
Pauper's Bible, 68
Peking, China, State Library, 227
Pennsylvania State Library, Harrisburg, 162
Pennsylvania, University of, 134, 149, 163, 243
Pergamum Library, 24, 34
Periodical indexes, 181, 224, 263-5
Periodicals, 95-6, 112, 125-6, 143, 148, 153, 182, 194, 196-7, 246-7, 261, 264-6, 286
Perry, Michael, 143
Peru, National Library, Lima, 206
Peter the Great, Czar of Russia, 94
Peterborough, New Hampshire, Public Library, 157-8
Petrarch, 57, 76, 216
Pfister, Albrecht, 80
Philadelphia Apprentices' Library,
154
Philadelphia College of Physicians Library, 179
Philadelphia Free Library, 237
Philadelphia Library Company, 136-8, 140, 170
Philadelphia Mercantile Library, 154, 237
Philip the Good, Duke of Burgundy, 58
Philip II, King of Spain, 53, 94
Philip V, King of Spain, 94
Philippines, National Library, Manila, 228
Philodemus, 38
Phonograms, 16, 20
Photo-copying, 244, 283, 286
Photo-engraving, 192
Piccolomini, Enea Silvio, 92
Pictographs, 15-6, 18-20
Pierpont Morgan Library, New York, 255
Pisistratus, 33
Pius XI, Pope, 215
Plantin family, 73, 81, 84
Playing cards, 66-7
Plutarch, 34
Pollio, Caius Asinius, 37
Poole, William Frederick, 170, 173, 181, 263
Portugal, National Library, Lisbon, 94, 218
Pratt, Enoch, 183
Pratt Institute Library School, Brooklyn, 180, 269
Prince, Thomas, 139, 172
Prince Edward Island, Canada, 202
Princeton University, 134, 147, 148, 175, 243
Printer, James, 119
Printing and printers, 64-81, 82, 84, 96-7, 100, 111-4, 118-31, 188-200, 286
Prints, 105, 191-2
Propaganda, 212, 214, 217, 220
Punched cards, 257, 284
Putnam, Herbert, 182
Pynson, Richard, 75, 81

Quills, 24, 26
Quipu, 14
Qumran library, 39-40

301

Radio, 198
Ranganathan, S. R. , 229
Rawlinson, Sir Henry, 18-20
Rawlinson, Richard, 102
Recorded knowledge, 6, 10, 30,
   287
Redwood, Abraham, 137
Redwood Library, Newport, R.I. ,
   137
Registrum Librorum Angliae, 56
Renaissance, 82, 84
Rhodes, Island of, 36
Ricardo, 118
Riessinger, Sixtus, 80
Rind, William, 142
Rittenhouse, William, 127
Rolls, 23, 25, 30-1, 37-40, 45,
   85
Rome, National Central Library,
   216
Rome, University of, 216
Rood, Theodoric, 80
Rosenwald Fund, 249
Rosetta Stone, 17-18
Rotary press, 114, 188-9, 192
Rotogravure, 192
Roulstone, George, 129
Royal Society Library, London,
   107
Roycroft, Thomas, 111
Rubrication, 48
Rumanian People's Academy,
   Bucharest, 221
Ruppel, Berthold, 80
Russia, Imperial Library, St.
   Petersburg (Leningrad), 94-5,
   219
Rustat, Tobias, Bishop, 101

St. Andrew's University, Scot-
   land, 101-2
St. John's College, Annapolis,
   Md. , 135
St. Louis Public Library, 269
St. Petersburg, Russia, Academy
   Library, 95
Saltykov-Shchedrin Library, Len-
   ingrad, 219
Sammonicus, Serenius, 38
San Lorenzo del Escorial Li-
   brary, Spain, 94, 218
San Marcos National University,
   Lima, Peru, 206

São Paulo, Brazil, Municipal Li-
   brary, 204
Sauer, Christopher, 126-7, 129
Schoeffer, Peter, 69-71, 76, 80
Schools, Medieval, 54
Scotland, National Library, Edin-
   burgh, 105-6, 208
Scoville Memorial Library, Sal-
   isbury, Conn. , 157
Scribner, Charles, and Sons,
   publishers, 196
Scriptorium, 48, 52, 83
Seager, F. S. , 113
Seals (cylinder seals), 64
Sears, Minnie E. , 266
Selden, John, 101
Semaphores, 8
Seneca, 38, 49, 76
Sensenschmid, Johann, 80
Sewall, Samuel, 139
Sharp, John, 139
Short, Thomas, 129
Signet Library, Edinburgh, Scot-
   land, 107
Silver Library, Königsberg, Ger-
   many, 88
Sloane, Sir Hans, 103
Smith, Lloyd Pearsall, 170
Smithson, James, 176-7
Smithsonian Institution Library,
   164, 169, 170, 172, 176-7
Snell, Johann, 73, 80
Society for the Propagation of
   the Gospel, 135, 137
Sorbonne, Robert de, 58
Sorbonne Library, Paris, 55-6,
   58
South Africa, National Library,
   Pretoria, 224
South Carolina State Library, 162
South Carolina, University of,
   150, 175
Spain, National Library, Madrid,
   94, 218
Special Libraries Association,
   275
Speech, 5, 7, 12-3
Spofford, Ainsworth Rand, 177,
   179
Stanford University, Stanford,
   Calif. , 175
Stanhope, Charles, Earl of, 188
State aid to libraries 171-2, 240,
   249-50

Stationers' Company, London, 110
Steel-plate engravings, 192
Stereotype, 188-9
Stiles, Ezra, 137
Sulla, 36-7
Sweden, Royal Library, Stockholm, 93, 217
Sweynheym, Conrad, 72, 80
Switzerland, National Library, 217
Symbols, 8-9, 13
Syracuse, New York, University Library School, 269

Tabula (waxed tablets), 26
Taiwan, National Library, Taipei, 227
Teaching machines, 251
Teletype, 197, 283
Television, 193, 198, 241, 251, 283, 287
Telstar, 198
Tennessee, University of, 150
Tennessee Valley Authority libraries, 239, 253
Texas, University of, 175
Text-books, 55, 60, 124, 134, 143, 195, 271
Textile printing, 68
Ticknor, George, 163, 172
Tilden, Samuel, 183, 236
Timothy, Anne, 128
Timothy, Lewis, 120, 127-9
Timothy, Peter, 128
Tokyo, Japan, Municipal Library, 227
Toronto, University of, 202
Tory, Geoffrey, 81
Trajan, Emperor of Rome, 37
Trinity College, Dublin, 102
Trow, John F., 190
Troyes, France, Municipal Library, 87
Turin, Italy, National Library, 84
Turkey, National Library, Ankara, 222
Tyler, John, 163, 173
Type and type-founding, 65, 70, 72, 74, 84, 111, 118, 127, 188-90
Typewriter, 197

Tyrannion, 36

Uffenbach, Johann F., 89
UNESCO, 207-8, 226, 230-1, 267
Union catalogs, 36, 92, 177, 209, 224, 244
United Nations libraries, 218, 256
U.S. Air Force Library Services, 253
U.S. Armed Forces Medical Library, 252
U.S. Atomic Energy Commission, 253-4
U.S. Department of Agriculture Library, 178. See also: National Agricultural Library.
U.S. Department of Interior Library, 178
U.S. Information Service Libraries, 213, 226, 231
U.S. Library of Congress, 152, 160-1, 163-5, 176-7, 182, 242, 252-3, 262, 266
U.S. Military Academy Library, 161, 253
U.S. National Youth Administration, 239, 244
U.S. Naval Academy Library, 161, 253
U.S. Navy Department, Library Services Branch, 253
U.S. Office of Education, 178, 181, 183, 238, 240, 248, 250, 268-9
U.S. Patent Office Library, 161
U.S. State Department Library, 161, 165
U.S. Surgeon General's Library, 178
U.S. Treasury Department Library, 161
U.S. War Department Library, 161
U.S. Works Progress Administration, 239, 244
Universities, Medieval, 54-5
University presses, 196
Uppsala University, Sweden, 90, 93
Usher, James, 102
Utrecht, Netherlands, University, 93

Van Buren, Martin, 163
Van Wert County, Ohio, Library, 171
Vance, Zebulon Baird, 163-4
Vanderbilt University, Nashville, Tenn., 175
Varela, Pedro, 118
Varro, Terentius, 37
Vatican Library, Rome, 58-9, 85-6, 90, 215
Vellum, See: Parchment.
Ventris, Michael, 19-20
Vermont, University of, 150
Vespasiano da Bisticci, 57-8, 60
Victoria State Library, Melbourne, Australia, 223
Victoria University Library, Manchester, England, 102
Vienna, University of, 93
Virginia Military Institute, Lexington, 173
Virginia State Library, Richmond, 161-2
Virginia, University of, 150, 175
Vivarium, 46-7

Waldfoghel, Procopius, 71
Wales, National Library, 106, 208
Wampum, 14-5
War damage to libraries, See: Libraries, Destruction of.
Warsaw, Poland, University of, 220
Washington, George, 142
Washington and Lee University, Lexington, Va., 173
Washington County, Maryland, Library, 171
Watterson, George, 160
Waxed tablets, 26
Webb, George, 129
Wells, William C., 129
Wesleyan University, Middletown, Conn., 149
West German Library, Marburg, 213
Western Reserve University Library School, Cleveland, 269
Wheeler, Joseph L., 273
Whittington, Richard, 57
Widener, Harry Elkins, 183
William and Mary College, Williamsburg, Va., 132-4, 148
Williamson, Charles C., 270-1
Wilson, H.W. Company, 196, 261-4, 266
Winchell, Constance M., 266
Winsor, Justin, 179
Winthrop, John, 132, 138
Winthrop, John, Jr., 139
Wisconsin State Historical Society Library, Madison, 178, 255
Wisconsin, University of, 150, 269
Wolfenbüttel, Germany, Duke's Library, 88-9, 91
Woodcuts, 64-6, 73-4, 76, 83, 113, 189, 191. See also: Block printing.
Wormesley, Ralph, 140-1
Writing, 5, 12-26, 51
Writing materials, 5, 17, 22-6, 66-7
Wynkyn de Worde, 75, 81

Yale, Elihu, 133
Yale University, 133, 147-8, 150-1, 174-5, 243, 245

Zainer, Gunther, 80
Zarotti, Antonio, 80
Zell, Ulrich, 80
Zenger, Peter, 123
Zenodotus of Ephesus, 35

DATE DUE

GAYLORD

PRINTED IN U.S.A.